EUROPE IN POEMS
THE VERSOPOLIS ANTHOLOGY

Europe in Poems
The Versopolis Anthology

Edited and introduced by
Patrick McGuinness

Beletrina

PUBLICATIONS

2020

Published by Arc Publications
Nanholme Mill, Shaw Wood Road
Todmorden, OL14 6DA, UK
www.arcpublications.co.uk

in collaboration with Beletrina Academic Press,
part of of the Versopolis project
https://www.versopolis-poetry.com/
www.versopolis.com

Design by Tony Ward
Printed by
Rotografika

Cover illustration:
'Vortex' (photomontage) © Jimmy Symonds

978 1908376 69 5 (pbk)

Co-funded by the
Creative Europe Programme
of the European Union

Supported using public funding by
ARTS COUNCIL
ENGLAND
LOTTERY FUNDED

Arc Publications
Anthologies in Translation
Series Editor: Jean Boase-Beier

VERSOPOLIS
is a unique, Europe-wide platform.
It gives emerging European poets
the chance to reach an audience beyond
the boundaries of the language they write in
by translating and publishing their poems
and inviting them to perform at festivals.

CONTENTS

INTRODUCTION

We are used to grand statements about poetry – discussions of poetry are the home of grand statements. We say that poetry crosses borders and unites people, forging communities across languages and national frontiers. We tell ourselves that it both resists translation and yet transcends it, and that whatever language we speak, poetry is the language that connects us. These are attractive thoughts, and we want them to be true. Maybe we think that saying them enough will make them true. However, fond as we are of celebrating poetry for its power to bring us together, we rarely create the spaces and the contexts in which these crossings and connections happen.

This is where Versopolis comes in, and where this anthology – a selection of sixty European poets from more than two dozen countries – makes its own contribution to turning the transnational ideal of poetry into something practical and realised.

Versopolis began in 2014, initially as a European poetry platform, and funded by the European Commission's Creative Europe Programme. It was founded by the Slovenian poet Aleš Šteger and the Ljubljana-based publishing house Beletrina, ten years after Slovenia joined the EU. The aim was to build an umbrella organisation in which Europe's poetry festivals could join together and exchange emerging poets and translators across a rolling programme of events. It was from the beginning conceived as a transnational community in a Europe that was growing and changing fast. As more festivals joined and hosted each others' writers, so more poets travelled, and more poems visited new destinations in the form of translations. The project is accompanied by the websites Versopolis Poetry and *Versopolis Review*, showcasing the poets and translators and publishing interviews and articles, which between them have a readership of over 200,000. By the end of 2020, Versopolis had hosted 271 poets from 32 languages and 39 countries. That number will grow in the coming years. It's an impressive figure, though not as impressive as the territory its festivals have covered (5.5 million square kilometres) or the number of people who have attended a Versopolis event since 2014 (800,000).

Versopolis has become an international co-operative of poets and translators keen to go beyond national boundaries, but also to share the uniqueness of their cultures. Because the paradox of all art – not just poetry – is that it expresses difference as well as sameness, and must be true to both what we share with others and what makes us irreducibly different. I have chosen the work of sixty poets, and aimed to give each poet and each translator sufficient space for their work to breathe.

I have also aimed to produce an anthology which showcases not just a wealth of poets and translators, but represents a feat of European intercultural exchange. It's what I think of as the Versopolis ethos: an extraordinary variety of themes, of styles, and of subjects, finding common ground in a shared idea not just of what poetry can be, but what a poetry community can be.

The poets range in age from their early twenties to their mid-fifties, and the anthology contains poetry in twenty-six languages. This is a Europe of new voices from old countries as well as old voices from new countries. It is also a Europe of minority languages with vibrant poetry cultures. Europe's recent history – as well as the history that stretches back centuries – has created languages without borders, whose literary traditions do not observe the parameters of the nation-state. In fact, they often predate the treaties that brought the states into being, and outlast them when new treaties are made. Colonialism, economic or political migrations, and the redrawing of states from the end of the Austro-Hungarian Empire to the still-evolving European Union, by way of the fall of communism, have altered the maps more than the territories. By some sad irony, the British poets in this anthology began as European poets and now, post-Brexit, no longer are. Thanks to Versopolis, however, and in these pages, they remain Europeans.

I began by questioning the happy clichés about poetry's reach and the airy rhetoric which those of us who love poetry all too often resort to. But the Versopolis project is not airy – or if it is, it's because its ambitions continue to rise... It is a solid, demonstrable, ongoing contribution to the creation of a transnational poetry community: a community of writers and translators, yes, but also of readers. The reader holding this book is one of them.

Patrick McGuinness

EUROPE IN POEMS
THE VERSOPOLIS ANTHOLOGY

RENATE AICHINGER (Austria)

Renate Aichinger (1976) lives in Vienna where she works as a writer and theatre director. She has published three books: Welt.All.Tag *(2012), and the poetry collections* wundstil *(2014) and* endeln *(2016). She has received several awards and scholarships including Rauriser Förderungspreis, Nestroy-Theaterpreis, VERSOPOLIS-poetess (Bratislava, Belgrade, Antwerp / Ghent) and residencies at Krakow, Paliano and Schwaz. She has worked at several theatres, including Junges Schauspielhaus Zürich and between 2016 and 2019 she was head of the Offene Burg department at the Burgtheater Wien.*

COLOUR PAINTING

I
once
imagined
what it would
what it would be like if
then the line went dead

Translated by Renée von Paschen

BUNTMALEREI

ich
hab
mir einmal vorgestellt
wie es wäre
wie es wäre wenn
dann ist die verbindung abgebrochen

MIND:GAP

it's that gap

in education
in consciousness
in the market

it's that gap
which separates
you

you
are
alienated

you & the police
you & the middle class
you & the next generation

it's that gap
which di
vides society

which carries us away like icebergs & separates
us like cracked eggs
yet there's no egg-white

there's no snowy froth
it's just you turning white
it's your future icing over

your perspectives are being managed
by a nice civil servant who doesn't
understand you
your prospects always worsening

soon we won't be able to see the opposite
bank
yet hope succumbs
to injury

Translated by Renée von Paschen

BEWUSSTSEIN:LÜCKE

es ist diese lücke

in der bildung
im bewusstsein
am markt

es ist diese lücke
die euch
trennt

ihr
entfremdet
euch

du & die polizei
du & der mittelstand
du & die next generation

es ist dieser riss
der die gesellschaft ent
zweit

der uns wie eisschollen davonträgt & trennt
wie aufgeschlagene eier
nur dass da nichts weiß

dass da kein schnee
dass nur du weiß vergreist
dass deine zukunft vereist

dass deine perspektiven weiterverwaltet
von einer netten beamtin die dich nicht versteht
dass die aussichten immer schlechter

bald können wir das andere ufer nicht mehr sehen
aber die hoffnung stirbt
verletzt

PEACE OF MIND:HE

will you charge my battery
when the world's shut out of my ears
by my white earbuds

will you fill my silence
when I can't hear my gut feeling
drowned by white noise

will you fill my emptiness
when I've closed my snail shell
with my white earbuds

long since grey

Translated by Renée von Paschen

SEELENSTILL:ER

füllst du meinen akku auf
wenn mir die welt mal wieder aus den ohren
mit weißen kabeln

füllst du meine stille auf
wenn ich mein bauchgefühl nicht hör
mit weißen bässen zugedröhnt

füllst du meine leere auf
wenn ich mein schneckenhaus zugestöpselt
mit meinen weißen kabeln

die längst grau

COLOUR FILTER

do you know
yesterday we looked forward to the future
watching black & white slides
in analogue astonishment
telling ourselves
tomorrow then

you know
today we're afraid of the future
watching synchronized
computer-generated horror scenes
telling ourselves
yesterday everything was better

know
tomorrow we won't have anything
not even any fear
preventatively putting retro-
filters over our immaculate digital iPhone images
& thus vacuuming up the dust of the past

Translated by Renée von Paschen

FARBFILTER

weißt du noch
gestern haben wir uns auf die zukunft gefreut
haben schwarz-weiß-dia
analog angestaunt
haben uns gesagt
morgen dann

weißt du
heute haben wir angst vor der zukunft
schauen synchron
auf computergenerierte horrorszenarien
sagen uns
gestern war alles besser

weiß
morgen werden wir nichts haben
nicht mal mehr angst
stülpen zur sicherheit retro
filter über unsere digitalmakellosen iphone-bilder
& saugen damit den staub der vergangenheit auf

NIKOLINA ANDOVA (North Macedonia)

Nikolina Andova Shopova (1978) has published two books of poetry, The Entrance is on the Other Side *(2013) and* Connect the Dots *(2014). Her first poetry book received the prestigious 'Bridges of Struga' award, and the UNESCO and Struga Poetry Evenings awards. In 2019 she received the 'Novel of the Year' award from the Foundation for Promotion of Cultural Values 'Slavko Janevski' for her first novel,* Someone Was Here. *She has also published short stories and picture books for children.*

EVERYTHING IS PIERCED

Everything here is pierced
the sky we spy through the lenses of the telescopes
and the folders on our office desks
the little windows in the ship cabins when we
travel
and the massive walls in the temples in which we pray

And the blankets of the secret lovers burnt from cigarettes
are pierced
and the world we see through the rings of the ancestors
the memories like cookie-dough when we shape
the targets in humans forms on which we practise shooting

everything, everything is pierced
the spy-holes on the doors closed for beggars
the earth from the ant's destroyed homes
god who we search through the circular openings of the domes

Translated by Elida Bahtijaroska and Gorjan Kostovski

СÈ Е ПРОДУПЧЕНО

Тука сè е продупчено
небото што го ѕиркаме низ леќите на телескопите
и папките на нашите канцелариски бироа
прозорчињата на кабините во бродовите кога патуваме
и масивните ѕидови во храмовите во кои се молиме

И ќебињата на тајните љубовници изгорени од цигара
се продупчени
и светот кој го гледаме низ прстените на предците
сеќавањата како тесто за колачиња кога ги обликуваме
метите во човечки облици на кои вежбаме пукање

сè, сè е продупчено
окцата на вратите затворени за питачите
земјата од растурените домови на мравките
бог што го бараме низ кружните отвори на куполите

ON PASSWORDS, BY GIBRAN

Fill each other's cup,
but drink not from one cup.
Give one another of your bread,
but eat not from the same loaf.
Sing and dance together and be joyous,
but let each of you be alone,
even as the strings of a lute are alone
though they quiver with the same music.

KHALIL GIBRAN

In one article on the internet
I read that many couples know
each other's e-mail passwords
and that they give them to each other
as a token of trust and security.

Had I been wise as Gibran
and I'm not
I would've added:

"Send e-mails to each other
but do not give away your passwords
for the man and the earth feed off each other
and yet, they keep the secret of their beginnings; each to their own."

Translated by Elida Bahtijaroska and Gorjan Kostovski

ЗА ПАСВОРДОТ, ПО ЏИБРАН

Полнете си ја еден на друг чашата, но не пијте од иста чаша
Давајте си еден на друг леб но не јадете од истата погача
Пејте и играјте заедно и бидете радосни
но нека секој од вас биде и сам
како што жиците на лирата стојат одвоено
а сепак треперат со истата музика

Калил Џибран

Во една статија на интернет
прочитав дека многу љубовни парови

си ги знаат пасвордите на мејловите
дека си ги разменуваат меѓусебно како знак
на доверба и сигурност

Да бев мудрец како Џибран
а не сум
ќе додадев:
„И праќајте си еден на друг мејлови
но не делете го пасвордот
зашто и човекот и земјата се хранат едно од друго
а ја чуваат тајната за почетоците, секој својата“

BLESSED IS THAT WHICH WE CANNOT TOUCH

Blessed are the distances and the places to which we will never go
and the tight smooth nightgown drying on the balcony across from us
Blessed is death that remembers the addresses
of all our unsent letters
and the gods we try to but cannot reach
like the cobwebs in the corner between the bed and the wall
Blessed is the Moon served on the sky
like the dish of someone who always dines alone
and the Sun reminding us
one can love from afar
Blessed is the freedom and our illusion that we have touched it
like we touch life through screens and displays
Blessed is the past that sticks to us
like long-lasting lipstick on our mouths
and the future smeared with red stains
resistant even to the most advertised of detergents
Blessed are the seas which we will never swim across
because of the water landmarks and the theories of safety
Blessed is the soft hair of a girl
that nearly, very nearly touched me
in a bus crowd

Translated by Elida Bahtijaroska and Gorjan Kostovski

БЛАГОСЛОВЕНО Е ОНА ШТО НЕ МОЖЕМЕ ДА ГО ДОПРЕМЕ

Благословени се далечините и местата на кои никогаш нема да
отидеме
и тесната мазна ношница што се суши на балконот спроти нас
Благословена е смртта која ги памти адресите
на сите наши неиспратени писма
и боговите кои се напрегаме но не можеме да ги дофатиме
како пајажините во аголот меѓу креветот и ѕидот
Благословена е Месечината сервирана на небото
како чинија на некој кој постојано вечера сам
и Сонцето што нè потсетува дека
може да се љуби и од далеку
Благословена е слободата и нашата илузија дека сме ја допреле
како што го допираме животот преку екраните и мониторите
Благословено е минатото што ни се лепи
како долготраен кармин на устата
и иднината извалкана со црвени дамки
отпорни и на најрекламираните детергенти
Благословени се морињата што никогаш нема
да ги препливаме
заради граничниците за вода и теориите за безбедност
Благословена е меката коса на една девојка
што за малку, сосема за малку ќе ме допреше
во една автобуска гужва

LIZ BERRY (UK)

Liz Berry (1980) was born in the Black Country, UK. Her debut collection,
Black Country *(Chatto & Windus, 2014), won the Forward Prize for Best
First Collection, Somerset Maugham Award and Geoffrey Faber Memorial
Prize. The title poem from her pamphlet* The Republic of Motherhood
(Chatto, 2018) won the Forward Prize for Best Single Poem.

SOW

"Dainty footwear turns a young lady into an altogether more
beautiful creature…"

Etiquette for Ladies – ELIZA SELL

Trottering down the oss road in me new hooves
I'm farmyardy sweet, fresh from the filth
of straw an' swill, the trembly-leg sniff

of the slaughter wagon. A guzzler, gilt.
Trollopy an' canting. Root yer tongue beneath
me frock an' gulp the brute stench of the sty.

I've stopped denying meself: nibbling
grateful as a pet on baby-leaves, afeared
of the glutton of belly an' rump. I've sunk
an when lads howd out opples on soft city palms
I guttle an' spit, for I need a mon
wi' a body like a trough of tumbly slop
to bury me snout in.

All them saft years of hiding at 'ome
then prancing like a pony for some sod to bridle
an' shove down the pit, shying away
from 'is dirty fists. All them nights,
me eyes rolling white in the dark when the sow I am
was squailin an' biting to gerrout.

Now no mon dare scupper me,
nor fancy-arse bints, for I've kicked the fence
an' I'm riling on me back in the muck,
out of me mind wi' grunting pleasure,
trotters pointing to the heavens like chimdey pots,
sticking V to the cockerel
prissy an' crowing on 'is high church spire.

BLACK COUNTRY / STANDARD
oss road / street
gilt / sow
canting / cheeky or saucy
guttle / chew
mon / man
saft / foolish
squalin / squealing or crying
bints / derogatory slang for girls

BLACK COUNTRY

Commuters saw it first, vast
on the hillside by the A41,
a wingless Pegasus, hooves
kicking road into the distance.

It had appeared over night.
A black shadow on the scrub,
galloping above the gates
of the derelict factories,

facing East, towards the pits,
mouth parted as if it would
swallow the sun that rose
from behind the winding gear.

Word spread. Crowds gathered.
Kids, someone said,
but when they examined its flanks
they found pure coal,

coal where none had been mined
in years, where houses
still collapsed into empty shafts
and hills bore scars.

A gift from the underworld,
hauling the past
from the dead earth. Old men
knelt to breathe the smoke

of its mane, whisper
in its ear, walked away
in silence, fists clenched,
faces streaked with tears.

THE YEAR WE MARRIED BIRDS

That year, with men turning thirty
still refusing to fly the nest,
we married birds instead.

Migrating snow buntings
swept into offices in the city,
took flocks of girls for Highland weddings.

Magpies smashed jewellers' windows,
kites hovered above bridal shops,
a pigeon in Trafalgar Square learnt to kneel.

Sales of nesting boxes soared.
Soon cinemas were wild as woods in May
while restaurants served worms.

By June, a Russian kittiwake wed
the Minister's daughter, gave her two
freckled eggs, a mansion on a cliff.

My own groom was a kingfisher:
enigmatic, bright. He gleamed in a metallic
turquoise suit, taught me about fishing

in the murky canal. We honeymooned
near the Wash, the saltmarshes
booming with courting bittern.

When I think of that year, I remember best
the fanning of his feathers
on my cheek, his white throat,

how every building, every street rang
with birdsong. How girls' wedding dresses
lifted them into the trees like wings.

PETR BORKOVEC (Czech Republic)

Petr Borkovec (1970) has published a number of poetry collections including bilingual editions (Czech / German) of Feldarbeit *(2001),* Nadelbuch *(2004),* Fünfter November und andere Tage *(2006) and* Liebesgedichte *(2014), all translated by Christa Rothmeier. He has received a number of literary accolades including the Jirí Orten Prize for poetry, the Hermann Lenz award and the Norbert C. Kaser award. Borkovec also translates poetry and plays from Russian.*

WINTER IN THE CITY

This morning Troy is already Achlan.
The things that you might hear there on the streets!
The things that you might see there on the streets!
On the right the victors stand, the left the vanquished
like different pictures and various alarums.
The snow plays round with people like a god.
What is the first thing that you might describe?
Enumerate the objects carried from the house?
Liken them to what, as they blacken on the snow?
All night the struggle, and now there's only hunger.
So they eat – roasted meats which they share out
on precious fabrics, bolting those patterns, glint
and shine from the jaws of circling dogs.
And space arranges itself around their faces.
What remains here that doesn't fall to them?
The final constellation is like a yoke.
The final stars resemble rings.
I think that of the others none now stands.
They all have bent their knees to tend the dead,
and all around them, that lament and grief,
the folds of sheets and curtains drawn in windows,
the whispers smelt in wax, walls behind beds,
are not the victors': they belong to the dead.
How could you describe the faces that are crying?
No, every one is hidden in palms of hands.
Look well on this, for you cannot know if these
are living faces in the hands of the dead,

or faces of the dead in the palms of those that live.
And from the vineyards where I stand, I see
the town looped tightly by its battlements
and looped more lightly still by the river,
and so far no-one has ridden out with news.

Translated by Justin Quinn

ZIMA VE MESTE

Dnes ráno je už Trója achajská.
Co všechno slyšel bys tam v ulicích!
Co všechno videl bys tam v ulicích!
Vpravo jsou vítezové, vlevo poražení,
jak ruzné obrazy a ruznorodý krik!
Ten sníh si hraje s lidmi jako Buh.
Což bys ty první mohl nejak popsat?
Vycíslit predmety, co vynášejí z domu?
A k cemu prirovnat, jak cernají se na snehu?
Boj trval celou noc, a ted je treba jíst,
tak snídají – peceni z ohnu, které rozdelali
na drahých látkách, hltají ty vzory, trpyt
i opar z tlam svých psu, co motají se kolem.
A prostor se jim skládá kolem tvárí.
Je neco, co jim nejde na ruku?
Poslední souhvedí je jako sprežení.
Poslední hvezdy jsou jako prsteny.
Z tech druhých, myslím, nikdo nestojí,
všichni si klekli u svých mrtvých,
a všechno kolem nich, ten nárek, plác,
záhyby prosteradel a zatažená okna,
šepot, který je cítit voskem, a zdi za lužky,
nepatrí vítezum, protože patrí mrtvým.
Což mužeš nejak popsat tváre placících?
Jsou prece všechny skryty v dlaních!
Dobre se podívej, vždyt nevíš,
zda jsou to živé tváre v rukou tech, co odešli,
anebo tváre mrtvých v dlaních tech, co žijí.
A odsud z vinic, kde ted stojím, pozoruji,
jak mesto svírá tesná smycka hradeb,
a za ní smycka reky, trochu volnejší,
a dosud nikdo nevyjíždí se zprávou.

HONEYCOMB PLAYGROUND

Mouse, leaf, snake and bird –
out of the ring of their changes, what calls
(whispering, rustling, hissing)
has fashioned everything around. Rust
on wiring is swallowed by the sun each moment,
then clouds and noise knit it back again.
Buck-bushes, lean elders are lying round,
left to the light's great vultures long ago,
and even they seem to have drifted off.
A wayward bolt of lightning twists a bush.
The sky is white, slippery, grading into grain –
on the right, it rises with the slope,
on the left, it swoops carefully down over the streets,
an even blue, all roar and thunder.
The sparks and shadows in between the pear-trees
net my whole vision, as they would a beast,
a small way off, down where the balls roll to a stop.
In space and time, a tree divides the downpour
as metre does the low, muddy murmurs
above the swirls of slag that run and flow
over the hardened en tout cas, baked like tiles.
You cannot hold it in you, not for a moment,
this hissing, gradual rustle of a word, the thing
so bare your eyes are watching (or maybe only
drifting over) – just as you would
something which, say, shunts into the hand,
takes up the strange rhythm, and fires it into stone.
The sand is mixed with twists of ivy
and trilling wire. There's a pole on which
a branch of acacia is firmly fixed,
and into this there thrusts the grey-white line
of an unseen aeroplane. The rain went quiet, suddenly,
without cause – like an exact lethargic machine.
And from everywhere now the small glossy machines.

Translated by Justin Quinn

HRIŠTE ÚL

Myš, list, had a pták –
to z kruhu jejich promen, co se ozývá
šramocením a sykotem,
je tady kolem všechno udeláno. Rez
pletiva každou chvíli polkne nemé slunce,
a vzápetí ji mrak a zvuky znovu propletou.
Vysáté, rozvalené pámely a bezy
vítr už dávno n
echal supum svetla,
a zdá se, že i ti už odtáhli –
zbloudilý záblesk ohne celý ker.
Nebe je bílé, kluzké, vysypané drtí,
vpravo se zdvíhá spolu se svahem,
vlevo se opatrne spouští nad ctvrt v údolí
do rovnomerné modri hukotu a hrmení.
A zvíre zraku sebou škube v síti
z jisker a stínu mezi hrušnemi,
tam vzadu, nad hrbitovem mícu.
Strom delí liják v prostoru a case
tak jako metrum nezretelné mumlání
nad šerpou škváry, která pretíná
antukový kurt, ztvrdlý na kachle.
Neudržíš to v sobe ani vterinu;
už zasycení,šramot slova, proste to,
co jenom pozoruješ – možná mín:
precházíš ocima – tak jako vec,
která se treba sune k ruce, sebere
studený cizí takt a strcí do pece.
Na stožár v písku, promíchaném
s šlahouny brectanu a zasvištením lanka,
je napíchnutá vetev akátu,
do které vráží šedobílou lajnu
neviditelné letadlo. Déšt ztichl, naráz,
bez príciny – jak presný letargický stroj.
A odevšad ted malé lesklé stroje.

ALEN BRLEK (Croatia)

Alen Brlek (1988) won the Na vrh jezika award for his first poetry book,
Metakmorfoze *(2014). His second poetry book,* Pratišina, *was published
in Serbia in 2017. His third book,* Sang, *was published in 2019 in Croatia
and awarded the Kirin Award for best poetry book. His poems have been
translated into numerous languages, most recently in Marko Pogačar's
selection of Croatian poetry* The Edge of a Page.

A DIVE

We don't build lighthouses, we've got phones –
the firebug's urge compressed into signal.
I don't like the bell in any form because on the other end
someone's eyes always lose focus. Waiting is a journey
into astigmatism.
I'm teaching myself to be close to the water every time it dives,
reach out with my palms facing away from the sky because
I don't trust the laws of the market.
I'm teaching myself to enter as if for the last time,
plant a pillow, exit as if I'd never entered at all.
To put Neptune to sleep. Cut into the night in all the right places.
Not to scratch my back every time it itches, not to forget
the details. To put more
trust in the depth of the dive.

Translated by Mirza Purić

ZARON

Više ne gradimo svjetionike, imamo telefone.
Nagon za piromaniju zbijen u signal.
Ne volim zvono ni u kojem obliku jer s druge strane
nečije oči uvijek gube fokus. Čekanje je put
u astigmatizam.
Učim se biti blizu vode svaki put kada zaroni,
pružati ruke dlanovima okrenutim od neba jer
ne vjerujem zakonima tržišta
Učim se ulaziti kao da ulazim zadnji put,
posijati jastuk, izlaziti kao da nikada nisam ušao
Uspavati Neptuna. Zarezati noć na pravim mjestima.
Ne počešati leđa uvijek kada zasvrbi, ne zaboraviti
detalje. Biti.
Vjerovati dubini zarona.

BREADLY

Suddenly, everything we do is a prayer,
all that is between us
an altar and swimming reflex. Tart
earth conquers us,
supplies the body with softness for a breadly tomorrow.
Tomorrow, your metals will forget the war,
tomorrow, my tongues will learn the art of wound cleansing.
Tomorrow, our lips will be botany and fish.

Translated by Mirza Purić

KRUŠNO

Odjednom je sve što radimo molitva,
sve između nas
oltar i refleks plivanja. Reska nas
osvaja zemlja,
snabdijeva tijela mekoćom za krušno sutra.
Sutra, tvoji će metali zaboraviti rat,
sutra, moji će jezici usvojiti znanje ispiranja rana.
Sutra će nam usne biti botanika i ribe.

DESCRIBING THE EXTRAORDINARY

Light was hollow this morning.
On the kitchen table, motionlessly
an onion levitated, and I wanted to say

I missed the ring of your voice.

Alongside water, thoughts boiled into

sugar are not awake, fast,
one should fast.

Translated by Mirza Purić

OPISIVANJE IZVANREDNOG

Svjetlost je jutros bila šuplja,
na kuhinjskom je stolu nepomično
levitirao luk, i htio sam reći

nedostaje mi kolut tvoga glasa.

Usporedno s vodom misli su proključale u

šećer se nije probudio, postiti,
treba postiti.

DESCRIBING THE MUNDANE

For days I've been trying to describe parquet. Parquet is
unvanquishable, it agrees only to scratching
and it's always potentially full of water.
Parquet is an indescribably harrowing version of the East,
a cherriless space. A journey of palms and
feet into the pain of a lonely man.
I shall not agree to dying above parquet level,
just as I don't agree to trams, lifts,
clocks and hate.
Parquet is an indescribably permanent absence of oxygen
and her.

Translated by Mirza Purić

OPISIVANJE SVAKODNEVNOG

Danima pokušavam opisati parket. Parket je
nesavladiv, pristaje samo na grebanje
i uvijek je potencijalno pun vode.
Parket je neopisivo mučna verzija istoka,
prostor bez trešanja. Putanja dlanova i
stopala u bol usamljenog.
Neću pristati na smrt iznad parketa,
kao što ne pristajem na tramvaje, liftove,
satove i mržnju.
Parket je neopisivo trajni izostanak kisika
i nje.

HELWIG BRUNNER (Austria)

Helwig Brunner (1967, Istanbul) is a poetry editor and co-editor of the literary magazine Lichtungen. *He has published twelve books of poetry as well as novels, short stories and essays. His work has appeared in numerous literary magazines and anthologies in Europe and beyond. He is the recipient of several literary prizes and was nominated for the Lyrikpreis Meran and the Dresdner Lyrikpreis.*

BACKYARD. MINOR FOREST MEMORY

The impassable is the path, the door of
the shed is stuck in the trampled snow.
I walk along the edge, where brushwood, old grass
grip the feet. There is the wren, rattling calls,
so mouse-brown in ice. Wood below the arm,
warmth is already told, the last word of the trees.

Translated by Monika Zobel

HINTERHOF. KLEINE WALDERINNERUNG

Das Unwegsamste ist der Weg, die Tür des
Schuppens steckt im glatt getretnen Schnee.
Ich gehe außen entlang, wo Reisig, altes Gras
die Füße halten. Da ist der Zaunkönig, ratternde
Rufe, so mausbraun im Eis. Scheite unterm Arm,
ist schon Wärme erzählt, das letzte Wort der Bäume.

ECHOLOCATION. AERIAL SCRIPT

The bats, reflecting on their sounds,
inaudible, thus eavesdropping on a
silence, which is none; they drag the gaze
through the twilight sky, the zigzag of their
flutter flight, satin-fur nearly birds
that see with their ears: listen to images.
A little later they diminish, vanish
behind the black blinds of night,
satiated by the blind spots of the echo
and I think how little I sound out
with trite words.

Translated by Monika Zobel

ECHOLOCATION. AERIAL SCRIPT

Die Fledermäuse, an ihre Laute gedacht,
unhörbar, das Horchen also hinein in eine
Stille, die keine ist; sie ziehn den Blick
in den Dämmerhimmel, das Zickzack ihres
Flatterfluges, samtpelzige Beinahvögel,
die mit den Ohren schaun: Bilder hören.
Wenig später sind sie entzogen, entflogen
hinter die schwarze Jalousie der Nacht,
gesättigt an den Blindstellen des Echos,
und ich denke sehr banal, wie wenig ich
auslote mit Worten.

VISION PROBLEMS

With glasses on your face, you quickly forget
that the watercolour strokes on the hill across
were vanishing just a moment ago in the moist sky.

Now the trees are instantly returning
to their growth. You see their sharp outlines
punched into your corrected vision,

brighter already, the air above the crowns
brightens where a bare branch, pulsing
like an artery, outgrows itself.

Translated by Monika Zobel

SEHFEHLER

Mit der Brille vor den Augen hast du rasch vergessen,
dass die Tuschestriche auf dem Hügel dort
eben noch zerronnen waren im feuchten Himmel.

Denn augenblicklich kehren die Bäume jetzt zurück
in ihren Wuchs. Randscharf siehst du ihren Umriss
in deinen korrigierten Blick gestanzt,

heller schon, aufgehellt steht über den Kronen
die Luft, wo ein kahler Zweig wie eine Schlagader
pochend über sich selbst hinausragt.

MASSAGE

the flesh sits loose around the head,
you can shift it, back and forth,

you can feel the jaw-bone
below, the cheekbone,

verify the slack coherence
the fragile syntax of life and death

Translated by Monika Zobel

MASSAGE

das Fleisch sitzt locker am Kopf,
du kannst es verschieben, hin und her,

kannst darunter den Kiefer-
knochen, das Jochbein fühlen,

den losen Zusammenhalt prüfen,
die brüchige Syntax von Leben und Tod

GEERT BUELENS (Belgium)

Geert Buelens (1971) is a poet, translator, cultural historian and academic, teaching at Utrecht University and Stellenbosch University. He has published four volumes of poetry: the prize-winning Het is / It is *(2002);* Verzeker u' / Be Insured *(2005);* Thuis / Home *(2014); and* Ofwa *(2020). He has performed at several international poetry festivals, is included in Italiano's & Wagner's* Grand Tour *anthology (2019) and has translated poems of Walt Whitman and Peter Gizzi.*

DOGMA

1. Speak in sentences
that understand people

2. Cut your life right
up to the line

3. Knock again
on the open door

4. Make the audience
your art

5. Restore order
until it breaks

Translated by Karlien Van Den Beukel

DOGMA

1. Spreek in zinnen
die een mens verstaan

2. Versnijd je leven
tot op de draad

3. Klop nogmaals aan
bij de openstaande deur

4. Maak het publiek
tot je kunst

5. Herstel de orde
tot ze breekt

ZERO HOUR

get past this point
then see
all that's left is sound
all that's left has been ground to grit
a grey carpet
you toss out the plumb and lower
it into what was once shaft four
there's a rumbling there
a band is no longer playing for a dance
the hesitation seems permanent

adjusted to high tension
its continuation
perhaps some kind of end

Translated by David Colmer

UUR NUL

wie hier voorbij is
dan zie
al wat overblijft is ruis
al wat overblijft is gruis vermalen
tot een grijs tapijt
je gooit het puntlood uit en zakt
ermee tot in wat eens schacht vier was
daar rommelt het
niet langer speelt een showorkest ten dans
de hapering lijkt permanent
op hoogspanning gesteld
dat dit blijft duren
zou dat een soort van einde zijn

CARMEN CAMACHO (Spain)

Carmen Camacho (1976), is a poet and aphorist, literary critic and creative writing teacher. She has published eight poetry collections and a personal anthology of her own poetic work, Las versiones de Eva *(2014). Her most recent poetry collection is* Deslengua *(2020). In 2011, she was awarded the* Premio Iberoamericano Fernando Quiñones. *Her work has been translated into numerous languages.*

TO DIE STANDING UP

We mannequins
abducted beings from an instant of life
look tired
sad
tense
bored
of cutting edge clothes
of pretending –

of making the gesture of those who have been
through it all
of dying of our own things
of concealing it
and continuing on our feet
in the never-ending
Sunday afternoons

Translated by Jacinto Pariente

MORIR DE PIE

A las maniquíes
seres raptados de un instante de vida
se nos nota cansadas
tristes
tensas
aburridas
de vestir a la última
de hacer como si –
de poner la mueca de estar
de vuelta
de morir de lo nuestro
disimularlo
y seguir en pie
en las interminables tardes
de los domingos

FINE PRINT

Some damages are not covered
by the combined home insurance, I know.
Missing calls, for example.
broken letters, the rope of silk,
the night that lies behind mirrors,
this plague of glass in my chest.
The ablation of my thirst.

That is the way I contracted the soap-bar disease.

That is why I loved him with abject horror.
Against a life on tenterhooks

I became a hole in his hole, cold in the glovebox,
still matter.
I let the walls of this house grow
with me inside.

Centuries, clock centuries, went by.

I will not elaborate further, madam.
I will only say that I tore the door up,
that I was merciful enough
as to throw the icing sugar
to the mud,
that now light enters my pantry.
The policy does not provide coverage for
love to third parties, solar storm,
street riot or ant mutiny, I know.

But this is a case of finesse majeure.

And I only called to tell you, dear madam,
that I have just granted myself
the fully comprehensive incertitude
of a wide-open life.

Translated by Jacinto Pariente with Richie McCaffery and Stefanie Van de Peer

LETRA PEQUEÑA

Hay daños que no cubre el seguro
combinado del hogar, lo sé.
Las llamadas perdidas, por ejemplo,
las cartas rotas, la soga de seda,
la noche que hay detrás de los espejos,
esta plaga de cristales en el pecho.
La ablación de mi sed.

Así contraje la enfermedad de los jabones.

Por eso le quise, con todo el hastío.
Contra la vida en vilo
fui hueco en su hueco, frío en la guantera,
materia inmóvil.
Dejé crecer las paredes de esta casa
conmigo dentro.

Pasaron siglos, siglos de reloj.

No abundaré en detalles, señorita.
Sólo diré que he arrancado la puerta de cuajo,
que he tenido la misericordia
de tirar al barro
el azúcar glasé,
que ahora me entra luz en la despensa.
Ya sé, tampoco contempla la póliza
el amor a terceros, el temporal de sol,
el tumulto en las calles ni el motín de la hormiga.

Pero este es un caso de delicadeza mayor.

Y yo sólo llamaba para decirle, amiga,
que me acabo de conceder
a todo riesgo
la incertidumbre de vivir
abierta de par en par.

ON FLIGHT (Bird Poetry)

I keep a metaphor in my fist. A warm body breathing in my hand:

1. The flying fish wants to live in the crack between the sky and the sea.

2. The finch alights on top of silence.

3. To touch a trace of the blind, vegetable butterfly.

4. Because I know the name of the bird, I see it.

5. To rip out the sharp eye out of an eagle will not cure your
                                        shortsightedness.

6. Some days the amputee bird has a flightache.

7. A raven barked and my wisdom teeth came out.

8. The canary dreams of his keeper wins the muteness award.

9. I whisper obscenities at the parrot so as not to sleep so alone.

10. Last spring the blackbird paid a visit. It was black but it was bird.

11. Clarity-chirping birds. Birds that would steal themselves
    from the tree on the square at sunset. Birds that
            can only sing at night.

12. The serin picks at a moonlight beam moving about the branches
            Moves its head like mad, laughs to itself. Sings.

13. The minute wave of water that the wasp sipped.

14. The song, I mean, the flight.

15. A non-flying bird
keeps his luck.

Translated Jacinto Pariente with Richie McCaffery and Stefanie Van de Peer

AL VUELO (Poesía pájaro)

Guardo una metáfora en el puño. Es un cuerpo caliente que
                        respira en mi mano:

1. El pez volador quiere vivir en la grieta que hay entre el cielo
                        y el mar.

2. El jilguero se posa en el silencio.

3. Palpar el rastro de una mariposa vegetal y ciega.

4. Porque sé el nombre del pájaro, lo veo.

5. Arrancar al águila el ojo avizor no remedia la miopía.

6. Algunas mañanas, al pájaro de las alas amputadas le duele el vuelo

7. Ladró un cuervo y me salieron las muelas del juicio.

8. Sueña el canario que su criador gana un certamen de mudos.

9. Susurro al loro palabras obscenas para no dormirme tan sola.

10 La primavera pasada vino a verme el mirlo. Era negro.
                        Pero era mirlo.

11. Pájaros que le pían a la claridad. Pájaros que se arrancarían del árbol de la
    plaza a la hora del crepúsculo. Pájaros que sólo saben cantar en la noche.

12. Pica el chamarín un haz de luz que se mueve entre las ramas. Mueve como loco la cabeza, se ríe para dentro. Trina.

13. La onda mínima del agua que libó la avispa.

14. El canto, quiero decir, el vuelo.

15. Pájaro que no vuela
guarda agüero.

VAHNI CAPILDEO (Trinidad and Tobago / UK)

Vahni Capildeo (1973, Trinidad) is a Seamus Heaney Centre Fellow at Queen's University Belfast (2019-20) and Writer in Residence at the University of York. Each of their seven books and several pamphlets explores a new poetic approach, from the autobiography in everyone else's voice of No Traveller Returns *(Salt, 2003) to the calligrams of* Simple Complex Shapes *(Shearsman, 2015) and immersive theatre of* Skin Can Hold *(Carcanet, 2019).* Odyssey Calling *(Sad Press, 2020) touches on the Odyssey, the Windrush, Buile Suibhne, and coffee.*

IN A DREAM

In what dream did I begin with you?
In what dream did I belong with you?
Every grey is edged with yellow,
this spit of narrow land is thrown
open between law and access,
the savage deliveries of sea.

One day I'll sleep   and that will be for a long time
and while I'm in a dream   all will have dream status
and while all's scheduled for dream   it will not matter
on the day of the longest dream   that you are part
in the dreaming   picking up where earlier glimpses
slipped painful perfections into which feet of sleep
walked   and as they walked   meadows began outspreading
slides of sleepscape   fourdimensional eyes of sleep
saw   and as they saw   you were there   more than spirit
easy   enduring   choosing our bodies' company
all the while you sang a trivial lyrical song
rhyming treasure   leisure   pausing to kiss and breathe

breathing being less required
Spirited away
I'll recall this sleep: reality. Like no dream
the years' complicated origami of hurt
in a dream   falling away   a puckered swan's fell
once blistered the maiden's skin inside   since   reely
tender to know   not to be urged to take   the air
dreaming   the false detachment of mornings cracked through
in its paper-lipped crudity of graph and talon   vivid line
grasping for its own excesses
One day of sleep the longest sleep and in a dream
so much will be suddenly unnecessary
shoes   when we're entering an ocean   obvious
for what has been obvious   our long-unseen dream

UTTER

First I tried to hide it from itself.
Then I tried to hide it from myself.
I tried quite hard to hide it from you,
even when we knew that was no use.
After all this hiding, no surprise
it's like a thing in translation:
eggshell-shy. A thumb's worth of glory,
nesting near the coastlines of your palm.

GOING NOWHERE, GETTING SOMEWHERE

How was it that till questioned, till displaced in the attempt to answer, I had scarcely thought of myself as having a country, or indeed as having left a country? The answer lies peripherally in looming, in hinterland; primarily in the tongueless, palpitating interiority. Trinidad was. Trinidad is. In the same way, some confident speakers do not think of themselves as having an accent. They will say so: "I don't have an accent! You have an accent!" In those accentless voices compass points spin, ochre and ultramarine flagella fling themselves identifiably towards this that or the other region. It is a motile version of that luxury, solidity, non-reflectivity that is the assumption of patria. So different is the expat from the refugee, who has her country on her back, or the migrant, who has countries at his back.

What would I have called home, before I began creating home? Before I had to learn to ravel up longitude, latitude, population, oil rigs, mobile phone masts, prayer flags, legality of fireworks, likely use of firearms, density and disappearance of forests, scarlet ibis, other stripes of scarlet, into a by-listeners-unvisited, communicable, substantial image of 'Trinidad'?

Language is my home. It is alive other than in speech. It is beyond a thing to be carried with me. It is ineluctable, variegated and muscular. A flicker and drag emanates from the idea of it. Language seems capable of girding the oceanic earth, like the world-serpent of Norse legend. It is as if language places a shaping pressure upon our territories of habitation and voyage; thrashing, independent, threatening to rive our known world apart.

Yet thought is not bounded by language. At least, my experience of thinking does not appear so bound.

One day I lost the words wall and floor. There seemed no reason to conceive of a division. The skirting-board suddenly reduced itself to a nervous gentrification, a cover-up of some kind; nothing especially marked. The room was an inward-focused container. 'Wall', 'floor', even 'ceiling', 'doorway', 'shutters' started to flow smoothly, like a red ribbed tank top over a heaving ribcage. Room grew into quarter. Room became segment. Line yearned till it popped into curve. The imperfections of what had been built or installed: the ragged windowframe or peeling tile: had no power to reclaim human attention to 'floor' or 'wall' as such. Objects were tethered like astronauts and a timid fringe of disarrayed atmosphere was the immediate past that human activity kept restyling into present. The interiority of the room was in continuous flow. Wall, floor became usable words again in a sort of silence.

I had the sense to shut up about the languageless perception. Procedure for living.

Language is my home, I say; not one particular language.

ELENI CAY (Slovakia)

Eleni Cay is a Slovakian-born poet living in England and Norway. Her award-winning collection of Slovak poems, A Butterfly's Trembling in the Digital Age, *was translated into English by John Minahane and published in the UK in 2017. Her English-language poems have appeared in many poetry journals and poems have also been published in French, Romanian and Filipino. Her filmpoems, dancepoems and innovative poetic combinations have been screened at international festivals.*

ORANGES ARE THE ONLY FRUIT

My grandfather unwrapped his first orange when he was nine.
He didn't wash his hands till Three Kings' Day,
the sweet essence lingering on his calluses.
He used to say grandma's hugs were like oranges in winter.

My parents plundered a few when they were young.
The bold sweetness of Valencias ignited a land
of opportunity inside their mouths. They gobbled the
flesh together with the skin, blinded by the flushed sun.

Mr McPhee bought as many as the words he wrote for *The New Yorker.*
Unsure whether to cut them into nine like planets or into quarters
like lunch for the businessmen. They tasted of a pre-dawn running,
pesticide-rich, fruitless manufactured concentrate to him.

I have experienced many. Too many for one person to carry.
I calorie-checked, Instagrammed, changed them beyond recognition.
With yellow nails you carved out the seeds, now the oranges are mine,
you said. *No one can put fruit back together once it is cut in half.*

Written in English

SOLDIERS' GRAVES

Inside the innocent poppy heads
there are billions of small black bullets.

Their unrequited kisses
leave empty spaces in-between the wild rye.

It doesn't matter how many you hurt in the combat.
The fleeting sunset does it every evening to the sky.

What unites us is the red blood,
setting out from the heart.

Written in English

WELCOME, DIGITAL!

A few years ago thoughts spoke
with pen and paper.
Now a small box can be their medium.
No need for tickets, dressing, scheduling:
from stage to auditorium,
when and wherever endlessly,
thoughts wing.

The digital holds everything, all sorts.
Chance meetings, lies, creeds, travellers' reports.

Maybe it's fine
that your message bleeps in the quiet of a wood.
One curses and the other thinks it good.
One photographs, the other writes some pages.
For their feelings people
always seek refuges.

So welcome, digital!
My fantasy's new well and source.
As if it went on water,
level, smooth,
an aircraft runs its course.
I welcome it and then,
dazzled by the hopes,
lose myself therein.

Translated by John Minahane

VITAJ DIGITÁLNO!

Pred pár rokmi ceruzkami a papierikmi
rozprávali sa myšlienky.
Dnes stačí im malá krabička.
Netreba lístky, róby, určiť hodinu.
Z nekonečného javiska do nekonečného hľadiska
kedykoľvek, kdekoľvek
myšlienky si lietajú.

A všetko, všetko do digitálneho sa zmestí.
Náhodné stretnutia, klamstvá, vyznania, cestovateľské zvesti.

Možno je to fajn,
že zapípa ti v tichom lese správa.
Jedného poteší, druhý nadáva.
Jeden odfotí, druhý napíše.
Vždy hľadalo ľudstvo
pre pocity skrýše.

Tak vitaj, digitálno!
Fantázie mojej nové žriedlo.
Ako po vodnej hladine,
rovnej a vyhladenej
rozbieha sa lietadlo.
Vítam ho s úsmevom,
omámená nádejou,
strácam sa v ňom.

KAYO CHINGONYI (UK)

Kayo Chingonyi (1987) is Assistant Professor in the Department of English Studies at Durham University. He is working on a PhD project exploring the influence of musical sampling on Black Atlantic poetry at Birkbeck, University of London. His debut collection, Kumukanda *(Chatto & Windus, 2017) won the 2018 International Dylan Thomas Prize and a Somerset Maugham Award.* A Blood Condition, *a new collection of poems, will be published in 2021 by Chatto & Windus.*

GRIEF

What became of the boy who called himself Grief?
The boy who, the story ran, harboured a gun
through the back-roads and alleyways of his teens
the boy who turned up as a footnote the night
we played *my ends are rougher than your ends*
in a flat overlooking London Road – frontline
of a post-code war from which we were
so far removed we chuckled when someone said
kebabs from the shop that wore a fresh batch
of memorial flowers were 'to die for'.
Grief was grit to lend the fable texture.
We never knew the name his mum called him
or what reduced him to plying the night trade
so white kids could say they *bun high grade*.
He is like those boys caught between commas
in news reports about youth crime, an image
fixed in place by someone else's language.

FOR THOSE ORPHANED LATE IN LIFE

What if the wind blowing through
the french doors of your childhood
is the house's way of saying goodbye
and when you call out, answering
yourself, greeting the gone out of habit
you hear, for the first time, the timbre
of your voice how someone else might?

ALTERNATE TAKE

When they laid our father out, mwaice wandi,
I want to say, I'm meant to say, soft light
played the skin of his spent face and the sobs
were, of course, a jangling kind of song.

If I could take you where the sandy earth
meets his final stone, tiled and off-white,
we might have learned to worship better gods.
He was known, in the shebeens, as *long John*.

At the wake relatives tried variations
on the words of the day: *I am sorry
for your grieving / your trouble / your loss.*
I've been weighing these apologies for years

that pass and retreat like disused stations.
I think of his walk becoming your quarry,
his knack for beguiling women, your cross.
It's enough to bring me here, past tears

to where his face simplifies to a picture:
the shrine in Nagoya, him stood, Sequoia
among lesser trees, looking good in denim;
every inch the charismatic spectre.

In his memory my voice bears his tincture –
saxophone played low slash boy raised on soya
porridge, chloroquine, a promise of heaven.
There are days I think I'm only a spectre

carrying him slowly to my own graveyard
and, standing at the lectern, rather than my son,
will be another copy: the same sharp
edge to the chin, that *basso profundo* hum.

Kid brother, we breathers have made an art
of negation, see how a buckled drum

is made from a man's beating heart
and a fixed gaze is a loaded weapon.

BROOMHALL

In light of what my aunt calls
the Arabic texture of my hair,
I'm Abdi outside the only shop
selling tamarind balls, Irish Moss,
Supermalt in decent quantities.

It is not enough to say I miss
the smell of cassava roasted
over open coals, expeditions
in want of Tilapia, Capenta,
assorted meats of questionable

provenance. *How much, auntie?*
Barter and bluff and rough hands
of stallholders glazed to a deep
blue shameless blackness that is
consigned, now, to another life

before this one of middle class
white boys in reggae bands, who
love roots and culture as if their
love is enough to know the code
that some of us live and die by.

At least these boys who call me
Abdi seem to be fond of Abdi.
They ask why I don't come
round no more, what it's like
in Leeds and maybe, today,
I can be Abdi and this shop
can be all the home I need.

ZEHRA ÇIRAK (Germany)

Zehra Çirak (1960, Istanbul) has published three poetry collections, two volumes of poetry and prose, and a book of short stories. She is the co-author of the bilingual volume, Die Kunst der Wissenschaft / The Art of Science, *published by Hans Schiler Verlag in 2017. Çirak has received multiple awards for her work including the Adelbert von Chamisso Award (2001) and the Amistade Multietnica Poeta Anima Istranza, Olbia (2005). Çirak often works with text accompanying sculptures by her late husband, visual artist Jürgen Walter.*

CLASSIC ATTEMPT

He hesitates he halts he hurries
belches and squelches
abandons himself to the skies
down below fingers spread by someone
earth tree roof
and hollow hand o'er the ground
he ponders yet a while
his best chances
above him the heavens expectant
below something else awaits
him with high hopes
No he can't ever do it
that can't work
not from this height
forcing Fortuna's arms
he stretches the tips of his lungs
sucks his eyes inward
and looks up once more.

Translated by Marilya Veteto Reese

KLASSISCHER VERSUCH

Er zagt er zögert er zeiteiligt sich
stößt auf und stößt ab
er übergibt sich den Lüften
da unten spreizt die Finger wer
Erde Baum Dach
und hohle Hand überm Boden
Er überlegt noch ein Weile
seine besten Chancen
über ihm Himmel erwartungsvoll

unten erwartet etwas anderes
ihn in bester Hoffnung
Nein das schafft er nie
das kann nicht gelingen
von dieser Höhe aus herab
Fortunas Arme zu bezwingen
er weitet seine Lungenspitzen
saugt die Augen nach innen
und schaut noch einmal nach oben

STRANGE WINGS ON ONE'S SHOULDERS

You are righthanded I am lefthanded
as if by nature then we dream of flying
you have a wing on your left shoulder
and naturally I have one on my right
so in beating our wings we would wish
shoulder grown closely to shoulder
for lift-off.

On solid ground
we have agreed here for a long time
but woe betide there in the skies we could
be torn to bits
and so dependably we hold each other's hand
my left hand in your right
and spend the evening mutually
scratching our itching shoulder blades.

Translated by Patricia Crampton

FREMDE FLÜGEL AUF EIGENER SCHULTER

Du bist Rechtshänder ich bin Linkshändin
wie selbstverständlich träumen wir vom Fliegen
du hast einen Flügel auf deiner linken Schulter
und ich natürlich einen auf meiner rechten
so beim gemeinsamen Schwingen wünschen wir
Schulter an Schulter verwachsen
abzuheben

Auf festem Boden
hier sind wir schon lange uns einig

aber wehe in den Lüften dort könnten wir
uns zerreißen
also halten wir verlässlich die Hände
meine linke in deiner rechten
und kratzen uns allabendlich
gegenseitig die juckenden Schulterblätter

VALENTINA COLONNA (Italy)

Valentina Colonna (1990) is a poet, composer and pianist. She has published three poetry collections, Dimenticato suono *(2010),* La cadenza sospesa *(2015) and* Stanze di città e altri viaggi *(2019) and her poetry has been translated and published in many countries. She is studying for her Ph.D. in Digital Humanities (Linguistics) at the Universities of Turin and Genoa. As a musician, she specialised in the Baroque repertoire at the ESMUC, Barcelona and is currently working at her PianoPoetry project, based on her original compositions.*

TURIN'S AVENUES

Turin's avenues
beginning of February when
the sun is warm, and yet,
plants cry.

Here in Sabotino Square
the number fifteen orange tram is covered
by the dust of workers' time,
of the old Lancia plant you know
it is a forsaken life
– with broken pink-blue glasses
that I stopped to console.

We return to the village, where
up the stairs, childhood reminds us
of the yellow smoke in the house, the tape
records sneaking through the door
to a bedroom to jump on a bed
on bed frames in front of the mirror

in that wardrobe full of
mothballs.

I spend every Monday suspending
my mind on tram cables and with every noise
I feel that your eyes
are looking down at the ground.
For years this tram has been connecting
the neighbourhoods of our passages.
It got stuck at each stop
along the way on wet tracks
and yet it endures despite snow:
its clanking
has always held us, exhaustedly
together.

Translated by Paweł Sakowski

I VIALI DI TORINO

I viali di Torino
i primi di febbraio quando
il sole è caldo eppure
le piante piangono.

Qui in piazza Sabotino
il quindici arancio ha
la polvere dei tempi operai,
della vecchia Lancia che sai
è una vita abbandonata
– coi vetri rosa-azzurri rotti
che mi fermavo a consolare.

Si torna nel borgo dove
l'infanzia ricorda su per le scale
la casa gialla di fumo, la bobina
registrare le fughe per la porta
verso camera da letto a saltare
sulle doghe davanti allo specchio
di quel mobile pieno
di naftalina.

Passare ogni lunedì è fermare
la mente sui fili e a ogni rumore

sentire chini i tuoi occhi
piegarsi per terra.
Questo tram ricuce da anni
i quartieri dei nostri passaggi.
Nel viaggio sui condotti bagnati
a ogni fermata incaglia
e pure nella neve prosegue:
è questo sferragliare
che da sempre ci tiene, sfiniti
insieme.

TONIGHT BARCELONA IS A SLEEPY TOWN

Tonight Barcelona is a sleepy town.
Hands are more naked
than cold and their smell reminds us
of embers but the windows
fill the streets of March.
A dog's shadow rises in silence
next to you driving,
while you can still hear the sea
from the back of some kitchen.

Tonight, like last night,
Barcelona is like stretched pincers
rummaging through garbage bins
to fill a cart.
It is the time of worn-out tools
stolen from nowhere and from nobody.
The empty can clangs against
the wheels of beds. Like stretchers
they travel to save sleep.

Translated by Paweł Sakowski

STASERA BARCELLONA È PAESI ASSONNATI

Stasera Barcellona è paesi assonnati.
Le mani sono più nude
che fredde e l'odore ricorda
di brace ma le finestre
riempiono le strade di marzo.

Sale l'ombra in silenzio
del cane a fianco a guidare,
mentre a tratti senti ancora il mare
di qualche cucina sul retro.

Stasera, come ieri,
Barcellona è tenaglie allungate
che frugano cassonetti
a riempire il carrello.
È l'ora dei ferri usurati
rubati allo spazio di nessuno.
La lattina vuota batte
alle ruote dei letti. Come barelle
viaggiano a salvare il sonno.

IN THESE YEARS I WAS BORN MANY TIMES

In these years I was born many times.

At least three silhouettes have cast
their colours on each other
which are no longer primary and are fading.

The first me is told about to the others:
I banged my head against the bars of my bed.
Whoever passed by along the years came out of the glass
to mix with the clouds.

The second me did cry
without that strength of a child.
Even then, I listened to Debussy
and my roof had
new edges of reason.

I have recently celebrated my third birth.
I registered late at the registry office
and I found out that being born
can only mean finding.

I will stop thinking that only the sum of them
is important but, if you really want

to count, don't get it wrong:
the sum subtracts.
                        I like neither clatter
nor ceremonial emptiness.

Who knows exactly when
I will again go to collect
leaves from the ground,
but this is certain: my leaves, I tied them well.

Translated by Paweł Sakowski

IN QUESTI ANNI SONO NATA PIÙ VOLTE

In questi anni sono nata più volte.

Almeno tre sagome hanno posto
l'una sull'altra a sommare i colori
che più non sono primari ma sfumano.

La prima la raccontano gli altri:
sbattevo la testa alle sbarre del letto.
Chi passava negli anni usciva dal vetro
a mischiare alle nuvole.

La seconda piangevo
senza ormai la forza bambina.
Anche allora ascoltavo Debussy
e il mio tetto aveva gli spigoli
nuovi della ragione.

Ho festeggiato di recente la mia terza nata.
L'ho registrata tardi all'anagrafe
e ho scoperto che nascere
può dire solo trovare.

Lascio pensare che sia importante
solo il totale ma, se si vuol proprio
contare, non si cada in errore:
la somma sottrae.
                        Non amo il chiasso
né il vuoto cerimonioso.

Chissà di preciso le volte
che ancora andrò a cogliere
foglie per terra,
ma è certo: le mie, le ho legate bene.

MOYA DE FEYTER (Belgium)

Moya De Feyter (1993) writes poetry, theatre scripts and prose. Her debut collection Tot iemand eindelijk / Until Someone Finally *(2018) was nominated for the Poëziedebuutprijs aan Zee and received an honourable mention in the C. Buddingh Prize. In 2019, she published her second book,* Massastrandingen / Mass Strandings, *a mixture of poetry, prose and dialogue. Recently, she founded Klimaatdichters, a community of Dutch and Flemish poets who want to raise their voice for the climate, inspired by Poets for the Planet.*

'ON CLOSER INSPECTION...'

on closer inspection we are not so easily singled out
in a library you can sit for a long time
on the ground between two stacks of books
waiting
without anyone choosing you
it can help to carry a heavy suitcase through town
it is clear then who you are
that is, someone carrying a heavy suitcase through town,
and what you possess

that is, a heavy suitcase
you are going somewhere, you have an intention
you are trying something out
that is, carrying the heavy suitcase from one place to another
that's quite clear to everyone

since you left, my room has grown exponentially
it now takes about forty minutes
to get from the door to the bed

we wake up in a body we did not choose ourselves
no, not everything is perfectible
no, people are not perfectible
sometimes heart valves open and don't close again

Translated by Paul Vincent

'BIJ NADER INZIEN...'

bij nader inzien zijn we toch niet zo aanraakbaar
in een bibliotheek kun je heel lang
op de grond tussen twee kasten vol boeken
zitten wachten

zonder dat iemand je kiest
het kan helpen om met een zware koffer door de stad te lopen
het is dan duidelijk wie je bent
namelijk iemand die met een zware koffer door de stad loopt
en wat je bezit
namelijk een zware koffer
je gaat ergens naartoe, je hebt een bedoeling
je bent iets aan het proberen
namelijk de zware koffer van de ene naar de andere plaats
brengen
dat is voor iedereen heel erg duidelijk

sinds jouw vertrek groeit mijn kamer exponentieel
het duurt nu ongeveer veertig minuten
om van de deur naar het bed te lopen

we worden wakker in een lichaam dat we niet zelf gekozen
hebben
nee, niet alles is maakbaar
nee, mensen zijn niet maakbaar
soms gaan hartkleppen open en niet opnieuw dicht

MOON-SHAPED SCARS

we know little about ourselves, for instance how we
would behave with a weapon lodged in our armpit
and an enemy charging towards us

obviously we need worldwide fancy-dress parties
to be able finally to leave our masks at home
tomorrow will be pale
tomorrow will be pale and angry

and still grazing horses
will stand unsuspecting in a meadow

(and whoever dies, everyone knows
that one day we'll have breakfast cereal
again)

Translated by Paul Vincent

MAANVORMIGE LITTEKENS

we weten weinig over onszelf, bijvoorbeeld hoe we
ons zouden gedragen met een wapen onder de oksel
en een vijand die komt aangestormd

blijkbaar hebben we wereldwijde verkleedfeestjes nodig
om onze maskers eindelijk thuis te kunnen laten

morgen zal bleek zijn
morgen zal bleek en boos zijn
en nog zullen er grazende paarden
nietsvermoedend in een weide staan

(wie er ook doodgaat, iedereen weet
dat we op een dag opnieuw
ontbijtgranen zullen eten)

PERHAPS THE REAL PEOPLE ARE ELSEWHERE

there are faces you can't simply
look at, conversations more urgent than wars
contraflows, we must go into the mountains

at the edge of the day the snow is melting
there are coal-black evenings, friends with no intention
of returning, it can only be a misinterpretation

of natural forces, these murky
bodies and nevertheless every day
new cells that awaken

a boy with flannel knees
longs keenly for a shadow coat

Translated by Paul Vincent

MISSCHIEN ZIJN DE ECHTE MENSEN ELDERS

er bestaan gezichten waarnaar je niet zomaar
kunt kijken, gesprekken dringender dan oorlogen
dwarsstromen, we moeten de bergen in

aan de rand van de dag is de sneeuw aan het smelten

er bestaan koolzwarte avonden, vrienden zonder voornemen
terug te keren, het kan toch alleen maar een verkeerd
begrip van natuurkrachten zijn, deze troebele
lichamen en desalniettemin elke dag weer
nieuwe cellen die wakker worden

een jongen met flanellen knieën
verlangt hevig naar een schaduwjas

MICHEL DELVILLE (Belgium)

Michel Delville (1969) is a poet, musician and essayist and teaches at the University of Liège. His books of poetry include Le troisième corps *(2005) / Third Body (English edition 2009),* Anything & Everything *(2016) and* Ali e t o lo ss *(w. Elisabeth Waltregny). Delville creates mixed-media projects featuring poetry with music, visuals and electronics and has received a number of awards and distinctions for his work. www.micheldelville.com*

ANDY WARHOL (I)

Why did he preserve his faith after so many years spent celebrating the canning of foodstuffs? The eye of the child scrutinizing the stained glass windows of the Church of Saint Jean Chrysostome already aspires to consolation, less to take refuge in them than to vanish completely, cancelling itself for a short while in the softness of the traits and the bright colours of the Byzantine frescoes. A few minutes later, the inferior senses take over. Bracing his flesh, muscles and nerves, he begins to stroll around the room, smells and gropes his way along the walls and columns, looking for a form of knowledge which would help him bear the pangs of consciousness. When fear gets the upper hand, he shrinks away from the most subtle dilemmas, the purity of torment, the blurring of the threshold between being and acting, depending on his current state of mental agitation. Later he will feed exclusively on his own breath, his own gaze, his own need to immerse himself in the world of images and reproduce them endlessly in order to enjoy them again and again. This game is so limpid that one sees oneself through it.

Translated by the poet

ANDY WARHOL (I)

Pourquoi avoir conservé la foi après avoir célébré la mise en boîte de l'aliment ? L'œil de l'enfant qui scrute les vitraux de l'Eglise de Saint Jean Chrysostome aspire déjà à la consolation, moins pour s'y réfugier que pour s'y évanouir complètement, s'annulant momentanément dans la douceur des traits et les couleurs vives des fresques byzantines. Quelques minutes plus tard, les sens inférieurs reprennent le dessus. Chair, muscles et nerfs tendus, il déambule, renifle, tâte, pourlèche les colonnes et les murs peints à la recherche d'une forme de connaissance du monde qui est à l'opposé du fardeau de la conscience. Quand la crainte domine, il se met à l'abri des dilemmes les plus subtils, des tourments les plus purs et des divisions les plus profondes de l'être et de l'acte, selon l'état d'agitation du moment. Par la suite, il vivra exclusivement de son souffle, de son regard, de son désir physique de jouir de l'image et de la reproduire sans fin pour en jouir encore et encore. C'est un jeu si limpide qu'on n'y trouve que soi.

F. T. MARINETTI

Vegetarian cubist square. A first splash followed by nationalist coquetries. The preciosity of anti-matter. Abolition of weight and volume. Mannerisms of tactilism and polymorphous orality. Raw meat brayed by trumpet blasts. A taste for metal that kills and pretends to awaken life's purpose. The terrorism of abjection.

Working their way towards a continuous display and a progressive synthesis of the dawning senses. Mixing conflicting flavours and colours, whipping the nerves to action, flattening forms, and whisking away the qualms of labour. Plenitude of covetousness, insatiable leagues of combat, preservative food additives in state of agitated merriment, extension of the realm of fight promotion, contingents sagging with fear. The antidote is to be found in the lower walls of the stomach, painted as they are with blazing savours. Gobbling up the whole world, with its milled rice stocks, its panettone, and its stuffed Milanese hams. Bring to a boil, then regurgitate in multicoloured sparks. Words in freedom, exploded body parts à la mode d'Adrianopolis. Fates dismissed by the world's only hygiene and the tyranny of innovation.

Translated by the poet

F. T. MARINETTI

Carré cubiste végétarien. Une première éclaboussure suivie de coquetteries nationalistes. Préciosités de l'anti-matière. Abolition des volumes et du poids. Maniérismes du tactilisme et de l'oralité polymorphe. Viande crue déchirée par des explosions de trompettes. Le goût du métal qui sème la mort sous prétexte de ranimer la vie. Terrorisme de l'abjection. Développement continu et synthèse progressive des sens en éveil. Mél ange des goûts et des couleurs qui se disputent et se confondent, fouettent les nerfs, secouent les viscères, allument les instincts, aplatissent les formes, et éloignent durablement du travail et de la douleur. Plénitude de la convoitise, insatiables fais ceaux de combat, agents conservateurs en état d'hilarité avancé, glissement du domaine de la lutte, affaissement des troupes dans le stupre et l'épouvante. En guise d'antidote, peindre les parois intérieures de l'estomac de saveurs fulgurantes. Engloutir le monde entier, avec ses réserves de riz, de panettone et de jambons farcis à la milanaise. Ensuite, les régurgiter en gerbes multicolores. Mots en liberté, membres éclatés saignants à la mode d'Adrianopolis. Destins congédiés par l'hygiène du monde et la tyrannie de l'innovation.

TO ABOLISH DEATH

We die from habit, finding refuge in leisure, in the style and passion of gigantic illuminated letters randomly drifting through our brains. Their message is simple, transparent. Meanwhile, we consent to the illusion that the living world, itself, becomes simply the effect of reduced vision. In the total clarity of those suburban insomniacs, we speak the same language. A language that must never relieve us from the need to feel close to each other and from expounding on the unlikely and painful privilege of being driven by an inner life.

Invoking Joyce, Loyola, Sade, Broodthaers, Duchamp, Ponge, Warhol and other fetishist saints, not to speak of all those major petit-bourgeois writers who console us by demonstrating that the real revolution is one of language and that the word is no more than a pretext for reassembling whatever's missing from stabilizing our fundamental relation to being.

Translated by Gian Lombardo

ABOLIR LA MORT

Nous mourons par habitude, trouvant notre salut dans le loisir, la mode et la passion des lettres géantes et lumineuses qui flottent librement sur nos têtes. Leur message est simple, transparent. Et nous consentons à l'illusion cependant que le monde animé, lui, devient le simple effet d'un trouble de la vue. Dans la clarté totale des insomniaques sous-urbains nous parlons tous la même langue. Celle qui ne doit rien nous enlever du besoin de nous sentir complices tout en nous évitant de disserter sur l'invraisemblable et douloureux privilège d'être mû de l'intérieur.

Invoquant Joyce, Loyola, Sade, Broodthaers, Duchamp, Ponge, Warhol et les autres saints fétichistes, sans compter tous ces grands écrivains petit-bourgeois qui nous consolent en démontrant que la vraie révolution est celle du langage et que la parole n'est qu'un prétexte pour rassembler toutes ces choses absentes qui stabilisent notre rapport fondamental à l'être.

VERONIKA DINTINJANA (Slovenia)

Veronika Dintinjana (1977) is a poet, translator and surgeon. Her first book, Rumeno Gori Grm Forzicij / Yellow Burns the Forsythia Bush *(2008) won the Slovenian Book Fair award for Best First Book. Her second book,* V Suhem Doku / In Dry Dock *(2016), received the Slovenian Writers' Association award for the best poetry published in the previous two years. Her published translations include the works of Louise Glück, Muriel Rukeyser, Denise Levertov, Ciaran O'Driscoll, Ursula K. Le Guin, Seamus Heaney and Pablo Neruda.*

CATHEDRAL LIONS

Rain, cold and heat have corroded
the
low-grade marble; they're like
the crest of a wave, for an instant
take form
and already
          dissolve into foam.

They smile.
Perhaps they know they are disappearing.

Translated by the poet with Rose Aasen

LEVI NA PROČELJU KATEDRALE

Tretjerazredni marmor so načeli dež,
mraz in vročina; podobni so
vrhovom valov, za hip
privzamejo obliko
in že se razpustijo
          v peno.

Smehljajo se.
Morda vejo, da kopnijo.

ST. FRANCIS

grow into the sky
until you become a tree

full of select rain and light soil

what can the wind do
when you dress up in blossoms

singularity is your sceptre

neither silver nor gold
have given their body
for a table, a bed

and when birds in your crown fall asleep
you stir no more

silence replaces the alphabet of signs

Translated by the poet and E. Underhill

SV. FRANČIŠEK

rasti v nebo,
dokler ne postaneš drevo

poln prebranega dežja in prhke zemlje

kaj ti more veter,
ko se odeneš v cvetje?

neponovljivost je tvoje žezlo

ne zlato ne srebro
nista dala telesa
za mizo, za posteljo

in ko pospijo ptice v tvoji krošnji,
se ne premakneš več

abecedo znamenj zamenja molčanje

THE ORANGE TREE IN FRONT OF THE HOUSE IS IN THE ZENITH

I listen to the absence of wind in the branches
and to the unpeopled afternoon.

For three things I have left the window shutters open,
for four I close the door.

For the glowing moon which hisses when the blacksmith sinks it in water,
for the morning which turns pale when the sun peers in its face.
For the day which blushes into night, and for the threshold –
there will no longer be feet to shine it, only petals.

Three ascend towards the heavens,
four have left without a slightest sound.

The filament blew in the light bulb,
a distracted line has vanished from my head.
Through a half-open window the cold came in,
and supper found its place at the table.

Four things I cannot comprehend,
three I cannot forget.

The round stone on the beach which taught me as a child
to tell my right knee from my left, one side of the road from the other.
The all-encompassing pain that left me a moment later.
The kindly sea I dream of every night, that waits for me at the door,
and by day sends seagulls and other messengers for an answer.

And the tree which is setting over the world.
You cannot tell which revolves and which is still.

By the shadow's length we set the sky's directions.
By the pace's length we know the time of night.

   Translated by the author and Ciaran O'Driscoll

ORANŽEVEC PRED HIŠO JE V ZENITU

Poslušam odsotnost vetra med listi
in neobljudeno popoldne.

Zaradi treh stvari puščam polkna priprta,
zaradi štirih zapiram vrata.

Zaradi lune, ki razbeljena zacvrči, ko jo kovač potopi v vedro.
Zaradi jutra, ki prebledi, ko ga v obraz pogleda sonce.
Zaradi dneva, ki zardi v noč, in zaradi praga,
namesto stopinj ga bodo obrusili cvetovi.

Trije se dvigajo v nebo,
štirje so šli brez najmanjšega šuma.

Šla je gorilna nitka v žarnici,
iz glave mi je ušla prekinjena vrstica.
Skozi priprto okno se je pririnil hlad
in za mizo si je prostor našla večerja.

Štirih stvari ne morem dojeti,
treh ne pozabiti.

Oblega kamna na obali, kot otroka me je naučil
razlikovati levo in desno koleno, levo in desno stran ceste.
Bolečine, ki je bila vseobsegajoča in je minila hip zatem.
Ljubeznivega morja, vsako noč ga sanjam, čaka me pred vrati.
Podnevi pošilja galebe in druge sle po odgovor.

In drevesa, ki zahaja nad svetom.
Ni moč videti, kdo se vrti okoli koga.

Po dolžini sence določamo smeri neba.
Po dolžini korakov, katera ura noči je.

SPARROW, THROUGH A HOSPITAL WINDOW

I saw death
sit down beside him on the bed and take off her slippers.
His blood pressure dropped,
his face paled, as she lay down.
His eyes were frightened.
I flew out. As I did not

have a share in his life,
it was only right not to have a part
in his dying.
Half an hour later I returned
to pick up the bread crumbs
left over from lunch.

Translated by the author with Ciaran O'Driscoll and Rose Aasen

VRABEC, SKOZ BOLNIŠNIČNO OKNO

Videl sem smrt,
kako je prisedla na posteljo in si sezula copate.
Pritisk mu je padel,
obraz je postal bel, ko je legla.
Oči prestrašene.
Odletel sem ven. Ker nisem imel
deleža pri njegovem življenju,
je bilo edino prav, da nimam deleža
pri njegovi smrti.
Čez pol ure sem se vrnil
po krušne drobtine,
ki so ostale od kosila.

ANA DRAGU (Romania)

Anna Dragu (1976) has published four poetry collections: larba pentru fiare / Grass for Beasts *(2004);* Păpuşa de ceară / The Wax Doll *(2008);* pazitoarea / The Guardian Woman *(2012); and* Bordeline *(2017). She has also published a book as the mother of an autistic child,* Maini cuminti. Copilul meu autist / Well-behaved Hands. My Autistic Child. *She is the founder and director of 'The Little Prince Centre of Resources and Reference for Autism' in Bistrita.*

FAMILY COUNCIL

not to switch on the central heating until late november
to consume more potatoes
sour soup stew paprikash with yoghurt
potatoes fried or baked
mashed, scalloped, stewed

French potatoes
for heavenly creatures

to accept old clothes for alms
new clothes are Chinese anyway
Fuck China! Fuck the invading winter!

I'll borrow the money for private lessons
and you know what, I said protectively
when I was little I wrapped my textbooks in paper,
not in shining covers
it was brown but now it also comes coloured
coloured paper!
you can change your favourite colour

there's nobody in the hall so don't leave the light on
I started saying
while my daughter pulled her pyjamas
towards the bed

that light doesn't keep you warm.

Translated by Radu Vancu

CONSILIU DE FAMILIE

să nu pornim centrala decât la sfârșit de noiembrie
să consumăm mai mulți cartofi
ciorbă tocană papricaș cu iaurt
cartofi prăjiți sau copți
piure, gratinați, răntăliți
cartofi franțuzești
pentru ființe cerești

să acceptăm hainele vechi de pomană
hainele noi sunt oricum chinezești
Fuck China! Fuck iarna invadatoare!

o să împrumut eu banii pentru meditații
și știi ce, i-am spus protectoare
când eram mică îmi înveleam manualele în hârtie,
nu în coperte strălucitoare
era maro dar acum există și colorată

hârtie colorată!
îți poți alege culoarea preferată

nu e nimeni pe hol deci nu lăsa becul aprins
am apucat să strig
în timp ce fiică-mea își târa pijamaua
spre pat

becul ăla nu ține de frig.

THE SECOND FRAME FROM A MOVIE ABOUT SILENCE

for one single morning
to have the certainty of the bread seller
her limpid blue eyes
blinking on the beat of the cash register

the ability to handle tens of knives
with my thoughts ever further from my hands
at the other end of the world where
you
falteringly step out of your bed

cross the hall and in front of the
mirror study the map
which the worn-out pillow case imprinted on your cheek:

I am alone
and things looked upon too long
slowly
lose
beauty.

Translated by Radu Vancu

AL DOILEA CADRU DINTR-UN FILM DESPRE LINIȘTE

într-o singură dimineață
să am siguranța vânzătoarei de pâine
ochii ei limpezi albaștri
care clipesc în ritmul casei de marcat

abilitatea de a mânui zeci de cuțite
cu gândurile tot mai departe de mâini
la celălalt capăt al lumii unde te ridici
tu
nesigur din pat

traversezi holul și-n dreptul
oglinzii studiezi harta
pe care fața de pernă uzată ți-a imprimat-o pe obraz:

sunt singur
și lucrurile privite îndelung
își pierd
încet
frumusețea.

2014-02-07 00:21 GMT+02:00

I was old but I'm good now
I'm telling the truth
the city is under snow I don't talk to myself any more nor with you
the future
as far as possible concerns me intensely
I have kids
so I don't take into account the chance offered by a nervous diseases hospital

in a moment of fear I caught myself cheering up with your voice
some words
I don't even remember if you ever said them or just
I imagine you have
I sit in my broken armchair and hear laughter from the kitchen
announcing the little eating bout

then comes the exhilaration
we'll get loans we'll pay bills with them
and mortgages and healthy food we'll have our stomachs full it'll be warm
we'll fill it up with fuel and travel around the block always around the block
ultrasophisticated
ultraaccommodated
possibly immortal

Translated by Radu Vancu

2014-02-07 00:21 GMT+02:00

am fost bătrână dar acum sunt bine
spun adevărul
orașul e sub zăpadă nu mai vorbesc singură și nici cu tine
viitorul
cât mai îndepărtat mă preocupă intens
am copii
deci nu iau în calcul șansa pe care ți-o oferă un spital de boli nervoase

într-un moment de frică m-am surprins încurajându-mă cu vocea ta
niște vorbe
nici nu mai știu dacă le-ai spus vreodată sau doar
îmi imaginez că le-ai spus
stau în fotoliul meu rupt și ascult râsete din bucătărie
anunțând mica beție alimentară

urmează înviorarea
vom obține credite cu ele vom achita facturi
și rate și alimente sănătoase vom avea burta plină va fi cald
vom pune benzină și vom călători în jurul blocului mereu în
                                        jurul blocului
ultrasofisticați
ultraadaptați
posibil nemuritori

RADNA FABIAS (The Netherlands)

Radna Fabias (1983) was born and raised in Curaçao. She is a graduate of HKU University of the Arts, Utrecht. She debuted as a poet with the poetry collection Habitus *(2018) which won all of the major poetry awards in the Netherlands & Belgium, amongst them the Herman de Coninck prize and the Grote Poëzieprijs. She was hailed as the Dutch literary talent of 2019 by the Dutch National newspaper* De Volkskrant. *Fabias' poetry has been translated into English, French and Spanish.*

OPENING SCENE

at the airport i take off
my shoes my belt and if
they ask my pants as well

i submit to being sniffed by dogs the weapons
are in my fingertips where i have also
stored the rapid heartbeat

i look smart i've done my hair
i smile like a sheep keep my eyes on the floor
the elastic of the mask
behind my ears

Translated by David Colmer

OPENINGSSCENE

op het vliegveld trek ik uit
mijn schoenen mijn riem en als
erom gevraagd wordt ook mijn broek

ik laat me door de honden besnuffelen de wapens
installeerde ik onder mijn vingertoppen ik heb daar
ook de versnelde hartslag opgeslagen

ik zie er keurig uit mijn haar zit goed
ik glimlach als een schaap ik kijk omlaag
het masker aan een elastiek
achter mijn oren gehaakt

BRIDE

like many women i always knew i would marry a man
a black man because that would go better with my dress
a question of contrast

the ceremony took place in a church where they profess a faith i do not adhere to
the priest like all the female guests wore a veil
white
he ended his sermon by asking who was going to call the police

on the altar were objects i knew from my childhood
a cactus, glowing coals, an axe for doing the weeding and a dead animal
presumably a stray dog

the floor was covered with corn flour
the interior recalled a beach bar
the incense smelled like midnight mass

the priest drew a seawater cross on my ash-covered forehead
i promised eternity in a language i didn't speak
i had only learned that one sentence

the bridegroom said the language didn't matter
everyone there looked vacant in a very specific way

i wasn't wearing a bra and was embarrassed by the nipple imprints in my lie
in my white white lie of a wedding dress
my groom whispered that marriage is a formality
for the reassurance of those who gave us birth

the women sang a song about my lost innocence
i apologized
it was a long sit
my veiled mother-in-law thanked me in advance for the grandchildren

on the way out the guests pelted us
with a range of seeds and grains:

aniseed for a sweet wedding night – as if we needed it – then rice
– because that was the done thing – then black dead-black sesame
seed according to my groom an important symbol and at the door
just before we stepped out of the church, buckwheat

Translated by David Colmer

BRUID

zoals veel vrouwen wist ik altijd al dat ik een man zou huwen
het werd een zwarte man omdat dat beter bij mijn jurk zou staan
een kwestie van contrasten
de zegening vond plaats in een kerk waar een geloof beleden
                              werd dat ik niet aanhing
de priester droeg net als alle aanwezige vrouwen een sluier
wit
zijn preek eindigde met de vraag wie de politie zou bellen
op het altaar lagen voorwerpen die ik uit mijn jeugd kende
een cactus, gloeiende kolen, een bijl om onkruid mee te wieden
                              en een dood dier
vermoedelijk een zwerfhond
de vloer lag vol met maïsmeel
het interieur deed denken aan een strandtent
de wierook rook naar kerstnacht
er werd met zeewater een kruis op mijn in as bedekte hoofd getekend
ik beloofde eeuwigheid in een taal die ik niet sprak
ik had alleen dat ene zinnetje geleerd
de bruidegom zei dat de taal er verder niet toe deed
de aanwezigen keken op een specifieke manier leeg

ik droeg geen bh en schaamde me voor de tepelafdrukken in mijn leugen
in mijn witte witte leugen van een bruidsjurk
mijn bruidegom fluisterde me toe dat het huwelijk een vormelijkheid is
ter geruststelling van hen die ons gebaard hebben
de vrouwen zongen een lied over mijn verloren onschuld
ik bood mijn excuses aan
het was een lange zit
mijn gesluierde schoonmoeder bedankte me alvast voor de kleinkinderen
onderweg naar buiten bekogelden de aanwezigen ons
met uiteenlopende zaden en granen:
anijs voor een zoete huwelijksnacht – alsof wij dat nodig hadden – toen
rijst – omdat dat hoorde – toen zwart doodzwart sesamzaad waarover
mijn bruidegom vertelde dat het een belangrijk symbool was en bij de
deur, ten slotte, voordat we de kerk uit stapten, met gort

ROOSTING TREE

on my way to the roosting tree
i water and manure one square mile of reddish-brown earth
it is an altruistic investment i'm making it
possible for someone else to put down roots expand disrupt the ecosystem
then i give my hands a good scrub
– long and painstaking –
i peel the prints from my fingers
– careful   i am careful –

i cut my hair because i am a victim
i dye my hair because i am a villain
i cultivate a moustache to match my forged documents
– i am calm   i am calm –

i fly the boeing through the turbulence in retrospect
to the man who casually and unintentionally begot me
i take a hostage, introduce him on arrival saying
this man reminds me of you i don't want him we need to talk it's tragic
that i am going to wear him
and i will wear him
i will wear him like a bearskin
like a cloak his skin
smells of desert heat fenugreek and open wounds

i am taking my mother back to the barren land because i love her
for the love of my mother i give all my kin back to the earth
i cast off my cloak because i love my mother
because i love my mother i ward off repetition from my clamped ovaries

my clamped ovaries are clean
my clamped ovaries are magnificent
my clamped ovaries are made of reactive metals

this is where i roost
i rust
i rest here
it ends here

Translated by David Colmer

ROESTPLAATS

onderweg naar de roestplaats
bewater en bemest ik één vierkante kilometer roodbruine aarde
het is een altruïstische invesering ik maak het mogelijk voor
                                                een ander om
wortel te schieten uit te dijen het ecosysteem te verstoren
dan was ik mijn handen
– lang en grondig –
ik trek de afdrukken van mijn vingers
– voorzichtig   ik ben voorzichtig –
k knip mijn ha ar omdat ik een slachtoffer ben
ik verf mijn haar omdat ik een schurk ben
ik kweek een snor voor bij mijn vaste papieren
– ik ben rustig   ik ben rusig –
de boeing vlieg ik door de turbulentie in retrospectief naar de man
                                die mij terloops en
onbedoeld verwekte
ik neem een gijzelaar, introduceer hem bij aankomst zeg
deze man doet me aan jou denken ik wil hem niet we moeten praten
                                het is tragisch
dat ik hem zal dragen
en ik zal hem dragen
als een berenvel
ik zal hem dragen als een mantel
zijn huid ruikt naar woestijnhitte fenegriek en open wonden

mijn moeder breng ik terug naar het barre land omdat ik van haar houd
vanwege mijn moeder geef ik iedereen die op mij lijkt terug aan de
                                aarde
ik werp mijn mantel af omdat ik van mijn moeder houd
omdat ik van mijn moeder houd bezweer ik de herhaling vanuit mijn
                                afgeklemde eierstokken

mijn afgeklemde eierstokken zijn schoon
mijn afgeklemde eierstokken zijn schitterend
mijn afgeklemde eierstokken zijn vervaardigd van reactieve metalen

dan rust ik
hier roest ik
hier stop het

ATHENA FARROKHZAD (Sweden)

Athena Farrokhzad (1983) is a Swedish poet, based in Stockholm. She works as a literary critic, translator, playwright and teacher of creative writing. Her debut collection Vitsvit / White Blight *(2013) has been translated into fourteen languages. She has published two further volumes of poetry,* Trado *in 2016 (with the Romanian poet Svetlana Cârstean) and* I rörelse *in 2019.*

'MY FAMILY ARRIVED HERE...'

My family arrived here in a Marxist tradition

My mother immediately filled the house with Santa knick-knacks
Weighed the pros and cons of the plastic Christmas tree
as if the problem were hers

During the day she distinguished between long and short vowels
as if the sounds that came out of her mouth
could wash the olive oil from her skin

My mother let bleach run through her syntax
On the other side of punctuation her syllables became whiter
than a winter in Norrland

My mother built us a future consisting of quantity of life
In the suburban basement she lined up canned goods
as if preparing for a war

In the evenings she searched for recipes and peeled potatoes
As if it were her history inscribed
in the Jansson's temptation casserole

To think that I sucked at those breasts
To think that she put her barbarism in my mouth

Translated by Jennifer Hayashida

'MIN FAMILJ ANLÄNDE HIT...'

Min familj anlände hit i en marxistisk idétradition

Min mor fyllde genast huset med prydnadstomtar
Vägde plastgranens för-och nackdelar mot varandra
som om problemet vore hennes

På dagarna skiljde hon mellan långa och korta vokaler
som om ljuden som kom ur hennes mun
kunde tvätta olivoljan ur huden

Min mor lät blekmedlet rinna genom syntaxen
På andra sidan skiljetecknet blev hennes stavelser vitare
än en norrländsk vinter

Min mor byggde oss en framtid av livskvantitet
I förortsvillans källarförråd radade hon upp konservburkar
som inför ett krig

På kvällarna letade hon recept och skalade potatis
som om det var hennes historia som fanns chiffrerad
i Janssons frestelse

Tänk att jag sög på de brösten
Tänk att hon stoppade sitt barbari i min mun

'MY FATHER SAID: YOU HAVE A TENDENCY...'

My father said: You have a tendency towards metaphysics
Still I schooled you in the means of production
when your milk teeth were intact

My mother said: Your father lived for the day of judgement
So did your mother, but she was forced to other ambitions

Translated by Jennifer Hayashida

'MIN FAR SA: DU HAR EN DRAGNING...'

Min far sa: Du har en dragning åt metafysik
Ändå skolade jag dig i produktionens beskaffenhet
när dina mjölktänder var intakta

Min mor sa: Din far levde för den yttersta dagen
Din mor likaså, men hon tvingades till andra ambitioner

'MY MOTHER SAID: IN YOUR FATHER'S SLEEP...'

My mother said: In your father's sleep you are executed together
In your father's dream you form a genealogy of revolutionaries

My father said: Your mother fed you with imported silver spoons
Your mother was everywhere in your face
frantically combed out the curls

Translated by Jennifer Hayashida

'MIN MOR SA: I DIN FARS SÖMN...'

Min mor sa: I din fars sömn blir ni avrättade tillsammans
I din fars dröm bildar ni en genealogi av revolutionärer

Min far sa: Din mor matade dig med importerade silverskedar
Din mor var överallt i ditt ansikte
kammade frenetiskt ut lockarna

'MY MOTHER SAID: FOR A LIFETIME...'

My mother said: For a lifetime I envied your father's traumas
until I realized that my own were far more remarkable

My mother said: I have spent a fortune on your piano lessons
But at my funeral you will refuse to play

Translated by Jennifer Hayashida

'MIN MOR SA: I EN LIVSTID...'

Min mor sa: I en livstid avundades jag din fars trauman
tills jag insåg att mina egna var långt mer anmärkningsvärda

Min mor sa: Jag har spenderat en förmögenhet på dina pianolektioner
Men på min begravning kommer du att vägra spela

'MY MOTHER SAID: FROM THE DIVISION OF CELLS...'

My mother said: From the division of cells
from a genetic material
from your father's head
But not from me

My father said: From the clash of civilizations
from a fundamental antagonism
from my tired head
But not from her

Translated by Jennifer Hayashida

'MIN MOR SA: UR CELLERNAS DELNING...'

Min mor sa: Ur cellernas delning
ur ett genetiskt material
ur din fars huvud
Men inte ur mig

Min far sa: Ur civilisationernas kamp
ur en grundläggande antagonism
ur mitt trötta huvud
Men inte ur henne

'MY FATHER SAID: IF IT WERE POSSIBLE...'

My father said: If it were possible to compete in martyrdom
your mother would do everything to lose
My mother said: The heart is not like the knee
that can be bent at will
My father said: Even the rooster who does not crow
gets to see the sun rise
My mother said: But if the hen does not lay an egg
she will be served for dinner

Translated by Jennifer Hayashida

'MIN FAR SA: OM DET GICK...'

Min far sa: Om det gick att tävla i martyrskap
skulle din mor göra allt för att förlora
Min mor sa: Hjärtat är inte som knäet
som kan böjas av fri vilja
Min far sa: Även den tupp som inte gal
får se solen stiga
Min mor sa: Men om hönan inte värper
serveras hon själv till middag

ANDY FIERENS (Belgium)

Andy Fierens (1976) has published two poetry collections, Grote Smerige Vlinder / Big Filthy Butterfly *(2009) which won the Herman de Coninck prize for best debut (2010) and* Wonderbras & pepperspray / Wonderbras & Pepper Spay *(2014). He is a key figure in Flemish performance culture. Fierens mixes vulgar and revolting impropriety in a seemingly naive way with light, tender beauty; attraction and repulsion are playing with each other. His poetry, which is sometimes described as social surrealism, is hard but not heartless.*

AT HOME I WALK THROUGH STREETS I DO NOT RECOGNISE

at home I walk through streets I do not recognise
it is cold there, I wear your breath like a winter scarf
and everything warm repels me like a burning monk

you whisper from afar when in the ridge of the world I coo your name
calm me with pollen in your hand when I splinter
if gnawed at by the rodent in the cradling straw

or no – strike me dead resuscitate me and strike me dead once more
romance is rubbish but I gave you my heart
and I presented it to you melting
until it stiffened in your hand and mouth

    do you know that book by gert vlok nel where he says
    I don't know if you've ever read a tintin book
    but tintin in tibet is the only book
    in which tintin has ever cried

sometimes I sense you in a bar, on a train
in a glance or a reflection and lash out
my fists burst in the blue around me

      come back   *come back*

but you are travelling through the immensities of space

I am waiting in the sun in a park with a dog

Translated by John Irons

THUIS LOOP IK DOOR STRATEN DIE IK NIET HERKEN

thuis loop ik door straten die ik niet herken
het is er koud, ik draag je adem als een wintersjaal
en al wat warm is stoot mij af als een brandende monnik

je fluistert van ver wanneer ik
in de nok van de wereld
je naam roekoe
sus mij met stuifmeel in je hand wanneer ik versplinter
als ik word aangeknaagd door het knaagdier in het wiegende stro

of nee sla me dood reanimeer me en sla me nog eens dood
romantiek is kul maar ik gaf je mijn hart
en ik schonk het je smeltend
tot het stolde aan je handen en mond

    ken je dat boek van gert vlok nel waarin hij zegt
    ek weet nie of jy ooit 'n tintinboek gelees het nie
    maar tintin in tibet is die enigste boek
    waarin tintin ooit gehuil het

soms vermoed ik je in een bar, op een trein
in een blik of een weerkaatsing en slaan
mijn vuisten barsten in het blauw rondom

    kom terug!   kom terug!

maar je reist door de onmetelijke ruimte

ik wacht in de zon in een park met een hond

MUMMIES AND DADDIES

mummies love daddies
daddies love mummies

usually a mummy gives
her love to one daddy
(the converse also applies)
day after day
she just gives her love
to the same daddy
or the same mummy

it sometimes happens
that the one contains
more love
than the other is
      equal to
we say about these others
that he / she is satiated
or quenched
the one (daddy / mummy) then has
a residue of love
and we sometimes call this
the surplus (that is jargon)

pay attention now
what follows is important

love has a limited shelf life
that means
that it can go sour
just like milk

what's such a daddy or mummy to do
with that surplus?
let it go bad?
let it languish in some corner?

or could they
perhaps
use it to make
someone else happy?
a daddy or mummy who is lonely?

no right-minded
person can
object to that
you might think

or?

but as you all know
with adults
you never know

imagine mummy gives her surplus
to another daddy
one of those who's lonely
then there's a big chance that your
daddy will call your mummy a whore
that means that daddy is not happy
that he

is ventilating his dis-satis-fac-tion

or imagine daddy gives some love
to some lonely mummy or other
then it's not unlikely that your mummy
runs through the house
screaming strange things
such as i'll milk you dry
to the last penny
or
just wait till you're asleep you bastard
and i'll smear
tar on your balls

that's terrible

it sometimes happens that a daddy gives
his surplus to another daddy

and sometimes things get patched up
between mummy and daddy
(but if daddy gives his surplus
to another daddy
usually not)

that's how it goes with adults

later when you've become an adult
and married
or live together with someone
or have a living-apart-together realisation

the chance is pretty big
that you'll notice sooner or later
that you've a surplus
then above all you must make
someone else happy with it

for life is short
and senseless without love

but you'll probably have to learn
to keep your mouth clamped shut

for silence is golden
and girls you don't want to be whores do you?
and boys you don't want tar on your balls do you?

but such worries are for the future
just start by looking up the meaning
of the word *jargon*

Translated by John Irons

MAMA'S EN PAPA'S

mama's houden van papa's
papa's houden van mama's

meestal geeft een mama
haar liefde aan één papa
(omgekeerd gaat het net zo)
dag na dag
altijd maar liefde geven
aan dezelfde papa
of aan dezelfde mama

soms gebeurt het
dat de een in zich
meer liefde heeft

dan de ander nog
        aankan
van die andere zeggen we
dat hij/zij verzadigd is
of uitgeblust
de een (papa/mama) heeft dan
liefde op overschot
we noemen dit ook wel eens
het surplus (dat is jargon)

let nu goed op
wat volgt is belangrijk

liefde heeft een houdbaarheidsdatum
dat wil zeggen
dat ze zuur kan worden
net als melk

wat moet zo'n papa of mama doen
met dat surplus?
het slecht laten worden?
het in een hoekje laten verkommeren?

of kunnen ze er
misschien
iemand anders
gelukkig mee maken?
een papa of mama die eenzaam is?

daar kan geen
weldenkend mens
iets op tegen hebben
zou je denken

toch?

maar zoals jullie weten
met grote mensen
weet je het nooit

stel je mama geeft haar surplus
aan een andere papa
zo een die eenzaam is
dan is de kans groot dat je
papa je mama een hoer noemt
dat betekent dat papa niet blij is
dat hij

on-ge-noe-gen ventileert

en stel je papa geeft wat liefde
aan zo'n eenzame mama
dan is het niet onwaarschijnlijk dat je mama
door het huis gaat lopen
en rare dingen schreeuwt
zoals ik ga je leegmelken
tot de laatste cent
of
wacht maar tot je slaapt rotzak
dan smeer ik
teer op je kloten

het is me wat

soms gebeurt het dat een papa zijn surplus
aan een andere papa geeft

en soms komt het ook weer
goed tussen mama en papa
(maar als papa zijn surplus
aan een andere papa geeft
meestal niet)

zo gaat dat bij grote mensen

later als je zelf groot bent
en getrouwd
of samenwoont
of een lat-realisatie hebt

dan is de kans groot
dat je vroeg of laat merkt
dat je zelf een surplus hebt
dan moet je daar vooral iemand
anders gelukkig mee maken

want het leven is kort
en zinloos zonder liefde

maar je zult wel moeten leren
om je mondje op slot te doen

want zwijgen is goud
en meisjes jullie willen toch geen hoer zijn?
en jongens jullie willen toch geen teer op jullie kloten?

maar dat zijn zorgen voor later
zoek nu eerst maar eens op
wat *jargon* betekent

THE SNORERS

Nothing is more precious to me
than my father's
snoring.

My father
like so many others
denied he was a snorer.

Not until I had taped
the rumbling sound
of his nocturne
did he admit the fact.

A couple of years later he died.

One of the few things
I still have of him
is the recording of his
sonorous breathing.

When the human race was still
in its infancy
the snorer was sacred.
He slept
on the outside of the circle
and with his chain-saw kept
wild animals
such as the
cave bear
at a distance.

Thus did he protect the tribe.

Today
recognisability makes
the snorer vulnerable.

Whenever in my youth
we went out camping
my father was
strictly forbidden
to enter the tent
before everyone else
was sleeping
like a log.

Is it mere chance that I
who in my whole life
had never snored
one single time
took over
the torch from him
after his death?

Not infrequently
when we are camping
I am now banished
at night by my own children
to the confined
acoustics of
the car.

Like my father
I am a snorer
whose fugue
is despised
by the tribe
he seeks to protect.

I am a tolerant man.
I can comply with
the whims of the woman
at my side.

There is though one rule
that I observe:
now and then
I ask her to stay awake
until I am asleep
and then softly
close to my ear
play the tape.

Then we snore together.

Two humming bees
who recognise each other
and in joy and merriment
dance through the night.

While snoring
harmoniously brought together
our hearts beat as one.

At last father and son.

Translated by John Irons

DE SNURKERS

Niets is mij zo dierbaar
als het gesnurk
van mijn vader.

Mijn vader
zoals zovelen
ontkende een snurker te zijn.

Pas toen ik op een bandje
het ronkende geluid
van zijn nocturne opnam
erkende hij de feiten.

Een paar jaar later stierf hij.

Een van de weinige dingen
die mij van hem resten
is de opname van zijn
sonore ademhaling.

Toen de mensheid nog
in de kinderschoenen stond
was de snurker heilig.
Hij sliep
aan de buitenkant van de kring
en hield met zijn kettingzaag
wilde dieren
zoals de holenbeer
op afstand.

Zo beschermde hij de stam.

Vandaag maakt
die herkenbaarheid
de snurker kwetsbaar.

Wanneer wij in mijn jeugd
uit kamperen gingen
was het mijn vader
streng verboden
de tent te betreden
voor alle anderen
de slaap van
Doornroosje sliepen.

Is het toeval dat ik
die in heel mijn leven
geen enkele keer
gesnurkt had
na zijn dood
de fakkel van hem
overnam?

Niet zelden
als wij kamperen
word ik nu bij nacht
door mijn eigen kinderen
naar de besloten
akoestiek van de wagen
verbannen.

Zoals mijn vader
ben ik een snurker
wiens fuga
veracht wordt
door de stam
die hij beschermen wil.

Ik ben een verdraagzaam man.
Ik kan mij schikken
naar de grillen van de vrouw
aan mijn zij.
Er is maar één regel
waar ik aan houd:
nu en dan
vraag ik haar te waken
tot ik slaap
en daarna zachtjes
bij mijn oor
het bandje af te spelen.

Dan snurken wij samen.

Twee brommende bijen
die elkaar herkennen
en in blijdschap vrolijk
dansen door de nacht.

Al snurkend
harmonieus samengebracht
kloppen onze harten synchroon.

Eindelijk vader en zoon.

TIZIANO FRATUS (Italy)

Tiziano Fratus (1975) lives at the foot of the Italian Alps where he deepens an everyday practice of zen meditation in the forest. He is author of many books inspired by the natural world: poetry collections, novels, manuals and travelogues. His poetry has been translated into ten languages and has appeared in anthologies and international poetry journals. His latest titles are Jonah of the Sequoias. A Trip among Red Giants in North America *(Bompiani, 2019) and* Cherry Flowers Sketcher's Dreams *(Aboca, 2020). Website: Studiohomoradix.com*

SAINT FRANCIS AT OXFORD STREET

in the litter there is always some cub that distinguishes itself,
that doesn't accept following the pack, survival can
mean camouflaging yourself: there are those who have counted from
                                                        one to seven
thousand two hundred and twenty seven: you need only admit to being
a bastion of contrariness, to invert mathematical logic, add
to accumulate – almost – never to subtract: and wake yourself one
morning in two thousand and one, wash your face, dry yourself, look
in the mirror, slap cheeks, leave to go to a
supermarket on oxford street and give away everything: birth
certificate, passport, house keys, car, works
of art: resetting the precipice of time, imploding
the complex equations of financial economics in the
bestial economic stew, attempt the road of anonymous
freedom, breaking the mirror into pieces and stopping it from reflecting
                                                        any image,
listening to the body breathe and stop
responding to the pressure of the absence of:
letting go the work of lawyers and bankers, returning to
hands painted on the walls of caverns, even if the birds,
probably, don't seem intent on dialogue

Translated by Francesco Levato

SAN FRANCESCO A OXFORD STREET

nel mucchio esiste sempre qualche cucciolo che si distingue,
che non accetta di seguire il branco, sopravvivere può
significare mimetizzarsi: c'é chi ha contato da uno a sette
mila due cento venti sette: bisogna pur ammettere di essere
bastian contrari, a invertire la logica matematica, aggiungere

per accumulare – quasi – mai per sottrarre: e svegliarsi una
mattina del duemilaeuno, lavarsi la faccia, asciugarsi, fissarsi
allo specchio, battersi le guance, uscire per andare in un
supermercato a oxford street e dare via tutto: certificato
di nascita, passaporto, chiavi di casa, automobile, opere
d'arte: azzerare il precipizio del tempo, implodere le
equazioni complesse dell'economia finanziaria nella
spremuta economia animale, tentare la strada della libertà
nell'anonimato, frangere lo specchio e smettere di riflettere
qualsiasi immagine, ascoltare il corpo respirare e smetterla
di rispondere alla pressione della mancanza di:
lasciare senza lavoro avvocati e banchieri, ritornare alle
mani dipinte sulle pareti di una caverna, anche se gli uccelli,
probabilmente, non sembrano intenzionati a dialogare

EVERY SEED CARRIES A JOURNEY WITHIN

Seeds
are journeys
whose destination is
already set at departure:
make yourself comfortable,
it's like going to school
by teleporta
-tion

Translated by by Gail McDowell

OGNI SEME HA DENTRO UN VIAGGIO

I
semi
sono viaggi
che hanno la meta
pronta in partenza:
ti puoi mettere comodo,
è come andare a scuola
con teletraspo
-rto

THE SEED OF GOD

The
seed falls
into the earth,
it moves when it is still
nothing, it generates life that has
yet to be. God invented it because
he wasn't able to become a tree, he
had too many tasks to be able to take
root in the form of stone. The
seed is God who's
unable to stay
still.

Translated by Gail McDowell

IL SEME DI DIO

Il
seme
cade nella
terra, si muove
quando ancora non
è niente, genera la vita
che non c'è. Dio l'ha inventato
perché non è riuscito a farsi albe
-ro, troppi impegni per radicarsi
sotto forma di pietra. Il seme
è Dio che non sa restare
immobile

DOGEN'S WORDS

At
the end
of the day,
I sat down in the centre
of nothingness: I allowed the "I,"
on which I had laboured so hard, to rust.
I saw that the water corrupted,
but I stopped caring. The
man who sat down
never stood back
up again

Translated by by Gail McDowell

PAROLA DI DOGEN

Alla
fine della
giornata mi sono
seduto al centro del vuoto:
ho lasciato che l'IO a cui tanto
avevo lavorato si arrugginisse. Ve
- devo che l'acqua corrompeva,
ma smisi di preoccuparmene.
L'uomo che si era se
-duto non si è
più rialza
-to

MARIJO GLAVAŠ (Croatia)

Marijo Glavaš (1986) has published three books of poetry, GrAD, Ciklona / Cyclone *(2012) and* Permutacije / Permutations *(2017), a novel and, online and in magazines, short fiction, literary criticism, essays and interviews with writers. He edited and hosted literary programmes for Croatian Radio-Television Split, is a member of the Croatian Writers' Society and is included in the English-language anthology* The Edge of a Page – New Poetry in Croatia, Generation 2010+. *He works for a Dutch IT company.*

PERMUTATION OF FREEDOM

It's about silence, the breaking of its back
the sound of water dripping from an old pipe
the chamber music from the apartment below or beside
the smell of people from an opened wardrobe
the electrified gas in a slowly brightening energy-saving bulb
a small number of read books
an unknown quantity of printed letters
time which enslaves the body through the aged face of ancestors
loneliness
the day which preceded today
the crossroads at which processions of flesh meet
blocking each other's way
the frequency with which breaking news is broadcast every hour, on the hour
the worn-out wiper blades on the windscreen
the thoughts before and after the national anthem
the finality of freedom which is being freely distributed in accordance with
                                                            the priorities

the importance of collective sports
the projects which await a signature and a consensus
the sound of breaking books every hour, on the hour
the chamber gas before and after the national anthem
an unknown quantity of the enslaved
the loneliness of ancestors
the crossroads at which priorities meet
the thoughts from the wardrobe
the silence of the consensus
the frequency of wiper blades on the windscreen
the importance of the finality of freedom
and the collective breaking of its back

Translated by Irena Škarica

PERMUTACIJA SLOBODE

Riječ je o tišini, lomljenju njene kičme
zvuku vode koji kaplje iz stare cijevi
komornoj glazbi iz stana ispod ili pored
mirisu ljudi iz rastvorenog ormara
naelektriziranom plinu u sporopalećoj štednoj žarulji
malom broju pročitanih knjiga
nepoznatoj količini otisnutih slova
vremenu što porobljava tijelo ostarjelim licem predaka
samoći
danu koji je prethodio današnjem
raskrižju na kojem se susreću kolone mesa i
jedna drugoj priječe put
frekvenciji koja emitira goruće vijesti na svaki puni sat
lošim metlicama brisača na vjetrobranskom staklu
mislima prije i poslije himne
konačnosti slobode koja biva slobodno raspodijeljena poštivajući prioritete
važnosti ekipnoga sporta
projektima koji čekaju jedan potpis i usuglašavanje
zvuku gorućih knjiga na svaki puni sat
komornom plinu prije i poslije himne
nepoznatoj količini porobljenih
samoći predaka
raskrižju na kojem se susreću prioriteti
mislima iz ormara
tišini usuglašavanja
frekvenciji brisača na vjetrobranskom staklu
važnosti konačnosti slobode
i ekipnom lomljenju njezine kičme

DISCRETION

To get a loan, to mortgage your flat, your car, your inheritance and kid
to sell your gold to the buyer with the prettiest shop window who
guarantees discretion
To check your account to see if it's still in
the red
To cross out this month, tear off another page of the
calendar and lay it on the pile
of withheld wages
To feel the hardness of the cardboard and the thickness of the
wooden handle of the placard which reminds you
of the pile of overdue utility bills

To feel yourself becoming untouchable,
disappearing understated, incomplete, half a man
To dig through your pockets, pits and stairwells
in order to realise you always have enough in your hand
to try to buy back love
from those who aren't selling it

Translated by Mirza Purić

DISKRETNOST

Podići kredit, založiti stan, auto, očevinu i dijete,
prodati zlato otkupljivaču s najljepšim izlogom i
zajamčenom diskrecijom
Provjeriti stanje na računu i jesu li brojke još uvijek
crvene
Precrtati i ovaj mjesec, otkinuti još jednu stranicu
kalendara i položiti je na hrpu
s preostalim neisplaćenim plaćama
Opipati tvrdoću kartona i debljinu drvene drške
transparenta koji te podsjeća
na dospjele rate struje
Osjetiti kako sve više postaješ nedodirljiv,
nestaješ, nesvršen, nedorečen, polučovjek
Prekopati džepove, jame i stubišta
kako bi shvatio da u ruci uvijek imaš dovoljno
da pokušaš otkupiti ljubav
od onoga tko je ne prodaje

MEN

V

Men have no fortune to be read from their palms
Their days are as long as the working
hours of the corner shops
On Sundays men live halftime lives
When the wall is wet they have to
stand
As if someone promised them something they
stand and wait
The next day it's all over again
Without men cities wouldn't have any doors

kids enter through the windows
Without men the walls would be empty

XIV

Men are something completely different
from anything that's ever existed from everything
that's so far been said
Not the same
Men are something else
as questionable as the white thing that's left
when you peel the rind off a tangerine
Hard core multi-layered men
Autumn doesn't mean they're any less busy
somebody still has to move the red
square on the calendar every morning
So
They don't get lost in the numbers
They know exactly and they know how much
They can mould time with their hands and speak
louder
The smell of Premium Unleaded erases the faintest
thought that they might remind one of someone
or something
There are theorems, exact mathematical calculations
which can prove this
Numbers don't lie
And men are different

Translated by Mirza Purić

MUŠKARCI

V

Muškarci nemaju sudbine na dlanovima
Dani su im jednake dužine kao rad
no vrijeme kvartovskih trgovina
Muškarci nedjeljom žive skraćeno
Kad je zidić mokar tada moraju
stajati
Kao da im je netko nešto obećao oni
stoje i čekaju

I onda sutra ispočetka
Bez muškaraca gradovi ne bi imali vrata
djeca prolaze kroz prozore
Bez muškaraca zidovi bi bili prazni

XIV

Muškarci su nešto potpuno drugačije
od ičega što je postojalo od svega
što je do sada izrečeno
Nisu isto
Muškarci su nešto drugo
upitni kao ono bijelo što ostane kad se
s mandarine oguli kora
Tvrdokorni višeslojni muškarci
Jesen ne znači da imaju manje obaveza
netko i dalje ujutro mora pomicati crv
eni kvadrat na kalendaru
Tako
I ne gube se u brojevima
Znaju točno i koliko
Rukama mogu ukalupiti vrijeme i govoriti
glasnije
Miris eurosupera 95 briše svaku i najmanju
pomisao da podsjećaju na nekoga
ili nešto
Postoje teoremi i precizni matematički izračuni
kojima se to može i dokazati
Brojevi ne lažu
A muškarci su drugačiji

THANOS GOGOS (Greece)

Thanos Gogos (1985) is the founder of publishing house and literary magazine Thraka, *and co-founder and director of the Thessalian Poetry Festival. He has published three poetry collections:* Frontier Playground *(2013),* Glasgow *(2014) and* Dakar *(2020). His poems have been widely published in literary magazines and anthologies and have been translated into Croatian, English, Russian and Slovenian.*

'THE HARDEST BREAST OF ALL...'

The hardest breast of all
was made from a small flower

Whatever you break on it now
it will exude
only
snow

Translated by Lena Kallergi

'ΤΟ ΠΙΟ ΣΚΛΗΡΟ ΑΠ᾽ΟΛΑ ΣΤΗΘΟΣ...'

Το πιο σκληρό απ᾽ολα στήθος
φτιάχτηκε από μικρό λουλούδι

Και ότι και αν σπάσεις τώρα πάνω
αυτό θα βγάζει
 μόνο
χιόνι

VI

My immune system worked wonderfully
Stronger than ever, I continue

MEMOIRS
OF THE FREEPENDENT POET

Budapest:

I sinned at the Acropolis
I laundered mafia money through cheap foreign currency

I separated Buda from Pest
I musically conducted the fountain in front of dozens of tourists
I hated goulash and every traditional dish
Drunk, I miaowed at the lions on the bridge
I survived Hungarian alcohol.
I refused entertainment via payment to thirteen whores

Budapostscript:

(One offered herself for free. She wanted to live a
complicated love affair. No luck.)

Berlin:

I chatted with Carl and Friedrich near Alexanderplatz
We disagreed on the transition to the last
stage of communism
I got angry and left.
I illegally photographed annoying
sandal-wearing Japanese tourists in two museums
I passed all the traffic lights on foot arousing
the fury of Jerry drivers
A vegetarian, I had lunch, a doner kebab in front of
the surprised eyes of my vegan companions
I peed standing up in all the toilets
Guilty!
I admit it. I am a sexist.
A scoundrel…

Berlinscript:

(The Turkish fella
A saviour
His chopped beef was holy
Radish there was even more tasteless
than in Greece.)

Translated by Lena Kallergi

VI

Το ανοσοποιητικό μου σύστημα δούλεψε υπέροχα
Πιο δυνατός από ποτέ συνεχίζω

ΑΠΟΜΝΗΜΟΝΕΥΜΑΤΑ
ΤΟΥ ΕΞΑΡΤΕΛΕΥΘΕΡΟΥ ΠΟΙΗΤΗ

Βουδαπέστη:

Αμάρτησα στην Acropolis
Ξέπλυνα χρήμα της μαφίας μέσω φθηνού συναλλάγματος
Ξεχώρισα τη Βούδα από την Πέστη
Διεύθυνα μουσικά το σιντριβάνι μπροστά σε δεκάδες
τουρίστες
Μίσησα την γκούλας και κάθε παραδοσιακό πιάτο
Νιαούρισα μεθυσμένος στα λιοντάρια της γέφυρας
Επέζησα του Ουγγρικού αλκοόλ
Αρνήθηκα τη διασκέδαση μέσω πληρωμής σε δεκατρείς πόρνες

Βουδαπεστερόγραφο:

(Μία μου προσφέρθηκε δωρεάν Ήθελε να ζήσει έναν
σύνθετο έρωτα – Καμιά τύχη.)

Βερολίνο:

Τα είπα με τον Καρλ και τον Φρίντριχ κοντά στην
Αλεξάντερπλατς
Διαφωνήσαμε ως προς τη μετάβαση στο τελευταίο
στάδιο του κομμουνισμού
Νευρίασα και έφυγα.
Φωτογράφησα παράνομα σε δύο μουσεία ενοχλητικούς
σανδαλοφόρους Γιαπωνέζους τουρίστες
Πέρασα όλα τα φανάρια πεζός προκαλώντας την οργή
γερμαναράδων οδηγών
Γευμάτισα χορτοφάγος ντόνερ κεμπάμπ μπροστά
στα έκπληκτα μάτια των vegan συντρόφων μου
Κατούρησα όρθιος σε όλες τις τουαλέτες
Ένοχος!
Το παραδέχομαι.Σεξιστής είμαι.
Παλιάνθρωπος.

Βερολινόγραφο:

(Καρντάσης ο Τουρκαλάς
Σωτήρας
Άγιο το κομματιασμένο μοσχάρι του
Τα ραπανάκια εκεί ήταν πιο άνοστα και από αυτά
της Ελλάδος)

LÜTFIYE GÜZEL (Germany)

Lütfiye Güzel is a poet and since 2014 has been publishing notes, novellas, poems and monologues under her own label, go-güzel-publishing. Lütfiye Güzel runs poetry workshops in schools and museums.

'WEATHER CONDITIONS...'

Weather conditions:
The sky glares grey.
Over shoulder.
It does it on purpose.
The writing and the message:
On walls. On columns. On T-shirts.
On jackets. On bags.
On people. Biographies. Typographies.
Reality labels.
The creator of irrelevance:
Existing your way through the neighbourhood.
A capella being.
The swallowed self.
Research:
Often, like when I'm eating, at a table
along a wall of windows, all I see
are monsters with serving trays, carrying ketchup
sachets and serviettes, seven
or eight of them. The total waste
plus plastic cutlery.
The people, for some reason always
a little malicious. Everything sealed.
Life administrated.

The perspectives stuffed into
all the cardinal points by a totality
that lives off it.
A permanent blackout. Audible.
Visible. Nothing left
to feel.
Four words.
(Four words are just four words):
It's time to sleep.
Little self-preservation strategy:
And if, as a reaction,
or a small act of rebellion,
I detach myself from the injections
of mum and dad and tell myself
I'm going to keep living in this tree, I am one
with everything that stays forever.
Forever and a day.
I celebrate my isolation with
gift ribbon and move about
on the footpath with my patchy knowledge
walking in zigzags from house number
to house number. Without colour levels.
And at every door I cease to
make an offering. Anti-climax.
Looking it up straight away.
Breakdown.

Translated by Joel Scott and Charlotte Thießen

'WETTERVERHÄLTNISSE...'

Wetterverhältnisse:
Der Himmel guckt grau.
Over shoulder.
Das macht er absichtlich.
Die Schrift und die Botschaft:
An Wänden. An Säulen. Auf T-Shirts.
Auf Jacken. Auf Taschen.
Auf Menschen. Biografien. Typografien.
Die Realität etikettiert.
Die Urheberin der Nichtigkeit:
Durch die Gegend existieren.
Das Sein a cappella.

Das verschluckte Ich.
Recherche:
Oft, so beim Essen, an einem Tisch
entlang einer Fensterwand, sehe ich
nur Ungeheuer mit Tabletts, darauf
Ketchup-Tuben und Servietten, sieben
oder acht. Die totale Verschwendung
plus Plastikbesteck.
Die Leute, irgendwie immer ein
bisschen bösartig. Alles besiegelt.
Das Leben verwaltet.
Die Betrachtungsweisen rein gepumpt
in alle Himmelsrichtungen, von einer
Ganzheit, die davon lebt.
Ein permanentes Black-out. Hörbar.
Sichtbar. Nichts mehr übrig
zum Fühlen.
Vier Worte
(Vier Worte sind nur vier Worte):
Es ist Zeit einzuschlafen.
Kleine Selbstschutz-Strategie:
Und wenn ich mich im Gegenzug oder
in einem kleinen Akt der Rebellion,
trenne von den Injektionen von Mutti
und Papa und mir sage, ich lebe
weiter in diesem Baum, ich bin eins
mit allem was für immer bleibt.
Für immer und einen Tag.
Ich feiere meine Isolation mit
Geschenkschleife und bewege mich mit
meinem Halbwissen auf dem Gehweg,
so im ZickZack-Lauf von Hausnummer
zu Hausnummer. Ohne Buntwerte.
Und an jeder Tür bringe ich kein
Opfer mehr. Antiklimax.
Sofort nachschlagen.
Absturz.

'I HAVE TO LEARN...'

i have to learn
how to dream
to spite
the non-dreamers

Translated by Joel Scott and Charlotte Thießen

'ICH MUSS LERNEN...'

ich muss lernen
wie man träumt
den nicht-träumern
zum trotz

'IT'S TIME...'

it's time
to radicalise
but first I need to stop
sweeping up the dust bunnies under the bed
& stocking up on water

Translated by Joel Scott and Charlotte Thießen

'ES IST AN DER ZEIT...'

es ist an der zeit
sich zu radikalisieren
dafür muss ich aber erst einmal aufhören
die wollmäuse unter dem bett wegzufegen
& mir einen vorrat an wasser anzuschaffen

'9:45 P.M....'

9:45 p.m.
watched a documentary
on beuys
& even though I know it all
in the end
& at the beginning too
I'm there
dangling a teabag
in the cup
the poems are useless
the poems are dead rabbits

Translated by Joel Scott and Charlotte Thießen

'21.45 UHR...'

21.45 uhr
eine dokumentation
über beuys gesehen
& obwohl ich das alles weiss
stehe ich am ende
& auch am anfang
wieder da
& hänge einen teebeutel
in die tasse
die gedichte werden nicht mehr
die gedichte sind tote hasen

'THEY GO INTO POLITICS...'

they go into politics
i go to bed

when you can't arrest anyone
for the course
of your own biography
& they have no idea
about suicide & good titles
when books turn into pamphlets
without page numbers
or delivery
then the wolf has survived

Translated by Joel Scott and Charlotte Thießen

'SIE GEHEN IN DIE POLITIK...'

sie gehen in die politik
ich gehe schlafen

wenn man niemanden verhaften kann
für den verlauf
der eigenen biografie
& sie nichts wissen
über suizide & gute titel
wenn dann aus büchern flugblätter werden
ohne seitenzahl
& auslieferung
dann hat der wolf überlebt

MICHAL HABAJ (Slovakia)

Michal Habaj (1974) is a poet and a literary scientist. He is the author of seven books of poetry, five in his own name and two under the pseudonym Anna Snegina. He is one of the co-authors of the experimental poetry project Generator X *and is also one of the co-authors of the international project* The European Constitution in Verse *(Brussels, 2009). His poetry has been included in multiple anthologies and collections.*

DO NOT FORGET: TODAY, TOMORROW, YESTERDAY

my body's bloody sword: is heading for your gates:
ancient sweetheart of the earthlings: my uprearing body's
bloody sword: bearing an item of information:
about me: chopped hands chopped nerves: sand mouth
sand heart: towards your gates: ancient: heading
ranks of bloody swords: our uprearing bodies:
in glittering space suits: in helmets and gauntlets:
concealing information: of the rusting implants:
of whirling memories: of the marsh of despair where
sorrow overcame us: you were still a young girl:
but already followed: by astronauts' glances: you were
more fragile and tender: but registered already:
by instruments on decks: you were she: whom I know:
only from hard discs: only from stories of old computers:
only from the sparse data given by taciturn proto-cyborgs:
you were: she whom still to this day I seek: alone
amidst the infinite universe of my solitude.

Translated by John Minahane

NEZABUDNÚŤ: DNES, ZAJTRA, VČERA

krvavý meč môjho tela: smeruje k tvojim bránam:
stáročná milenka pozemšťanov: krvavý meč
môjho vzpínajúceho sa tela: nesúci informáciu:
o mne: uťaté ruky uťaté nervy: piesočné ústa
piesočné srdce: k tvojim bránam: stáročná: smerujú
šíky krvavých mečov: naše vzpínajúce sa telá:
v ligotavých skafandroch: v helmách a rukaviciach:
ukrývajúcich informáciu: o hrdzavejúcich implantátoch:
o zavírených pamätiach: o močiari beznádeje kde
nás premohol smútok: bola si ešte mladé dievča:
ale už sledovaná: pohľadmi astronautov: bola si

krehkejšia a nežnejšia: ale už zaznamenávaná:
prístrojmi na palubách: bola si tou: tou ktorú poznám:
iba z harddiskov: iba z rozprávaní starých počítačov:
iba zo strohých informácií zaryto mlčiacich prvokyborgov:
bola si: ktorú dodnes hľadám: sám
uprostred nekonečného vesmíru svojej samoty.

EDEN'S APPLES OF REMEMBRANCE

to call up a smile on the face of a girl: call it up like a pupil
to the board: like a film negative: like the spirit of Marilyn Monroe:
during nights like this: announcing itself in the depths of our hearts:
all I hear is her murmuring songs: I see only blotches of her face:
mammy: but she's only wheezing: mammy: but she has no colours:
connect the sound connect the picture: in your neon technohead:
you'll hear divine Marilyn's laughter and Frankieboy's velvet voice:
when in a silent forest of monitors: together with James Dean
she saves the world: and yet it moves! and yet it moves:
tape in a projector: their naked stars fall from the screen
to earth: soft memories easy dreams: and Kate Moss:
when she doles out smiles draped in the dictate of secret keyboards:
and Vanessa Paradis: with chewing gum wound round her finger:
stands in the empty metro: and she sees: a striding
sable youth: a leaf falling from the tree: high school girls
trustfully clutching the butts of mobile telephones:
and she sees: herself seen: she calls up memories: faces
of her lovers: she calls up a smile on the face of the girl:
who she once was: and who she will ever remain:
deep in our hearts: deeper in the film negatives.

Translated by John Minahane

RAJSKÉ JABLKÁ SPOMÍNANIA

vyvolať úsmev na tvári dievčaťa: vyvolať ho ako žiačku
k tabuli: ako negatív filmu: ako ducha Marilyn Monroe:
za nocí ako je táto: sa ohlasuje hlboko v našich srdciach:
počujem iba šum z jej piesní: vidím iba šmuhy z jej tváre:
mami: veď ona iba chrčí: mami: veď ona nemá farby:
pridaj zvuk pridaj obraz: v tvojej neónovej technohlave:
počuješ smiech božskej Marilyn a zamatový hlas Frankieboya:
keď v mĺkvom lese obrazoviek: s Jamesom Deanom

zachraňujú svet: *a predsa sa točí! a predsa sa točí*
páska v premietačke: ich nahé hviezdy padajú z plátna
na zem: mäkké spomienky ľahké sny: a Kate Moss:
keď rozdáva úsmevy zahalené diktátom tajných klávesníc:
a Vanessa Paradis: keď so žuvačkou namotanou na prste:
postáva uprostred prázdneho metra: a ona vidí: kráčajúce
sobolie mláďa: list padajúci zo stromu: stredoškoláčky
dôverne sa chytajúce za končeky mobilných telefónov:
a ona vidí: sama videná: vyvoláva si spomienky: tváre
svojich milencov: vyvoláva úsmev na tvári dievčaťa:
ktorým kedysi bola: a ktorým navždy zostane:
hlboko v našich srdciach: hlbšie na negatívoch filmu.

WHAT REMAINED OF ALL THAT

they depart: leaving behind them a dustbowl: burning
horses: dead tanks: swords and keyboards: chopped like bloody
hands: in grass and thicket: bare brushwood of bodies: now small and
invisible robot systems: buzz and become airborne:
the mechanical flies the digital ladybirds: armed aerial
forces: new bombarders: who sits there and guides from the cockpit
the death-bringing warheads the engines of time? I fear: that never
more will your hand huddle in mine: when our memories
are dying away: of the naked body's beauty: deep under the spacesuit
of the prisoner: under more and more layers of matter:
I do not hear your heart: I do not hear your blood: *deep
deep: faraway faraway:* on the dead plateaux:
we grope: two amorphous beings embracing
through layers of memories: from all sides: arrive
the fighting systems: where shall we hide from danger
if not in our hearts?

Translated by John Minahane

ČO ZOSTALO Z TOHO VŠETKÉHO

odchádzajú: zanechávajúc za sebou spúšť: horiace
kone: mŕtve tanky: meče a klávesnice: uťaté ako ruky
krvavé: v tráve a tŕstí: nahé chrastie tiel: už malé a
neviditeľné robotické systémy: bzučia a vzlietajú:
mechanické muchy digitálne lienky: ozbrojené vzdušné

sily: nové bombardéry: kto v nich sedí a riadi z kokpitu
hlávky smrtonosné stroje času? bojím sa: že už nikdy
tvoja dlaň v moju sa neschúli: keď odumierajú nám
spomienky: na krásu nahého tela: hlboko pod skafandrom
väzneného: pod novými a novými vrstvami hmoty:
nepočujem tvoje srdce: nepočujem tvoju krv: *hlboko*
hlboko: ďaleko ďaleko: na mŕtvych planinách:
sa potácame: dve amorfné bytosti objímajúce sa
cez vrstvy spomienok: zo všetkých strán: prichádzajú
bojové systémy: kam sa schováme pred nebezpečenstvom
ak nie do svojich sŕdc?

SANNA HARTNOR (Sweden)

Sanna Hartnor (1986) lives and works in Malmö. Apart from being a poet,
she has worked with music and performance theatre. In her debut Hamnen
/ The Harbour *(2014), she decodes the architecture of a new, exclusive*
residential area by the sea. The collection is sharp and humorous – a satirical
contemporary fairy tale. In 2015, Hamnen *was nominated for the Katapult*
Prize, the Swedish Writers' Union award for the best debut of the year, and
in 2017 Sanna Hartnor recieved the Mare Kandre Award.

'THE FREELANCER TOOK A STEP BACK...'

the freelancer took a step back and was off
she slid like a seal
on her soft belly
over the stainless steel dining table

then she went
up the stairs to the sleeping loft
and wrote an ad copy

Translated by Željka Černok

'FRILANSAREN TOG SATS...'

frilansaren tog sats
hon kanade som en säl
med sin mjuka mage
över matbordet av rostfritt stål

sen gick hon
alla trappstegen upp till sovloftet
och gjorde copy

'PENCILS WERE BROUGHT TO PAPER...'

pencils were brought to paper
drew houses and horses
lists
suns
maps over the area

plans
lines that looked like lines
were really
heating cables
the water's way through the walls

the heating cables' way
through the ground
were really
lines in the plumber's dreams

the lifeline in
the plumber's hand
was really
a sun
a horse
a house

pencils were brought to paper
some searched
the face
in the mirror
for something familiar
searched for a
nose

found it
and drew

others saw nothing but
colours

Translated by Lars Ahlström

'PENNOR FÖRDES TILL PAPPER...'

pennor fördes till papper
gjorde hus och hästar
listor
solar
kartor över området

ritningar
linjer som liknade linjer
var egentligen
värmekablar
vattnets väg genom väggarna

värmekablarnas väg
genom marken
var egentligen linjer
i vvs-killens drömmar

livslinjen i
vvs-killens handflata
var egentligen
en sol
en häst
ett hus

pennor fördes till papper
en del tittade efter
i ansiktet
i spegeln
letade efter
något välbekant
letade efter en
näsa
hittade den
och ritade

andra såg bara
färgerna

'LAKES ARE PREDICTABLE…'

lakes are predictable
and smooth like mirrors
lakes are black and seas are grey
the sea slept
with one eye open

from that eye
a hardiness shone
so old that it had
an extinct and altogether
unknown colour

the sea was there
when the colours came
the light and eye sockets for the light
to throw itself into
colours were novelties
you wore their names
like hats

Translated by Lars Ahlström

'SJÖAR ÄR BERÄKNELIGA…'

sjöar är beräkneliga
och blanka som speglar
sjöar är svarta och hav är grå
havet sov
med ett öga öppet

ur det
lyste en tålighet
så gammal att den nu bar
en utrotad och alltigenom
okänd färg

havet var där
när färgerna kom
ljuset och ögonhålorna för ljuset
att kasta sig i

färgerna var nymodigheter
man bar deras namn
som hattar

'THE STAFF MANAGER LAY DOWN...'

the staff manager lay down on the shore
in the wet sand close to the sea

for a long time
she had been waiting
glancing
she wanted
to feel the sea
throb
roll back and forth

she had been falling asleep to the sound
of waves
and she had been longing

the staff manager had been longing for porn

she spread her legs wide
kept her eyes open
and let the sea lick her
decisive and unwitting
unsentimental the way it
drowns some and saves others
she wanted

the whole ocean inside
she wanted to be infected with something
unrelenting

the staff manager had been looking at pictures
of the sea in sunset
and the sea in rain

blushing
clear wild idle
all kinds
she had been drinking seawater

she had gone out into the storm collecting waves in a bucket
gone home and poured them over her face
googled the depths
sorted them among bookmarks
deeper and deeper
the Mariana trench had made her
come each time

so now it was just her
and the sea
the staff manager closed her eyes and saw
how her womb was a port
filled with expensive sailboats
tankers cargo ships icebreakers submarines
ferries
battleships

and she lay there until she saw
how they all sank

and how their hulls cracked
into just as expensive
indistinguishable splinters

Translated by Lars Ahlström

'PERSONALCHEFEN LA SIG...'

personalchefen la sig en kväll i sanden
den fuktiga närmast vattnet
hon hade väntat länge
sneglat
hon ville
känna havet
dunka
rulla ut och in

hon hade somnat till ljudet
av vågornas svall
och hon hade längtat

personalchefen hade längtat efter porr

hon särade benen brett
behöll ögonen öppna
och lät havet slicka henne
resolut och ovetande
osentimentalt på samma vis som det
dränker en del och räddar en del
hon ville ha
hela stora havet inuti
hon ville bli smittad av något
obevekligt

personalchefen hade tittat på bilder
av havet i kvällssol
och havet i regn
rodnande
klart vilt lojt
alla sorter
hon hade
druckit havsvatten

gått ut i stormen samlat vågor i en hink
gått hem och hällt dem över sitt ansikte

googlat djupen
ordnat dem bland bokmärken
djupare och djupare
marianergraven hade fått henne
att komma varje gång

nu var det alltså bara hon
och havet
och för sin inre syn såg personalchefen
hur hennes livmoder var en hamn
full av dyra segelbåtar
tankfartyg lastfartyg isbrytare ubåtar
bilfärjor
slagskepp

och hon låg kvar tills hon såg
hur de alla gick under
och skroven sprack till
precis lika dyra
flisor av oigenkännlighet

MONIKA HERCEG (Croatia)

Monika Hercog (1990) has published three poetry books: Početne
koordinate / Inital Coordinates *(2018),* Lovostaj / Closed Season
(2019) and Vrijeme prije jezika / Time Before Language *(2020).*
Winner of a number of prestigious literary awards including the Goran for
Young Poets, the international award Bridges of Struga, three more awards
for Initial Coordinates *and the Na vrh jezika award for* Lovostaj, *she has*
been translated into more than ten languages. Her selected poems were
published in French as Ciel sous tension *(L'Ollave, 2019).*

HEREDITARY DISEASES

a ring a spring another ring and some coins
is what the x-ray found in grandma's stomach
we stared long at the picture and couldn't agree
whether insanity was hereditary or contractible

for years afterwards she kept to herself
she was a demi-doe grandma
with muddy hooves
we were afraid she would soil our clothes
she would plant us with seeds of autumn
that would overgrow us like weeds

keeping my father's vows
behind her navel
she told me she had had many lads and stags
one time she was found they say
with the priest
by the brook

Translated by Mirza Purić

NASLJEDNE BOLESTI

prsten feder još jedan prsten i nekoliko kovanica
sve su to pronašli u bakinom trbuhu na rendgenu
dugo smo gledali u sliku i nismo se mogli složiti
je li ludost nasljedna ili zarazna

još godinama poslije nije nam prilazila
bila je polusrna polubaka
s blatom na papcima
bojali smo se da će nas zamazati
da će u nas posaditi sjemenje jeseni
koja će nas obrasti kao korov

čuvajući zavjete mog oca
iza pupka
rekla mi je da je imala puno momaka i jelena
jednom su je našli priča se
i s popom
kraj potoka

SECOND-RATE FATHER

London fog is a concept I know nothing about
although I've always thought I would travel
Admit the world into my hair,
shave it off and flush the shavings, New York, Brač and Niagara Falls
down the drain
That I would dissect motorways, as cocky as an election campaign,
bend them up into the tube of my inflexible vulva

But these days I feel like fog with a stern British accent
And I weigh as much as all the soil I never bonded with
Plants are reluctant to bloom near me
lest I irreversibly infect their seductiveness
Trees are chary of spitting out shoots
lest I eat their acrid foetuses

For months I've been dancing on Sunday's edge though I should
serve it to my family with my marinated eyes and drumsticks
The truth is I'm lonely and in waiting rooms I adopt
every courteous granddad and his old man skin

Poor Persephone, airing your heart chambers avails nothing
As does soothing yourself with imaginary pomegranate pips I playfully
push into my navel
As if each were a little Pluto, no man's place in the vacuum
A sky stripped down to the blue skips in the aorta as if to re-flood the planet
You know, I sometimes dream of us walking in the park
You hold my hand like an excellent father
You're so considerate when I dream of you

For six months, Zeus
For six months you
let them strip me and rape me
in the weightless dark

Translated by Mirza Purić

DRUGORAZREDNI OTAC

Londonska magla je koncept o kojem ne znam ništa
iako sam uvijek mislila da ću putovati
Zaprimati svijet u dlačice,
depilirati ga i puštati šume, New York, Brač, Niagarine slapove niz
odvode
Da ću samouvjereno kao predizborna kampanja secirati autoceste
i savijati ih u cijev svoje nerastezljive rodnice

Ali ovih dana osjećam se kao magla strogog britanskog naglaska
i težim kao cijela Zemlja koju nisam prisno upoznala
Biljke se boje rascvasti kraj mene
jer ću im nepovratno zaraziti zavodljivost
Stabla se boje pljunuti pupove iz vršaka
da im ne pojedem kisele zametke

Mjesecima plešem na oštrici nedjelje mada bih je trebala poslužiti
obitelji uz svoje marinirane oči i batake
Istina je da sam usamljena i u čekaonicama posvajam
svakog uglađenog djeda i njegovu staračku kožu

Jadna Persefona, ništa ne pomaže provjetriti komore srčanog mišića
Niti tješenje izmišljenim košticama nara kojima se igram gurajući ih u pupak
kao da su svaka mali Pluton, ničije mjesto u vakuumu
Nebo oguljeno do plave preskakuje u aorti kao da će ponovno potopiti planet
Znaš, sanjam nekad da šetamo parkom
Držiš me za ruku poput izvrsnog oca
Tako si pažljiv kad te sanjam

Šest mjeseci si, Zeuse
Šest mjeseci puštao
da me skidaju i siluju
u bestežinskom mraku

ESCAPE

we started locking our room at night when
we saw granddad's shadow standing by our bunk with a knife
he said he could hear steps near the house
and was keeping an eye lest they drag us into the woods forever

soon after he spoke with the dead
for the first time
and escaped by scaling
the tall fence round our yard
that was the neighbours' account
four days later we found him
at the other end of the city
hiding in a ditch

he said he was on the run afraid to return
somebody beheads men
plants the heads in the forest
to grow an army

Translated by Mirza Purić

BIJEG

počeli smo noću zaključavati sobu vidjevši
djedovu sjenu s nožem kako stoji kraj naših kreveta
rekao je da čuje korake oko kuće
i pazi da nas zauvijek ne odvuku u šumu

nedugo zatim je prvi put
razgovarao s mrtvima
i pobjegao preskočivši
visoku ogradu našeg dvorišta
tako su svjedočili susjedi
nakon četiri dana našli smo ga
na drugom kraju grada
skrivenog u jarku

rekao je da bježi i ne smije se vratiti
netko siječe ljudima glave
i sadi ih u šumi
da uzgoji vojsku

BROTHER

he had polio as a kid
and they tossed him in freezing water all the time
to cool off his incandescent organs
but he took a breath and he burnt
as if he'd taken the nuclear reactions of stars under his roof

st anthony may have jumped in later
since god couldn't be bothered
and brother started to walk again though by then they'd read
three more sicknesses from his spongy skeleton

in his head he grew unnamed birds
talked with them more often than with people

there are remnants of the sun's incandescent corona
underneath his inexperienced skin
and sometimes
when no one is looking
he glows in the dark

Translated by Mirza Purić

BRAT

imao je dječju paralizu kao mali
i bacali su ga neprestano u mrzlu vodu
da ohlade njegove užarene organe
a on je tek udahnuvši gorio
kao da je udomio nuklearne procese zvijezda

možda je kasnije uskočio sveti ante
kad se bogu nije dalo
pa je prohodao makar su pročitali još tri bolesti
u njegovom spužvastom kosturu

u glavi je uzgajao neimenovane ptice
s kojima je pričao češće nego s ljudima

ostalo je još nešto od užarene sunčeve korone
ispod njegove neiskusne kože
i ponekad
kad nitko ne gleda
svijetli u mraku

TRAINS

when the first train passed
the villagers thought the night was a candle
lit up and put out
at the will of the roaring machine
and nothing was quiet and holy
any more

only kata loved the noisy metal caterpillars
on tuesdays she grazed her sheep
and cows by the tracks
and observed obediently
as they spoke with god

Translated by Mirza Purić

VLAKOVI

kad je prošao prvi vlak
učinilo se seljanima da je noć svijeća
koja se pali i gasi
prema volji glasnog stroja
i ništa više nije ostajalo
sveto i tiho

samo je kata voljela bučne metalne gusjenice
utorkom je vodila ovce i krave
na ispašu kraj pruge
i promatrala poslušno
kako razgovaraju s bogom

MERERID HOPWOOD (UK / Wales)

Mererid Hopwood (1964) writes mainly in Welsh and is the only woman to have won the three main prizes for poetry and prose in the Eisteddfod, Wales' national cultural festival. She has been Children's Laureate for Wales and won the Tir na n'Og award for children's literature in 2018. Her collection Nes Draw *won the poetry section of the Welsh Book of the Year Awards, 2016. She has collaborated with visual artists, composers and dancers and has taken part in literature events world-wide.*

HAFN Y GLO

So this is Hafn y Glo.
A sharp-edged fissure on my list
between the might of Dyffryn yr Allorau
and the softness of Dôl y Plu.
Hafn y Glo.
I'm searching
on the margins of recognition
for the imprint of the fern
that stretches its fingers from the ages
before the ages that went before.
Hafn y Glo.
I'm listening for the scent of the dew,
or the whistle of the awakening in the tendril strings
at the hour when the green violin unwound its head.
Hafn y Glo
with its cold light.
Hafn y Glo,
an edge, a sword,
a cove of secrets
like an ever-existing memory.
Hafn y Glo.
There's an older name than this
in embers somewhere, I suppose.
Hafn y Glo.
It takes my breath away.

Translated by Tim ap Hywel

NAMES GIVEN BY THE WELSH TO PLACES ON THE PAMPAS:
Hafn y Glo / Coal Creek
Dyffryn yr Allorau / Altar Valley
Dôl y Plu / Feather Meadow

HAFN Y GLO

A dyma Hafn y Glo.
Hollt finiog ar fy rhestr
rhwng cadernid Dyffryn yr Allorau
a meddalwch Dôl y Plu.
Hafn y Glo.
Rwy'n chwilio
ar ymylon adnabod
am stamp y rhedyn
sy'n estyn ei fysedd o'r oesoedd
cyn yr oes o'r blaen.
Hafn y Glo.
Rwy'n gwrando am arogl y gwlith,
neu chwiban y dihuno yn llinynnau'r awr
pan ddadweindiodd y ffidil las ei phen.
Hafn y Glo
a'i golau oer.
Hafn y Glo
yn fin, yn gledd,
yn gilfach cyfrinach
fel cof erioed.
Hafn y Glo.
Mae enw hŷn na hwn
mewn marwydos rhywle, sbo.
Hafn y Glo.
Mae'n dwyn fy anadl.

RUSSIAN PROVERB

a wide road leads to war, a narrow path leads home

Come, Mother, come to the door,
tidy my hair with your comb;
a wide road leads to war,
a narrow path leads home.

Come, Mother, come, cry no more,
it's time for your son to roam;
a wide road leads to war,
a narrow path leads home.

Come, Mother, come as before,
pray 'neath the whispering dome;
a wide road leads to war,
a narrow path leads home.

Come, Mother, tell me who tore
the page that said in the tome:
a wide road leads to war,
a narrow path leads home.

Oh, They tore the page, my Son,
They took it away to hide;
come home, the war is done,
and the path is coffin wide.

Translated by Tim ap Hywel

FFORDD LYDAN, FFORDD GUL

Dere, Mam fach, dere at y ford,
mae'r llestri yn disgwyl te –
ffordd lydan sy'n arwain at faes y gad,
ffordd gul sy'n dod tua thre.

Dere, Mam fach, dere at y drws,
criba fy ngwallt nôl i'w le –
ffordd lydan sy'n arwain at faes y gad,
ffordd gul sy'n dod tua thre.

Dere, Mam fach, a phaid llefen mwy,
rwy'n mynd, er na wn i i ble –
ffordd lydan sy'n arwain at faes y gad,
ffordd gul sy'n dod tua thre.

Dweda, Mam fach, pwy chwalodd y gair
mai cariad yw'r Duw sy'n y ne'? –
ffordd lydan sy'n arwain at faes y gad,
ffordd gul sy'n dod tua thre.

Nhw chwalodd y gair â chelwydd, fy Mab,
arweinwyr y dillad parch,
mae'r rhyfel ar ben, der' adre fy Mab,
ar y ffordd sydd mor llydan ag arch.

BEAM

What is the forest but a twig? – And the great
cold snow? Only a flake.
And all the world? A beam
Of God's light in the mind of man.

Translated by Tim ap Hywel

LLYGEDYN

Beth yw'r goedwig ond brigyn? – A'r eira
mawr oer? Dim ond plufyn.
A'r byd i gyd? Llygedyn
O olau Duw ym meddwl dyn.

OLENA HUSEINOVA (Ukraine)

Olena Huseinova (1979) has published two poetry collections. Her first, Vidkrutyi Raider / Open Rider *(2012) was ranked in the top 10 books of the Ukrainian Book Arsenal Fair and placed in the top 20 of the Lviv Publishers' Forum. Her second,* Superheroi / Superheroes, *was published in 2016 and received a number of design and illustration awards. She is currently working at the National Public Broadcasting Company of Ukraine. Her poems have been translated into English, Polish, Czech, Slovak, Lithuanian and Russian.*

'THE CITY COULD HAVE BEEN CALLED ZHERONO...'

The city could have been called Zherono
It could have been called Syracuse
It could have no name at all
(I press my finger
to the imaginary map of the world
and you're there, right beneath my fingertip)

Now I don't care
whether the wine was
red or white
Today
I could
turn it into water
or pomegranate juice
(homemade)
Today
I could
differentiate
when the "o" is only a cry
or when the "o" is the beginning of a name
(by ear)
Today
I could
hide
(until the next time)
the cherry-coloured atlas
And the strokes
of Chinese hieroglyphs
long as the road to the Windy Mountain.

Translated by Karo Caren

'МІСТО МОГЛО НАЗИВАТИСЯ ЖЕРОНОЮ...'

Місто могло називатися Жероною
могло називатися Сирак'юс
могло взагалі не називатися
(я притискаю палець
до уявної карти світу
і ти – там – під моєю пучкою)
мені байдуже зараз
яке було вино
червоне чи біле
я сьогодні
змогла б
обернути його на воду
або гранатовий сік
(по-домашньому)
я сьогодні
змогла б
відрізнити

коли «О» тільки зойк
й коли «О» початок імені
(на слух)
я сьогодні
змогла б
заховати
(до наступного разу)
вишневий атлас
і довгі як дорога в Голу Пристань
стовпчики
китайських ієрогліфів.

'YES, MY LOVE, THIS IS MEXICO...'

Yes, my love, this is Mexico.
We came here
on foot.
Don't you remember? Don't you believe?
In all honesty,
We got a car
in San Diego.
I wanted a Dodge Aries,
but just as at home, you trusted
Alan Mullally alone.
The 1982 Ford Granada
was the colour of coffee with milk,
and for this I made peace with it –
all the way to Mexico.
When we were crossing the border,
The engine
broke
(the wind wheel, the water wheel,
the swinging weight?)
We left the car.
We walked on foot
across the Gila Desert.
I covered
my hair with a bandana,
took off my red boots,
and trod right behind you
step by step.

You turned around,
and blew
kisses at me,
with a million of the tiniest sand grains,
and you yelled:
"From this angle you resemble
the wife of Gaspar de Portola, my love."
"Who is she?"
"Mrs Portola, I think."
We slept in the desert,
although the city of Alamos
was alight with fires on the horizon.
In the morning I gathered some agave and said:
"I'll make Mezcal for you"
"Why not tequila?"
"Because we don't have any sugar."
When the Sea of Cortez
hit our faces with
a breeze of iodine and salt,
you said:
"Stop"
I took off my T-shirt
and jeans.
You kissed my lips,
entangled in your legs,
caressed,
drew closer,
held tight,
cuddled.
You smudged the wet sand of El Vizcaino
on my breasts
and my inner thighs.
"Yes, love, this is Mexico,
The Scammon's Lagoon –
People cannot stay here."
"We're just waiting –
for the sea lions,
the sea turtles,
the grey whales,
the blue whales,

the common seals,
don't be afraid, my love."

Translated by Karo Caren

'ВІРШ, В ЯКОМУ БАГАТО ВЛАСНИХ НАЗВ…'

Вірш, в якому багато власних назв і мало географічної достовірності
Так, любий, це Мексика.
Ми прийшли сюди
на своїх власних.
Не пам'ятаєш, не віриш?
Якщо чесно,
в Сан-Дієго
ми взяли машину.
Я просила Dodge Aries,
але ти, як і вдома, довіряв
тільки Алану Малаллі.
Ford Granada 1982 року
був кольору кави з молоком,
і це мене з ним мирило –
аж до Мехікалі.
Коли ми перетинали кордон,
всередині зламався
двигун
(вітряне колесо, водяне колесо,
гирьовий механізм?).
Ми кинули машину.
І йшли пішки
через
пустелю Хіла.
Я насунула
на волосся хустку,
зняла червоні черевички
і ступала за тобою
слід в слід.
Ти обертався,
відправляв мені
повітряний поцілунок,
з мільйоном найдрібніших піщинок,
і кричав:
– Чуєш, люба, звідси ти схожа
на жінку Гаспара де Портоли.
– Хто вона?
– Думаю – пані Портола.
Ми ночували в пустелі,
хоча місто Аламос

світило своїми вогнями на горизонті.
Зранку я збирала агаву і промовляла:
– Я зварю тобі з неї мескаль.
– Чому не текілу?
– Бо в нас немає цукру.
Коли море Картеса
вдарило нам в лиця
диханням з йоду і солі,
ти сказав:
– Зупиняйся.
Я скинула кофтинку
і джинси.
Ти цілував мене в губи,
обплітав ногами,
обсотував,
пригортав,
стискав,
тулив.
Мокрий пісок Ель-Віскаіно
налипав на груди
і внутрішній бік стегон.
– Так, любий, це Мексика,
лагуна Скаммонс –
людям тут бути не можна.
– Ми просто чекаємо –
морських левів,
морських черепах,
сірих китів,
синіх китів,
звичайних тюленів,
не бійся, люба.

'THE PERSON IN ME GROWS SMALLER...'

The person in me grows smaller,
curls up in a ball,
wraps in a colourful wrapper.
A chocolate-covered prune.
Bitter, sugary, smoky,
marks the fingers
with the black, abrasive stain –
that's how you'll recognize your kin,
that's how you'll distinguish
between black and white.

My entire person may be eaten in one go.
Open your mouth wide,
clench your jaw tight,
swallow once.
The person in me
will squeak, crumble, and halt.
And already without her –
with marble-like confidence
– I will hold back
the cargo carriages,
the distant roads,
the barbed wires,
the tall fences,
the perpetual snow.
And those
with bones in their throats,
those with crossed fingers
behind their backs,
the shady dealings of a military man,
a horse made of damp, fireproof wood,
and a berry – round and poisonous.

Translated by Karo Caren

'ЛЮДИНА В МЕНІ МЕНШАЄ…'

Людина в мені меншає,
згортається калачиком,
обгортається кольоровим фантиком.
Чорнослив в шоколаді.
Прогірклий, приторний, димний.
Лишає на пальцях
чорний в'їдливий слід,
за яким впізнаєш своїх,
за яким відрізняєш
чорне від білого.
Людину в мені можна
з'їсти нараз.
Вистачить одного
широко відкритого рота,
одного міцного притиску щелеп,
одного ковтка.
Людина в мені
скрипне, розтрощиться, стане.

І вже без неї –
з мармуровою певністю –
я триматиму
вагони товарні,
дороги далекі,
дроти колючі,
огорожі високі,
вічні сніги.
І тих,
у кого кістка в горлі,
хто тримає за спиною
схрещені пальці,
темне підступне військо,
коня з вогкого незаймистого дерева
і ягоду – круглу, отруйну.

DAVOR IVANKOVAC (Croatia)

Davor Ivankovac (1984) has published three poetry books: Rezanje magle
/ Cutting Through the Fog *(2012),* Freud na Facebooku / Freud on
Facebook *(2013) and* Doba bršljana / Season of the Ivy *(2018). He has won
a number of prestigious literary awards including the Goran for Young Poets
for* Freud na Facebooku *and his poems have appeared in English, German,
Italian, French, Greek, Romanian and Slovenian translation.*

A NON-SENTIMENTAL STORY OF RAIN

I don't know about other places, but this is how it is here:
houses have gutters. OK,
I know about other places, just a figure of speech.
What matters is, rainwater flows from the roofs into the gutters
and on into the four downpipes at each corner of the house
then straight down, out of the spout and into the drain.
Or it just pools into a puddle in the yard, as the case may be.

I don't know about other people's, but our gutters for a long time stood
riddled with shrapnel, here and there severed by direct hits.
Rainwater leaked, gushed, spurted and dripped,
always in a regular manner, depending on the intensity of precipitation
and the size and position of the holes. That is how it was.
With time I memorised the workings of the whole system

always looking for regularities.
They mattered, irregularities did, as they lent meaning to all things
and every time it rained and I saw them I was reassured that
everything was fine, all things in their proper place.

Leaking left and right, like life, Nan was wont to say.
On endless quiet twilit afternoons we sat about doing
whatever, shelling beans, chopping green beans, listening to the leaking.
To the patter of drops dripping into the bowls scattered round rooms
                                                    from ceilings
patched up with planks and poly.
Waiting for better days without rain or bombardment.

I don't know about other people's houses, but ours was hit
by over twenty shells.
By the tail and by the size of the hole one could
determine the calibre. Father filled the craters in with a shovel
or simply scraped soil in with his boots.
Which one is this in a row, I asked one day flipping the fins in my hand.
He shrugged, I stopped counting at fifteen.
Pity, I thought, now we'll never know the exact number.
Because I, too, had lost count and I was afraid
that wasn't the end of losing.

And it wasn't. They're both dead now,
I am alone.
Years later, we mended the roof and the ceilings, the refurbishment
included new gutters. Now the rainwater flows nicely down
into the metal troughs girdling the roof,
on through the downpipes at the house corners straight
through the spout and into the ditches...
All is dull and dreary again,
and we gave the shrapnel-riddled gutters to the Gipsies.

But, no, wait, I must confess something.
The gutters with the holes are still there, leaking left and right.
I don't know about other places, but this is how it is here.
You may think I'm embellishing and raving, but really,
when it drizzles or pours I stand and I look and I see.
Leaking left and right, like in the old times.

This makes me happy.
For I am alone now.
And that's the way it's going to be until
the end.

Translated by Mirza Purić

NESENTIMENTALNA PRIPOVIJEST O KIŠI

Ne znam kako je drugdje, ali ovdje kod nas je ovako:
kuće uokolo imaju rine. Dobro,
znam kako je drugdje, tako se samo kaže.
Ono bitno je da se kiša s krovova slijeva u njih i
otječe dalje, sve do okomitih zatvorenih cijevi na svakome
ćošku kuće i spušta se ravno dolje, kroz otvor u kanaliće.
Ili ostaje ležati u dvorištu, kako kome.

Ne znam za druge, no naše su rine dugo vremena stajale
izbušene gelerima, gdjegdje i potpuno prekinute izravnim pogocima.
Kiša je iz njih curila, šikljala, poskakivala, kapala,
uvijek pravilno, a ovisno o intenzitetu padalina i
veličini i položaju rupe. Tako je to bilo.
S vremenom sam cijeli sustav naučio napamet i
uvijek pratio otkrivajući pravilnosti.
One su bile bitne, te pravilnosti, jer svemu su davale smisao
i kada bih ih pri svakoj kiši opet iznova zapazio bio sam siguran
da je sve u redu i na svome mjestu.

Puštaju na sve strane, kao život, znala je govoriti baka.
Za beskrajnih polutamnih i tihih popodneva sjedili smo
radeći štogod, čisteći grah, narezujući mahune, i slušajući curenje.
Kapanje u zdjele raširene po sobama, s navrat nanos
najlonima i daskama pokrpanih stropova.
Čekajući bolje dane, bez kiše i granata.

Ne znam za druge, na našu kuću i okućnicu tresnulo ih je
više od dvadeset.
Prema repiću projektila i veličini oštećenja mogao se precizno
odrediti kalibar, a rupe u zemlji otac je zatrpavao lopatom
ili naprosto zagrtao čizmama.
Koja je ova, pitao sam jednom prevrćući repić po rukama.
Slegnuo je ramenima, od petnaest više ne brojim.
Šteta, pomislio sam, sad nikad nećemo znati točan broj.
Jer i ja sam se izgubio u brojanju i uhvatila me bojazan
da bismo se i drugdje mogli pogubiti.

Tako je to bilo, doista. A sada su oboje mrtvi,
ostao sam samo ja.
Godinama kasnije, osim stropova i krova, s obnovom smo
dobili i nove rine. Kiša se opet uredno slijeva
u metalne žljebove duž krova,
odatle kroz okomite cijevi na ćoškovima i ravno dolje
kroz otvor u kanaliće...
Sve je opet jednolično i monotono,
a izbušene rine odavno smo razdijelili Ciganima.

Ali ne, čekajte, priznat ću vam nešto.
Te su izbušene rine još uvijek tu, na kući, i puštaju na sve strane.
Ne znam kako je drugdje, ali kod mene je tako.
Mislite da pretjerujem i bulaznim, ali doista,
kad rominja ili pljušti ja stanem i gledam, i sve jasno vidim.
Puštaju na sve strane, kao nekad.
To me veseli.
Jer sada sam ostao sam.
I tako će biti do
kraja.

FIVE MINUTES TO WINTER

I go out for a walk and I find him at the cemetery.
What am I doing here, I surprise myself with the question.
What are you doing here, I surprised me.
What by-roads of the subconscious had brought me here?
What guilt led me through streets and junctions,
by prickly bushes and feral dogs?
It's easier to realise that flashing is – lightning.
Hesitant as if in the hallway of a stranger's house
I wait for the other to speak up, point out the obvious.
Across the plain, dark rolls like an avalanche.
If one could only go home like that, without thinking
of the roots of the weeds on the grave.

Translated by Mirza Purić

PET MINUTA PRIJE ZIME

Izađem u šetnju i zateknem se na groblju.
Otkud ja ovdje, iznenadim se pitanjem.
Otkud ti ovdje, iznenadi ja mene.
Kakvi su me to podsvjesni puteljci doveli čak ovamo?

Kakva krivnja me vodila kroz ulice i raskrižja,
kraj bodljikavog grmlja i podivljalih pasa?
Lakše je spoznati da je sijevanje –munja.
Neodlučan kao u predsoblju strane kuće
čekam da drugi progovori, gestom ukaže na očito.
Preko ravnice, poput lavine, kotrlja se mrak.
Kad bi se tako moglo nazad, da se ne pomisli na
korijenje grobnog korova.

TICK-TOCK

Maybe it's the sound of non-occurrence
the syntax of time running through a mechanical amplifier
hanging on the wall. Maybe, as we sit in silence,
we listen to the drops dripping evenly onto
the window-sill, between drowsing and waking with a start,
or is it the beeps of hospital machines making
their way to the darkness of our deep unconsciousness
like the drip of a drip.
Maybe, as we lie by the window, time's joints
crackle with strain.
Why is the time of sickness so slick and sharp?
A nick on the pad, a letter driven under the fingernail.
Morning rays on the wall, the calendar reflects
black days and red Sundays, all things are ossified,
scentless,
white
only a half of the heart still beats.
And it's hard to cope
        with those sixty small silences
in each minute.

Translated by Mirza Purić

KUCANJE ZIDNOG SATA

Možda je to zvuk nedogađanja,
sintaksa vremena kroz mehaničko pojačalo
okačeno na zid. Možda, dok sjedimo u tišini,

osluškujemo ravnomjerno kapanje na prozorsku dasku,
iz polusna, iz buđenja, između dvaju trzaja,
ili nam se u tamu duboke nesvjestice probija
kao kapanje infuzije
odbrojavanje bolničke aparature.
Možda, dok ležimo kraj prozora, uslijed naprezanja
pucketaju zglobovi vremena.
Zašto je vrijeme bolesti tako glatko i oštro?
Mali rez na jagodici, slovo zariveno pod nokat.
Jutarnje zrake na površini zida, kalendar reflektira
crne dane i crvene nedjelje, sve je okoštalo,
bezmirisno,
bijelo,
samo otkucava još polovica srca.
I dok traje, teško se nositi s tih
šezdeset malih tišina
u svakoj minuti.

NETTLE POEM

In the unpredictable yet familiar geometry of
pavements and paths
where walking is permitted
I find my own ageing plan every day.
Ageing isn't dying, it is the state
sloughing its skin,
slowly supplanting an excess of self, of all things,
robbing space to pay time.
Morning daze lacks accuracy,
I lack accurate thoughts for hard, dry words,
the daze is the bark of an old oak,
a damp hollow in a moor and a moldy landscape.
The geometry leads me where the state permits,
the concrete has been spilt, the ground stomped,
a training range stretches
by the roads to the medicinal herb plantation,
everything is as I presage.

Translated by Mirza Purić

PJESMA KOPRIVA

U nepredvidljivoj a poznatoj geometriji
pločnika i puteva
po kojima je dozvoljeno kretanje
svakodnevno pronalazim vlastiti plan starenja.
Starenje to nije umiranje, to je polagano
mijenjanje kože države,
polagano popunjavanje prostora suviškom sebe, svega,
oduzimanje prostoru da bi se dalo vremenu.
U jutarnjoj omamljenosti nedostaje preciznosti,
nedostaju mi precizne misli za suhe tvrde riječi,
omamljenost je kora starog hrasta,
vlažna udolina u ravnici i pljesnivi krajolik.
Geometrija me vodi kamo država dozvoljava,
razliven je beton i ugažena zemlja,
rasprostire se tjedan poligon,
kraj putova plantaže ljekovitog bilja,
sve je kako predosjećam.

HELEN IVORY (UK)

Helen Ivory (1969) is a poet and visual artist. Her fifth Bloodaxe collection,
The Anatomical Venus, *was winner of the East Anglian Writers 'By the
Cover' Award, and shortlisted in the 2019 East Anglian Book Awards
poetry category. A book of collage / mixed media poems,* Hear What the
Moon Told Me, *and a surrealist chapbook* Maps of the Abandoned
City, *were published in 2019. She edits the webzine* Ink Sweat and Tears
and teaches for UEA / NCW online.

IN A TIME BEFORE MAPS

Long ago when the city was an infant
it lay on its back on a big white sheet
transfixed by the tiny articulations
of its own small hands.

Constellations of eyes beheld from the sky –
the city grew vivid, grew hearty,
grew schools and grew graveyards
and when these were replete, it grew more.

Straw begat sticks, then sticks begat brick
so the wolf packed its bags
and decamped to the forest.
The city sprouted a gate and then locked it.

Even the city became lost in those days –
took itself for a wander inside its own head
and simply vanished. Something had to be done.
The cartographer stepped from a fold in the sky.

STREETS OF THE ABANDONED CITY

The Street of the Candlemaker runs slant to the river
where time is detained in slight tallow bodies,
moored up in ragboats awaiting the tide.

The Street of the Illusionist was never there,
or so it would have you believe;
an empty black bag in a vat full of pitch.

The Street of the Graveyard is lined with books,
with symbols and scorings no one can decipher
and carvings of cherubs too weighty to fly.

The Street of the Birds is a vault of locked cages,
each inhabitant rendered to feather and bone.
Wind blusters through keyholes to parody song.

The Street of the Kings wears a crown of eye teeth
plucked from the jaws of anonymous dogs.
The Street of the Dogs was scratched from the map.

NIGHTS IN THE ABANDONED CITY

Dark comes home to the abandoned city
and heaves off its boots by the fire.
It is astonishing how weary the dark is from its work,
its commute through choking towns and encampments.

It talks to the flames of the things it has seen
of the stilled hearts it has held
between finger and thumb.
It unburdens itself of all human sorrow.

And the fire, pretending for now,
it is a hearth at the centre of a church house,
listens like a priest and bites its own tongue,
imbues the parlour with cloying incense.

In the shadowplay, the dark is a plague doctor's mask,
a bone-saw, a gathering of spat-out teeth.
Soon, fire will describe a still life of eyeglasses:
their tiny infinities – all their dashed lenses.

LUNCHEON IN THE ABANDONED CITY

There have been no hands
to wind clocks for months now,
thus, restaurants rely on instinct
and the shadows on pavements
to signal when to prepare for service.

Only salt and pulses remain
so, ladles spend the morning
meting them out in melancholy portions
onto row upon row
of poker-faced plates.

At noon, cutlery goes through the motions –
a mechanical dance of luncheon
gnashing salt into powder
agitating the pulses
till the gong shudders
            and they all fall down.

THE BIRDS

During the final days of those final days
the city gate was propped open for stragglers
dragging their suitcases through windy streets –
civilization's chip-wrappers jamming their wheels.

And then a rustling of a million feathers
as all the sky's birds
put their shoulder to the gate
and closed it, as if closing a tomb.

A whirlwind of litter baffled about the city –
until a crow with one blue eye
rose, gave an ushering caw,
and thence the assembly swooped.

For six days and six nights they worked
with unstinting precision
to garner each cast-off wrapping, each scuttling drink can,
each motley fragment of plastic.

On the seventh day, urged on by the crow,
they conjured a structure from this debris,
a structure surpassing any manmade fabrication.
A nest, a glorious nest reaching out to the high heavens!

THE CARTOGRAPHER UNMAKES

It's snow that gives her the idea,
bleaching parks of desire lines
and blotting out coffin paths.
With a white paintbrush
she makes a halo of the ring road
and cancels out the tower blocks and castle.

And when there is no one left
to remember the City,
when all has turned to fireside yarns and myth,
a traveller will open out
some spotless pages of the map
and imagine lady fortune shines on him.

KATERYNA KALYTKO (Ukraine)

Kateryna Kalytko (1982) is a writer, translator and author of two books of short stories and six poetry collections, for which she has received numerous literary awards. Her poetry has been translated into English, German, Polish, Armenian, Lithuanian, Slovenian, Serbian, Italian and Hebrew. As a translator from the Balkan languages, she was awarded the prize of the magazine The Kryvbas Courier *and the independent translation award* METAPHORA.

APRIL 6

You are not just sleeping with this one man, but with his whole life,
and sometimes it wakes you up and snatches him out of your arms.
For, you see, war often comes along and lies down between you like a child
afraid to be left alone in the dark.

War, he says, involves many numbers, let's see –
two relatives equal one sack of bones,
one thousand three hundred and ninety-five days of siege,
three packages of humanitarian aid: butter, canned goods,
powdered milk, three bars of soap.

Four armed men come for you,
show you their orders and then escort you out into the night.
During the walk across the city
you hear missiles flying over your head – twice.

… Five times they take you out of the barracks
to a ditch where forty-three lay rotting
and each time you think: I will finally die
and tell God that it was a lame joke.

But they throw you face down into the dirt
and take their sweet time pressing a gun to your head.
Since then, he says, I don't like to dream,
these kinds of memories, they aren't fitting for a man.

You run through the woods, they shoot at your back,
a bullet hits your thigh but all you feel is this dirt on your face.

That's when a leafless tree of pain grows
in your chest, pulsating.
And I don't respond because what do you say to that
I just keep wiping the dirt off his face, over and over again,
even while he's sleeping,
even while he's away.

Translated by Olena Jennings and Oksana Lutsyshyna

ШОСТЕ КВІТНЯ

Спиш не лише з одним оцим чоловіком,
а й з усеньким його життям.
І часом воно заважає вам спати чи просто собі обійматися.
Скажімо, часто приходить війна і лежить між вами, немов дитя,
яке боїться лишатись на самоті у темній сусідній кімнаті.

У війни, каже він, в арсеналі багато чисел:
двоє родичів – один мішок із кістьми,
тисяча триста дев'яносто п'ять днів облоги міста,
три пакунки з гуманітаркою: масло, консерви, сухемолоко, три
                                        брусочки мила.
По тебе приходять четверо, кожен зі зброєю на плечі.
Показують список, ведуть тебе під конвоєм
через місто нічне. Два рази, ідучи,
чуєш снаряди, що пролітають високо над головою.
…П'ять разів із бараку виводять під зливу вночі
до відкритої ями, в якій вже гниють сорок троє,
і щоразу думаєш: от я нарешті зараз помру
і зізнаюся Богові – це був невдалий жарт.
А вони вас кидають всіх долілиць у бруд
і тицяють у потилицю дуло, і мусите довго лежати.
І відтоді я розлюбив, каже він, дивитися сни –
всі ці спогади, знаєш, не дуже-то й чоловічі,
коли ви біжите через ліс, вам у спину стріляють вони,
коли куля в стегні, а ти все відчуваєш оте багно на обличчі.

Ось тоді велике безлисте дерево болю проростає йпульсує в грудях,
і ти не відповідаєш, бо що на таке відповісти.
І стираєш, стираєш, стираєш йому з обличчя той бруд,
навіть крізь сон.
І навіть
коли на відстані.

'THIS LONELINESS...'

This loneliness could have a name, an Esther or a Miriam.
Regiments fall to the ground with an infant's cry.
Words hardly fit between water and salt.
Under the flag at half-mast, hundreds of hoarse voices

laugh, pricked by the splinters of language.
This loneliness is vast, bottomless, and so chilling
that even a stranger turns away. Restless children wander
out of the school, stand by the sea, as if in front of a tribunal.

Dried tree branches crackle in the air like transmitters.
Somebody keeps calling out the name of the city turned into ashes.
This loneliness could be named Sevgil or Selima.
The names of the abandoned are salty and deep.

She comes out, fumbles with the knot
of her black headscarf; her lips are pale.
Who is there, she says, do you read me? Does anyone hear us?
Just a moment ago somebody called out our names.

Do you read me, son, try and listen to me, to me –
they have all left the shore, look for them in the sea.

Translated by Olena Jennings and Oksana Lutsyshyna

'ЦЮ САМОТНІСТЬ...'

Цю самотність могли би звати Естер або Міріам.
З немовлячим плачем лягають у землю полки.
Між води та солі давно затісно словам.
Під приспущеним прапором регочуть сотні хрипких
нетутешніх пельок, скалками мови поколотих.
Ця самотність холодна, розверста й така бездонна,

що й чужак не бере.
Неприкаяні діти зі школи
вибрідають, стоять над морем, як перед судом.
Тріскотить у повітрі зв'язку пересохле гілля,
хтось уперто вигукує позивний попелища.
Цю самотність могли би звати Селіма або Севгіль,
імена покинутих солоні й завжди найглибші.
І виходить вона, нервово пальцями мне
чорний вузол хустини, губи в неї бліді:
хто це, каже. Прийом, чи хтось іще чує нас?
Щойно хтось викликав нас і називав імена.
Ну ж бо, синку, прийом, послухай мене, мене:
всі пішли із берега, пошукай у воді.

HE WRITES

They were disliked on earth and forsaken among the clouds.
Yuri Andrukhovych

Mother, you haven't sent me a single photograph
so I almost forgot what your face looks like.
You'll cry, I know, I have caused you distress
but each trouble is just a tiny speck of blood
on a Sunday dress.

Life is a house on the side of the road,
old-world style, like our peasant house, divided into two parts.
In one, they wash the dead man's body and weep.
In the other, they dress a bride.

Mother, I want you to have a dream in which I come
and sit in the part with more light.

You cry so much mother, you don't stop sobbing.
I can't see your face well, but faces don't matter much,
Your hair, I still remember, smells of cornflowers.

They all want something from us and keep stirring
the anthill of the army, in which the country lies like a rotting fish.
I wrote to Andrew, a long soulful letter,
but didn't get a reply, maybe I got the address wrong.

And before that Andrew wrote: how he remembers the taste of
the toffee that Dad used to bring from town, also the slippery ravine
behind our house. Peter, he wrote, if we ever return, it will be on
stretchers.
Mother was right – we should have remained fishermen.

Rain drums loudly, mud covers the front lines.
We march hopelessly along rivers and under the clouds.
I'm forgetting everything, as if memories were leaking out of me.
… Mother, does that girl Hafiya still sing in the church choir?

Translated by Olena Jennings and Oksana Lutsyshyna

ВІН ПИШЕ

Їх не любили на землі й забули серед хмар.
Юрій Андрухович

Мамо, Ви мені не надсилали із себе фото,
і тому я майже забув, які Ви з лиця,
Ви заплачете, знаю, це-бо я додаю вам гризот,
але кожне горе –тільки кривава цятка
на святочній сорочці.

Життя – придорожня хата,
старовинна подільська, наша, на дві половини,
тут голосять, покійника обмиваючи, там – квітчають
дівку на свято,
хай Вам, мамо, насниться, що я прийшов у гостину,
і сиджу на тій половині, де більше світла.

Ви ще плачете, мамо, ридань ніяк не вколошкати,
але що те обличчя, із нього води не пити,
а волосся Ваше – я ще пригадую – пахне волошками.

Всі щось хочуть від нас і ворушать мурашник війська,
у якому країна лежить, ніби тухла риба.
Я писав Андрієві – довго, розлого, по-свійському,
а від нього нічого, може, адреса хибна.

Перед тим він писав: пам'ятає смак тягучих конфет,
що привозили з міста тато, за хатою мокру балку,
а додому, Петрусю, тепер хіба на лафетах,
мама правду казали: краще були б рибалками.

Злива б'є в барабани, болото попід фронтами,
ми йдемо вздовж річок і під хмарами, безнадійно.
Я усе забуваю, з мене наче витекла пам'ять.
Чи співає ще, мамо, в церковному хорі Гафія?

SANNA KARLSTRÖM (Finland)

Sanna Karlström (1975) has published five books of poetry, the first of which,
Taivaan mittakaava / Heaven's Magnitude, *won the Helsingin Sanomat*
Literature Prize for the best debut work of literature in 2004. Her third book
of poetry, Harry Harlow'n rakkauselämät / The Love Lives of Harry
Harlow *(2009) received the Tanssiva karhu Poetry Prize and also the Kalevi*
Jäntti Prize. Karlström's poetry has been translated into ten languages.

'AFTER NINE IN THE EVENING...'

After nine in the evening
the landscape decreases
by thirty percent.
When darkness comes, everything is sold off.

Once I stood at the seashore.
On the horizon an island crumbled like a vast croissant,
but much slower.
I felt like rowing there,
to see if it was still for sale.
But of course I didn't have a boat.
Or money, its favourable wind.

Translated by Pauli Tapio

'ILTAYHDEKSÄN JÄLKEEN...'

Iltayhdeksän jälkeen
maisema vähenee
kolmellakymmenellä prosentilla.
Kun tulee pimeää, kaikki myydään pois.

Kerran seisoin meren rannalla.
Horisontissa saari mureni kuin valtava voisarvi,
mutta paljon hitaammin.
Minun teki mieli soutaa sinne,

jos se vielä olisi kaupan.
Eihän minulla ollut venettä.
Eikä rahaa, sen suotuisaa tuulta.

'O OMNIPOTENT...'

O omnipotent
your world, beautiful as steak and wrong

There are the potatoes, onions, herbs.
There is the shade, sun-dried tomatoes,
shelves so deep the hand can't reach the farthest jar.

O stupendous sowing machine
in the beginning I was a sleeve and a couple of trouser legs.

You said: here are the other garments.
Here the sewing box of the heart.

Translated by Pauli Tapio

'OI KAIKKIVOIPA...'

Oi kaikkivoipa
maailmasi kaunis kuin pihvi ja väärin

Tuossa perunat, sipulit, yrtit.
Tuossa hämärä, aurinkokuivattuja tomaatteja,
niin syvät hyllyt ettei käsi tavoita taaimmaista purkkia.

Oi suuri saumuri
alussa olin hiha ja pari lahjetta.

Sanoit: tuossa loput pukimet.
Tuossa sydämen ompelurasia.

'DEEPLY I INHALED...'

Deeply I inhaled a little bunch of basil,
scented like a forest.
Forests spread uncontrollably
somewhere around the chest, I nearly got lost there.

Someone took whatever they wanted.
The money clomped back and forth in the cash-register,
like one who is troubled paces a room.

Translated by Pauli Tapio

'MINÄ HENGITIN SYVÄÄN...'

Minä hengitin syvään pientä basilikaa
joka tuoksui kuin metsä.
Metsät leviävät hallitsemattomasti
jossain rinnan alueella, olin eksyä sinne.

Joku poimi koriinsa mitä halusi.
Raha louskutti kassakoneessa edestakaisin,
niin kuin se, jolla on huoli, kulkee huonetta.

'I DRIFT ALONG THE CORRIDORS OF THE ALEPA...'

I drift along the corridors of the Alepa in search of content,
the shopping trolley's chain clinked gaily, I didn't know what to take.

Three marinated broilers lay in a heated display case.
I, too, wanted to procreate there and then.

I took an egg from its case, plucked it like a bilberry,
put it under my wing, without asking, became a little better right away

and the sand began to close up where it had been struck.

Translated by Pauli Tapio

'MINÄ HARHAILIN ALEPAN KÄYTÄVILLÄ...'

Minä harhailin Alepan käytävillä etsien sisältöä,
kärryn kahle kilisi iloisesti, en tiennyt mihin tarttua.

Lämpövitriinissä makasi kolme marinoitua broileria.
Minunkin teki mieli heti lisääntyä.

Otin kennosta munan, poimin sen kuin mustikan varvusta,
panin siipeni alle, kysymättä, olin heti vähän parempi

ja hiekka alkoi umpeutua siitä mihin oli isketty.

AUŠRA KAZILIŪNAITĖ (Lithuania)

Poet and philosopher Aušra Kaziliūnaitė (1987) is author of five poetry books: The First Lithuanian Book *(2007);* 20% Concentration Camp *(2009);* The Moon is a Pill *(2014);* I am Crumbled Walls *(2016) and* There is No Sea *(2020). Kaziliūnaitė's poems have been translated into 16 languages and in 2018, her selected poems,* The Moon is a Pill, *was published in English by Parthian Books in Rimas Užgiris' translation. She was invited to the International Writing Program 2018 in the USA.*

WARDROBE

i saw another person's dream
try you on for size

it washed and ironed you
hung you in the closet
then threw you away
– you were just too big –

occasionally i meet
the homeless man
who wears you now

finally, there is light in his eyes

Translation by Rimas Uzgiris

APRANGA

mačiau kaip tave apsirengė
kito žmogaus sapnas

kaip kabino į spintą
skalbė ir lygino
kaip išmetė
– nes per didelis –

kartais sutinku
tą benamį
kuris vilki tavim

jo akys pagaliau švyti

HOLIDAY MAKE-UP

I saw angels with automatic rifles in their hands
staring sadly at the floor in airports and stations

waiting

I saw eight-year-olds sent by their parents
running up to human rights activists
shouting – give us back the rainbow –

giggling

I saw men who thought they were real men
and women who thought they were real women
saying instead of a name in greeting
– I am so and so's woman –

I saw emptied villages, forests felled
dammed rivers and steeples of small towns

in the mirror

Translation by Rimas Uzgiris

ŠVENTINIS MAKIAŽAS

Mačiau angelus su automatais rankose
jie liūdnai žvelgė į grindis oro uostose ir stotyse

lūkuriavo

Mačiau tėvų siųstus aštuonmečius
kurie pribėgę prie žmogaus teisių aktyvistų
šaukė – gražinkit mums vaivorykštę –

kikeno

Mačiau vyrus, kurie manėsi esantys tikri vyrai
ir moteris, kurios manėsi esančios tikros moterys
susipažindamos vietoj vardo jos sakydavo
– esu to ir to moteris –

Mačiau ištuštėjusius kaimus, kertamus miškus
užtvenktas upes ir mažų miestelių bažnyčias

veidrodyje

FROM THE MEMOIRS OF A SAD GOD

I cut a person out of the river

I took the first stencil into my mitts
that came walking down the street –
the shadow that was created earlier
than the one who cast it

and I cut and I cut
and I sawed –

a round head
two arms of similar length
two legs of similar length

I cut a person out of the river

he flows in waves
sputters and
doesn't move

but
you won't step twice
into him

Translation by Rimas Uzgiris

IŠ LIŪDNOJO DIEVO MEMUARŲ

iš upės aš iškirpau žmogų

ėmiau į leteną pirmą pasitaikiusį
gatve žengiantį trafaretą –
šešėlį kuris buvo sutvertas anksčiau
už jį metusį

ir kirpau kirpau
ir pjoviau –

apvali galva
dvi panašaus ilgio rankos
dvi panašaus ilgio kojos

iš upės aš iškirpau žmogų

jis teka banguoja
šnypščia ir
nejuda

bet
į jį du kartus
neįbrisi

INVISIBLE METAMORPHOSES

would you love me
if suddenly my gender
changed or my scent
the colour of my skin
the time of year

would you still love
if I were a flower and a stone
or a flower growing
among stones

and
generally
do you love me

in those blinks of an eye
when I am truly
there

Translation by Rimas Uzgiris

NEMATOMOS METAMORFOZĖS

ar mylėtum mane
jei staiga pasikeistų
mano lytis kvapas
odos spalva
ar metų laikas

ar mylėtum
jei būčiau gėlė ir akmuo
arba gėlė užaugusi
tarp mažų akmenėlių

ir
apskritai
ar myli mane

tomis trumpomis akimirkomis
kai iš tiesų
jais būnu

BARBARA KLICKA (Poland)

*Barbara Klicka (1981) made her debut in 2000. Her second collection,
same same (2012), was nominated in the 'Book of the Year' category of
the Wrocław Poetry Award 'Silesius'. Her subsequent book* nice *(2015)
won two of the most important Polish poetry awards: the Wrocław Poetry
Award 'Silesius' and the Gdynia Literary Award. She is the author of the
poetic drama* Primer, *staged at the National Theatre, Warsaw. In 2019,
she was again nominated for the Gdynia Literary Award for her first
novel,* Zdrój.

EASTER

A start like a recipe for spring. I was going on a long journey in
a fast car. Everywhere there were clouds, I appreciated the value
of the sun-roof. We passed some storks, so I said:

look, storks. He said: you're happy like a little kid. Stupid, I said,
I'm happy like a little kid, because you're speaking to me like to
a woman in April, be my friend, I want to be aglow from that.
Then

I called the witnesses on the spot, e-mails, ballets. All in pretty big quantities, because nothing stubbornly would do for me. Doesn't matter, because the calendar resurrection's on the way

for this I'll bring the world a cheesecake.
Let them all love me, since you can't.

Translated by David Malcolm

WIELKANOC

Początek jak z przepisu na wiosnę. Jechałam w długą podróż szybkim samochodem. Wszędzie były chmury, doceniałam walor szyberdachu. Mijaliśmy bociany, więc powiedziałam:

patrz, bociany. Powiedział: cieszysz się jak dziecko. Głupi, powiedziałam, cieszę się jak dziecko, bo mówisz do mnie jak do kobiety w kwietniu, bądź mi przyjacielem, chcę od tego świecić. Potem

wezwałam na świadków miejscowych, maile, balety. Wszystko w dość dużych ilościach, bo nic uparcie nie chciało mi starczać. Ale nic, nadciąga bowiem kalendarzowe zmartwychwstanie

z tej okazji niosę światu sernik.
Niech kocha mnie każdy, skoro ty nie możesz.

SUE RYDER FROM THE SQUARE

Sue Ryder – she encountered misfortune early on, when along with her mother she visited hospitals and the gravely ill.
www.dom-seniora.ovh.org

Greetings to you, Sue Ryder from the square, on which no window of mine looks out. Greetings to you, because I don't want to go back to my place today. You're in the snow, and I'm in a strange kitchen, my dear Sue Ryder, in the Wild West.

Not long till high noon now, so I'm meeting you, we're meeting, Sue Ryder, I'll bring the cigarettes. Now I'm scraping paint from the windowsill with my nail, then I do it the other way round – do you like manicures?

I like them though I shouldn't, since it's possible to do so many serious things, and here there's the bishop's violet in a brushstroke across the nail bed and you have to watch out for, fear the consequences. There awaits us, my dear, *a silent cloud in the earth*

– the square behind the bus stop needs work. Dear Sue Ryder, and even then you can't be sure, since the toilets by it will stay triangular – someone might find that ugly photo of you on google.

Greetings to you, Sue Rider, masterless cow-girl. Already we're away from everywhere – the address books of mothers, our own beds, at the ends of the nerves of enemies from many nights, of brothers from just one.

Already we're away from everywhere, so don't look round, my sad Sue Ryder, you're nowhere to be found.

Translated by David Malcolm

SUE RYDER OD SKWERU

Sue Ryder – z nieszczęściem zetknęła się wcześnie, kiedy razem z matką odwiedzała szpitale i ciężko chorych.
www.dom-seniora.ovh.org

Bądź pozdrowiona Sue Ryder od skweru, na który nie mam okien. Bądź pozdrowiona, bo nie chcę dziś wracać do siebie. Ty jesteś w śniegu, a ja w obcej kuchni, moja droga Sue Ryder, na dzikim zachodzie.

Niedługo samo południe, więc się z tobą spotkam, spotkamy się Sue Ryder, wezmę papierosy. Teraz paznokciem zrywam z parapetu lakier, potem zrobię na odwrót – lubisz manicury?

Ja lubię, chociaż nie wypada, bo można by robić tyle ważkich rzeczy, a tu róż biskupi pędzelkiem po płytce i trzeba uważać, bać się konsekwencji. Czeka nas, kochana, *cichy obłok w ziemi*

– na skwer za przystankiem trzeba zapracować. Kochana Sue Ryder, a nawet wtedy nie możesz być pewna, bo szalety przy nim zostaną trójkątne – ktoś może znaleźć w googlach twoje brzydkie zdjęcie.

Bądź pozdrowiona, Sue Ryder, bezpańska kowbojko. Już wszędzie nas nie ma – w kapownikach matek, w naszych własnych łóżkach, na końcówkach nerwów wielonocnych wrogów, jednonocnych braci.

Już wszędzie nas nie ma, więc się nie rozglądaj, moja smutna Sue Ryder, nie ma gdzie się szukać.

POSSESSIONS

It was your evening, odd boy. Your eyes get smaller as evening comes on. Long ago I was taught not to hold out my hand, so when I come home by some chance taxi, I'm thinking of kissing, thinking of the platforms we could say goodbye on, if by some miracle we'd met.

Oh, no exaggeration – I feel God's will in these bright nights. But in my home, drought and withered ferns, no one calls by. To close my eyes here means to look at paws smeared with juicy fat, means to face up to the fancy floor above, means to horn over. You can come into me like into a swamp.

Odd boy, right behind the lilac in the square – all my lymph; the shroud drawn from lips.

Translated by David Malcolm

DOBYTEK

To był twój wieczór, nieparzysty chłopcze. Maleją ci oczy z wieczornym przypływem. Dawno oduczono mnie wyciągać ręce, więc kiedy wracam do domu przypadkowym taksi, myślę o całowaniu, myślę o peronach, na których moglibyśmy się żegnać, gdybyśmy jakimś cudem jednak się spotkali.

Och, to nie przesada – czuję wolę bożą w te zorzyste noce. Lecz w moim domu susza i zwiędłe paprotki, nikt tu nie zachodzi. Zamknąć tu oczy znaczy patrzeć na łapki z soczystą słoniną, znaczy mierzyć się z okazałym piętrem, znaczy rogowacieć. Mógłbyś wejść we mnie tak jak w trzęsawisko.

Nieparzysty chłopcze, tuż za bzem na skwerze cała moja limfa; całun z ust dobyty.

KRISTINA KOČAN (Slovenia)

Kristina Kočan (1981) has had three poetry collections published – Šara / Junk (2008) nominated for the Best Debut Award, Kolesa in murve / Bicycles and Mullberies *(2014) and* Šivje / Stitchery *(2018) – and a multimedia poetry book* s|prehod / r|amble *(2018). Her poetry has been translated into more than ten languages and published in foreign publications. She holds a PhD in American Poetry. Her translation of selected poems by Audre Lorde was published in 2009.*

WALNUTS

the holidays have brought us
a bit closer again
we baked
cookies together
so that it'd smell nicer
in the apartment we touched more
so that it'd be warmer
in the apartment we were constantly
quiet even new year's eve passed
the first day of the new year
was behind us we didn't fall asleep
even as Brvar's lovers
fall asleep at least as siamese twins
conjoined at their backs we again
fell asleep on opposite
sides with our backs against each other
at least one other couple
could sleep between us tomorrow
I'll go to the farmers' market
to get two kilos of walnuts
we'll crack them
and we'll see

Translated by Jernej Županič

OREHI

praznki so naju spet
nekoliko zbližali
skupaj sva
pekla kekse
da bi bolj dišalo

v stanovanju se več dotikala
da bi bilo bolj toplo
v stanovanju sva bila ves čas
tiho je minilo še silvestrovo je
bil za nama že prvi dan
novega leta nisva zaspala
niti kot brvarjeva ljubimca
zaspita vsaj kot s hrbti zraščena
siamska dvojčka sva midva
zaspala spet vsak na svojem
robu s hrbtom drug proti drugemu
bi vmes lahko spal
še vsaj en drug par jutri
bom šla na trg
po dve kili orehov
jih bova trla
in bova videla

RUINS

doors have fallen off their hinges and there are no windows
the air is always fresh pleasant
a precise and unexpected beauty
can be found in such a house a leaning tree
perhaps a mulberry a linden or a walnut
this beauty is not for anything or
anybody the streaks of sunlight caress
those who on mornings walk into these rooms
empty and the floors composed of
patterns of ivy and other weeds
a precise and unexpected freedom
can be found in such a house within you
peace

Translated by Jernej Županič

RUŠEVINE

vrata so se snela z okov in ni več oken
zrak je vedno svež prijeten
natančna in nepričakovana lepota
je lahko v taki hiši v poševnem drevesu
morda murva ali lipa ali oreh
ta lepota ni za nič in za

nikogar prameni svetlobe božajo
tistega ki vstopa ob jutrih v sobe
prazne in tla sestavljena
iz vzorcev bršljana in plevela
natančna in nepričakovana svoboda
je lahko v taki hiši v tebi
mir

TRAINS

sometimes at night we hear
trains invading our
bedroom especially distinct
in summer we sleep with the window open
they are often slow
squeaking as they brake not letting
me sleep as I listen to them I have always
lived in places where
on summer nights one could hear
the trains in childhood
the tracks were the farthest
on the other side of the brook
with frogs ribbitting
louder than the night whistles
later the tracks were
a bit closer but were
drowned out by owls now
only cricket sounds blend
with the clashing iron
at night unable
to ever drown it out

Translated by Jernej Županič

TIRJE

včasih se ponoči slišijo
vlaki vdirajo v najino
spalnico to je zlasti slišno
poleti spiva pri odprtem oknu
so pogosto počasni
škripajoče zavirajo mi ne

dajo spati poslušam jih vedno
sem živela v krajih kjer so se
v poletnih nočeh slišali
v otroštvu je bila proga
najbolj oddaljena
vmes je bil potok
v katerem so regljale žabe
so preglasile nočne piske
kasneje so bili tiri
bližje vendar so bile
glasnejše sove zdaj se
z železnim jekom ponoči
meša le čirikanje čričkov
ki ga ne zmore
nikoli preglasiti

HALYNA KRUK (Ukraine)

Halyna Kruk (1974) is an award-winning poet, translator, children's writer and literary critic. She holds a PhD in Ukrainian Literature and is currently researching Ukrainian medieval literature. Her writing includes five poetry books – Journeys in Search of a Home, Footprints on Sand *(both 1997),* The Face Beyond the Photograph *(2005),* Co(an) existence *(2013) and* An Adult Woman *(2017) – a collection of short stories and four books for children. Her poems and children's books have been translated into more than twenty languages.*

'POETS DON'T HAVE GENDER...'

poets don't have gender
    just faint words embossed on their flesh
        like secondary sexual characteristics,
a many-years-old growth of impressions
    which is never fully expressed,
shave it off or leave it for its charm?
bearded Hemingway hunts down his death –
a lazy lioness in a broken trajectory of flight
pounces on him swiftly and heavily
    like tropical rain after a long drought,
how long did he have to wait for her
        hidden, craving,

feeding the mosquitoes of routine with his own blood?!
after all, who has to wait for whom
    in this unwritten code of existence
        who is hunting whom?
poets don't have gender
    solitude's hermaphrodites
incomprehensibly wanting every time the other the Other,
in torture giving birth to only themselves
        which are repeated,
a repetition of a repetition
    repeat please
        a repetition of a repetition,
how does one escape these hula-hoops of bodies?
reconciling these differences within oneself
        smoothing genitalia,
everything will go smoothly, Hemingway
        without any snags,
the last boundaries of self-identification are crossed,
Gordian knots of mutual obligations are hewn,
Sisyphus' stone of life is pushed from the summit,
genius doesn't have gender
    just a throat raw from shouting
        between the legs

Translated by Olena Jennings

'ПОЕТИ НЕ МАЮТЬ СТАТІ...'

поети не мають статі
лише недолугі випуклини слів на тілі,
як вторинні статеві ознаки
багаторічний заріст вражень,
яких ніяк не вдається виповісти
зголити його чи лишити для шарму?
бородатий Гемінгвей упольовує свою смерть –
ліниву левицю у заламаній траєкторії польоту
вона падає на нього стрімко і важко,
як тропічна злива після довгої посухи
скільки ж він мусив чекати її,
спраглий, зачаєний,
годуючи власною кров'ю москітів буденності?!
зрештою, хто кого мусить чекати
в цьому неписаному кодексі екзистенції,
хто кого упольовує?

поети не мають статі
гермафродити самотності
незрозуміло прагнучи щоразу іншого Іншого,
народжують в муках тільки самих себе,
вкотре повторених
повторення повторення
repeate please
повторення повторення
як вирватися із цих хула-хупів тілесної визначеності?
погоджуючи в собі відмінності
згладжуючи геніталії
все буде гладко, Гемінгвею,
без жодної зачіпки
перейдено останні рубікони самоідентифікації
розрубано гордієві вузли взаємних зобов'язань
відпущено згори сізіфів камінь життя
геніальність не має статі
лише роз'ятрене від крику горло
поміж ногами

'SHE WILL NEVER BECOME THEIR IDOL…'

she will never become their idol
even if she climbs to the highest peak
and in the book of records
they dedicate a separate line to her
even if enamoured housewives
recognize her in supermarkets
and she signs
their crumpled shopping lists
acknowledging her inability to live in their world
maybe for that reason she won't become their idol
besides, she lacks the drive –
that heated pacing of blood through the veins
she can't feel where it is thin reality's
paper curtain tears
behind which all these dirty mechanics are hidden
all these entrails of true motives –
unsuccessfully
in her exaltation as in her exile –
everywhere foreign land and her language no one understands
and with a twist of fate

all the more-or-less sincere words
lead to a proposition of intimacy
yet even if they carry her in their arms some day
it will only be on her final journey
and so won't mean anything to her
in the end, just like today
when again (yet again!) she did not succeed
in grabbing God by his blue beard

Translated by Olena Jennings

'ВОНА НІКОЛИ НЕ СТАНЕ ДЛЯ НИХ КУМИРОМ...'

вона ніколи не стане для них кумиром
навіть якщо зіпнеться на найвищу вершину
і в книзі рекордів
їй присвятять окремий рядок
навіть якщо захоплені домогосподарки
впізнаватимуть її в супермаркетах
і вона розписуватиметься
на їх зімнутих списках продуктів
у власному невмінні жити в їхньому світі
може тому вона не стане для них кумиром
їй бракує драйву –
цього цілеспрямованого вештання крові по жилах,
вона не вміє відчути, де тонко і рветься
паперова завіса реальності,
за якою заховано всю цю брудну механіку,
всі ці тельбухи справжніх мотивів
безуспішно
у своєму визнанні, як у вигнанні –
де скрізь чужина і ніхто не розуміє її мови,
і за іронією долі
всі більш-менш щирі слова
зводяться до пропозицій інтиму
ба, навіть якщо вони колись понесуть її на руках –
то тільки в останню дорогу
для неї тоді це не матиме жодного значення,
зрештою, як і нині,
      коли їй знову (вкотре!) не вдалося
            схопити бога за синю бороду

PSYCHOANALYSIS

Halka, my sunshine, don't block the light
                    there's hardly any as it is,
life is beautiful
                but sooner or later must end
on a couch between Freud and Lacan
                    Halka, the last war exorcized
women, children and the elderly from our bodies
                            as prayer did the devil,
what followed was nothing to fear
                    it was a vaccination against
the sappy pathos of peace
                    and the nations' safe sex,
listen, Halka, millions have already died of AIDS
more than in the last war
but, you and me, we're alive –
this has to mean something,
after long separations we become estranged from tenderness
and everything becomes habit, quick and eager,
so a happy ending in life just as in this, not the last war,
is difficult to imagine
but I'm telling you truthfully, Halka, believe me –
life is beautiful…

Translated by Olena Jennings

ПСИХОАНАЛІЗ

Галко, сонце, не стій над душею,
                    і так того світла катма
життя прекрасне,
            та мусить рано чи пізно скінчитись
на кушетці між Фройдом й Лаканом
                    Галко, остання війна
виганя з наших тіл дітей, жінок і старих,
                        як біса – молитва
після неї – нічого страшного
                    вона – вакцинація від
слинявого пафосу миру,
                безпечного сексу націй

слухай, Галко,
у світі вже стільки мільйонів померло на СНІД,
      більше, ніж в останній війні
а ми з тобою живі – і це щось таки значить!..
після довгих розлук відвикаєм від ніжності і
все стається зазвичай так швидко і передчасно
що ж – happy end у житті,
як і в цій неостанній війні,
штука малойомовірна
хоч по правді кажу тобі, Галко, повір –
життя прекрасне…

AURÉLIA LASSAQUE (France / Occitan)

Aurélia Lassaque (1983) is a bilingual poet in French and Occitan. Often cooperating with visual artists, videomakers, dancers and musicians, she has performed all over the world. Her poetry collection Pour que chantent les salamandres *(2013) has been published in German (2020), Spanish (2019), Norwegian (2015), Hebrew ((2014), Dutch (2014) and English (2012).* En quête d'un visage *(2017) has been published in Spanish (2019). Aurélia Lassaque works as scriptwriter and is also a literary adviser for festivals in France, Italy and Africa.*

DAYDREAM

There's a chill in my soul
Romantic and jaded.
Me,
I'd have taken the boat in Greece.
Slipped down
To the sea at Santorini
On the back of a donkey.
Hung my lantern
From the branch of an olive tree
And in a white stone house
Made love to devout fishermen
And defrocked cenobites.

Translated by Madeleine Campbell

PANTAIS

Fai freg dins mon anma
Es romantic e desuet.
Ieu
Auriái presa la nau en Grècia.
A Santorin auriái limpat
Sus l'esquina d'un ase
Fins a la mar.
Auriái penjat mon lum
A la branca d'un olivièr.
E dins un ostal blanc
Auriái aimat de pescaires esperitals
E de monges desfrocats.

ORPHEUS DREAMS

In the nether worlds, where men
Are only shadows,
Inside your body, I will become shadow.

I will build cities of sand
To swallow the river from which none return.

We will dance on towers invisible to our eyes.

I will be your tongue torn out that cannot lie.

And we'll curse the love that betrayed us.

Translated by Madeleine Campbell

LO SÒMI D'ORFÈU

Dins los infèrns que los òmes
Son pas mai que d'ombras,
Me farai ombra al dedins de ton còs.

Bastirai de ciutats de sabla
Qu'agotaràn lo flum que degun ne tòrna.

Dansarem sus de torres que nòstres uèlhs veiràn pas.

Serai ta lenga trencada que sap pas mentir.

E maudirem l'amor que nos a perduts.

HER SKIN WARM AND OPAQUE...

Her skin warm and opaque
Is a summer's night
Stretching until it fools the dawn
As her wild mare's body
Begins to unfold anew
Revealing in the darkness of her limbs
A bird-caller's paradise.

Translated by Madeleine Campbell

SA PÈL ESCURA E CAUDA...

Sa pèl escura e cauda
Coma una nuèch d'estiu
S'estira fins a fintar l'alba
Quand son còs de cavala fèra
Tornamai s'alanda
E cava dins la prigondor de sas cambas
Un paradís d'auselaire.

HE DRANK HIS MOTHER'S MILK...

He drank his mother's milk
Dined on his wife's flesh
Fried his children's brains
But knows not his own solitude.
His house drinks rain
His soil devours rocks.
And still he reigns king of the story he tells
Such is in the gift of monsters here below.

Translated by Madeleine Campbell

DE SA MAIRE BEGUÈT LO LACH...

De sa maire beguèt lo lach,
De sa femna manjèt la carn,
De sos dròlles cremèt lo cervèl,
Pr'aquò compren pas sa solesa.
Son ostal bèu la pluèja,
Sa terra engolís las pèiras.
Demorarà lo rei de l'istòria que conta,
Es lo privilègi dels mostres d'aiçaval.

LULJETA LLESHANAKU (Albania)

Luljeta Lleshanaku (1968) is the author of eight poetry collections in Albanian and fourteen other collections published in translation. She was the recipient of 'Kristal Vilenica 2009' award in Slovenia. Her last poetry collection in English, Negative Space, *published by Bloodaxe Books in the UK and New Directions in the USA, was a winner of an English PEN award, and a finalist in the Griffin International Poetry Prize 2019, PEN America, 2019 and the Best Translated Book Awards, 2019.*

THE MYSTERY OF PRAYERS

In my family
prayers were said secretly,
softly, murmured through sore noses
beneath blankets,
a sigh before and a sigh after
thin and sterile as a bandage.

Outside the house
there was only a ladder to climb
a wooden one, leaning against a wall all year long,
ready to use to repair the tiles, in August before the rains.
No angels climbed up
and no angels climbed down –
only men suffering from sciatica.

They prayed to catch a glimpse of Him
hoping to renegotiate their contracts
or to postpone their deadlines.

"Lord, give me strength," they said
for they were descendants of Esau
and had to make do with the only blessing
left over from Jacob,
the blessing of the sword.

In my house praying was considered a weakness
like making love.
And like making love
it was followed by the long
cold night of the body.

Translated by Henry Israeli

MISTERI I LUTJEVE

Në familjen time
lutjet bëheshin fshehtas
me zë të ulët, me një hundë të skuqur nën jorgan,
gati mërmëritje,
me një psherëtimë në fillim dhe fund
të hollë, e të pastër si një garzë.

Përreth shtëpisë,
kishte vetëm një palë shkallë për t'u ngjitur
ato të drunjtat, të mbështetura gjithë vitin pas murit,
për riparimin e tjegullave në gusht para shirave.
Në vend të engjëjve,
hipnin e zbritnin burra
që vuanin nga shiatiku.

Ata luteshin duke u shikuar sy më sy me Të,
si në një marrëveshje kryezotësh
duke kërkuar nje shtyrje afati.

"Zot, me jep forcë!" e asgjë më shumë,
se ishin pasardhësit e Esaut,
të bekuar, me të vetmen gjë që mbeti prej Jakobit,
– shpatën.

Në shtëpinë time
lutja ishte një dobësi,
që nuk përflitej kurrë,
si të bërit dashuri.
Dhe njësoj si të bërit dashuri
pasohej nga nata e frikshme e trupit.

OLD NEWS

In the village nestled between two mountains
the news always arrives one month late,
cleansed in transit, glorified, mentioning only the dead who made

it to paradise,
and a coup d'état referred to as 'God's will'.

Spring kills solitude with solitude, imagination
the sap that shields you from your body. Chestnut trees
awaken, drunken men
lean their cold shoulders against a wall.

The girls here always marry outsiders and move away
leaving untouched statues of their fifteen-year-old
selves behind.

But the boys bring in wives
from distant villages,
wives who go into labour on heaps of grass and straw in a barn
and bear prophets.
Forgive me, I'd meant to say 'only one will be a prophet'.
The others will spend their lives throwing stones
(that is part of the prophecy, too).

At noon on an autumn day like today
they will bolt out of school like a murder of crows stirred by the
smell of blood
and chase the postman's skeleton of a car
as it disappears around a corner, leaving only dust.

Then they will steal wild pears from the 'bitch's yard'
and nobody will stop them. After all, she deserves it. She's sleeping
with two men.

Between the pears in one boy's schoolbag
lies a copy of *Anna Karenina*.
It will be skimmed over, impatiently, starting on the last page
cleansed and glorified, like old news.

Translated by Henry Israeli

LAJME TE VONUARA

Në fshatin midis maleve, lajmi vjen një muaj me vonesë.
Gjate rrugës pafajësohet: ai që vdiq shkoi doemos në parajsë,
e një grusht shteti "është vullneti i zotit".

Përroi mbyt vetminë me vetmi. Imagjinata është rrëshirë
që të mbron nga trupi. Përndryshe, pylli i rëndë i gështenjave dhe
     burrat e dehur,
gdhihen me shpatulla të ftohta ngjeshur pas murit.

Vajzat preferojnë martesat larg
për të lënë prapa, të paprekur,
bustin e pesëmbëdhjetëvjeçares.

Dhe përtej pesë fshatrave vijnë nuset,
nuset që do të lindin femijë- profetë
midis sanës dhe kashtës në plevicë. Ah, desha të them
vetëm njëri prej tyre do të jetë profet;
të tjerët do të praktikohen për të gjuajtur me gurë
(kjo është gjithashtu pjesë e profecisë).

Në një mesditë vjeshte si kjo,
ata do të dalin nga shkolla si një tufë e trazuar sorrash prej erës se gjakut,
per t'iu vënë pas makines- rrangallë të postës
deri në kthesë, kur ajo të zhbëhet në pluhur.

E pastaj do të shkojnë të vjedhin dardhët e egra në "oborrin e kurvës"
Askush nuk i ndalon. "Grua me dy burra... hak e ka!"
Midis dardhëve të egra në çantë- një roman,
me porosinë për t'u mbajtur mirë. Një "Ana Kareninë"
që do të lexohet me padurim duke filluar nga faqja e fundit,
e pastër dhe e fisnikëruar si një lajm i vonuar.

VERTICAL REALITIES

Waking is an obligation:
three generations open their eyes every morning
inside me.

The first is an old child – my father;
he always chooses his luck and clothes one size too small for him.

Next comes grandfather… In his day, the word 'diagnosis' did not exist.
He simply died of misery six months after his wife.
No time was wasted. Above their corpses
rose a factory to make uniforms for dockworkers.

And great-grandfather, if he ever existed,
I don't even know his name. Here my memory goes on hiatus,
my peasant origins cut like the thick and yellow nails
of field-workers.

Three shadows loom like a forest over me
telling me what to do
and what not to do.

You listened to me say 'good morning'
but it was either an elephant pounding on a piano
or the seams coming apart in my father's little jacket.

Indeed, my father, his father, and his father before that
are not trying to change anything
nor do they refuse to change anything; the soap of ephemerality
leaves them feeling fresh and clean.

They only wish to gently touch the world again
through me, the way latex gloves
lovingly touch the evidence
of a crime scene.

Translated by Henry Israeli

REALITETE VERTIKALE

Të vazhduarit, në rastin tim, nuk është zgjedhje por detyrim
qëkur tri breza zgjohen njeherazi brenda meje.

I pari është një fëmijë i plakur; im atë.
Fatin dhe veshjet i zgjedh gjithmone nje numër më të vogël.

E pastaj gjyshi. Në kohën e tij nuk njihej fjala "diagnozë",
ai thjesht vdiq nga dëshpërimi gjashtë muaj pas së shoqes
E pa humbur kohe, mbi trypat e tyre
komuniteti ndërtoi nje punishte uniformash prej doku.

E stergjyshi. Nese ka ekzistuar nje i tille
une nuk ia di as emrin, ketu kujtesa pëson hiatus,
– prejardhja fshatare e prerë si thonjtë e fortë
e te zverdhur. nga puna ne arë.
Te tre perkulen si një pyll sipër meje
e me diktojne se cfare duhet te bëj
e çfare nuk duhet.

Sapo degjove prej meje nje te tillë "mirëmëngjes"
si e dale prej nje elefanti me putra mbi piano
apo prej shqepjeve te xhaketes se im eti.

Ata nuk po orvaten te ndryshojne ndonje gjë
e as te kundervihen; ndjehen te freskët
ashtu te larë me sapunin e lirë të perkohësisë.

Ata thjesht e riprekin boten permes meje
si me nje palë doreza plastike
për të ruajtur të paprekur shkakun
në vendin e krimit.

PRISONERS

guilty or not
always look the same when they are released –
patriarchs dethroned.

This one just passed through the gate
head bowed despite not being tall
his gestures like a Bedouin's
entering the tent
he carried on his back all day long.

Cotton curtains, stone walls, the smell of burnt lime
take him back to the moment
the cold war ended.

The other day his sheet was hung up in the courtyard
as if to flaunt the blood stain
after a wedding night.

Faces tarnished by sun
surround him, all eyes and ears:
'What did you dream of last night?'
A prisoner's dreams
are parchment
made sacred by its missing passages.

His sister is still discovering his odd habits:
the bits of bread hidden in pockets and under his bed
the relentless chopping of wood for winter.

Why this fear?
What can be worse than life in prison?

Having choices
but being unable to choose.

Translated by Henry Israeli

TË BURGOSURIT

Të burgosurit,
të fajshëm e të pafajshëm
kur dalin, kanë të gjithë të njëjtën shprehje në fytyrë -
patriarkun a saporënë nga froni.

Kur kapërceu pragun
ai përkuli kokën, pavarësisht gjatësisë së tij mesatare.
Të njëjtën gjë bëjnë beduinët
kur futen në tendën
që kanë mbartur gjithë ditën mbi shpinë

Muret, perdet e pastra dhe aroma e gëlqeres
ndjellin ndjesinë e luftës së ftohtë
kur lufta sapo ka marrë fund.

Dhe të nësërmen çarçafët e tij u varën për ajrosje
në mes të oborrit, si pas natës së parë të dasmës,
njollat e virgjërisë.

Fytyra të nxira nga dielli
e rrethuan gjithë sy e veshë
"Ç'ëndërr pe mbrëmë?"

Ëndrrat e të burgosurit
janë pergamena
që shenjtërohen prej kapitujve të humbur.

E motra, sapo i zbuloi një zakon të ri:
copa të fshehura buke nëpër xhepa e nën shtrat
dhe të prerit pa pushim dru për dimër.

Ç"ishte gjithë ky panik?
Çfarë mund të ishte më e keqe se vitet e burgut?

E drejta për të zgjedhur
Duke mos mundur.

EVA LUKA (SLOVAKIA)

Eva Luka (1965) studied interpreting-translating English and Japanese and now writes, translates, draws and paints, and teaches Japanese. Her first poetry collection, Divosestra / The Wild Sister *(1999) won the Rubato, Krasko, Literary Revue and Haľamová awards. Her second book,* Diabloň / The Devil Tree, *was published in 2005 and her third,* Havranjel / The Ravenangel, *in 2011. Her award-winning fantasy novel for children and adults with her own illustrations appeared in 2018 and her poetry collection,* Jazver / I-animal *was published in 2019.*

THE OLD WOMEN

The old women wearing grey suits, sweaty
former nursemaids, bearers
of snakes and medusas, foster-mothers of bald
teddy bears in their
empty wombs. The old women
without wombs. The old women
who have forgotten: they collect
only what is. Toadstools
and small change, rain-worms.
Grey-haired; not our mothers,
not us. High heels
on varicose legs; a face – the posthumous
mask of Marilyn.

That's not us. We still
regularly gaze into the face
of the bloody moon in the toilet
bowl. Youth, you howl
like a dog; you depart
on a very strange road.

Translated by James Sutherland-Smith

STARÉ ŽENY

Staré ženy v sivých kostýmoch, upotené
bývalé varovkyne, nositeľky
hadov a medúz, pestovateľky vyplešivených
medvedíkov vo svojej
vyprázdnenej maternici. Staré ženy
bez maternice. Staré ženy,
čo zabudli: zbierajú
už iba, čo je. Muchotrávky
a mince, hlístočky.

Sivovlasé; nie naše matky,
nie my. Vysoké podpätky
na kŕčovitých nohách; tvár – posmrtná
maska Marylin.

Nie sme to my. My ešte
pravidelne pozeráme do tváre
krvavému mesiacu v záchodovej
mise. Mladosť, skučíš
ako pes; odchádzaš

veľmi čudnou cestou.

RAVENANGEL

Every night
he comes to me with laboured
wings, drenched with rain. I make a place
for him in my bed, on my thighs feeling
the coldness of his embrace; I strive
to hug his black-sad head to my breast.
It takes so long to become used to the burden, which

he grants me as a gift, it takes so long to warm
my solitary legs. With resignation
my pale skin accepts the transparent moistness of water,
of a ravenangel's sperm and spit. Who's to say where he wanders when
night has fallen? What might have happened to him, cast out
against his will into the horror of life? I forgive him
this coldness, this... dampness; relieved
of my daily grind I accept everything.
I pity.
I try to feel his
pulse, to stroke
his exhausted nape.
He brings me nothing, except slime,
sleep with its very own after-taste,
traces of bitter-tender efforts through which
he hopes to overcome futility
and the night.
In the morning I find by my head
a shed, grey feather. I draw a bath,
slowly, as when they lower, on thick ropes
into a grave, a last
posthumous rose. I open
a window.
The ravenangel regards me
from the wilderness of the day;
and at midday I sense in me
our mutual,
black children pushing forward
into relentless life.

Translated by James Sutherland-Smith

HAVRANJEL

Každú noc
ku mne prichádza, so sťažknutými
krídlami, zmáčanými dažďom. Ja mu urobím
v posteli miesto, na stehnách pocítim
chlad jeho objatia; pokúšam sa
pritisnúť si k hrudi jeho čiernosmutnú hlavu.
Dlho mi trvá, kým si zvyknem na ťažobu, ktorú
mi dáva do daru, dlho trvá, kým si zohrejem

osamelé nohy. Moja bledá koža
odovzdane prijíma priezračnú vlhkosť vody,
havranjelích spermií a slín. Ktovie, kadiaľ sa túlal, odkedy
začala noc; čo všetko sa mu stalo, vyvrhnutému
bez vlastnej vôle do hrôz života. Odpúšťam mu
ten chlad, aj vlhkosť, zbavená svojej
zvyčajnej urputnosti prijímam všetko,
súcitím;
usilujem sa nahmatať mu
pulz, pohladiť
uštvanú šiju.

Neprináša mi nič, okrem slizkého,
rozličné pachute ponúkajúceho spánku,
okrem stôp trpko-milostných pokusov, ktorými
dúfa prekonať márnosť
a noc.

Ráno nachádzam pri svojej hlave
jeho opŕchnuté sivé pierko. Napustím si vaňu,
pomaly, ako keď do hrobu na hrubých lanách
spúšťajú poslednú
posmrtnú ružu, otváram
okno.

Havranjel sa na mňa pozerá
z pustatiny dňa;

i na poludnie v sebe cítim
naše spoločné,
do neúprosného života sa derúce

čierne deti.

NATALIA MALEK (Poland)

Natalia Malek (1988) is a Polish poet, literature curator and book reviewer. She published three collections of poetry: Pracowite popołudnia / Busy afternoons *(2010),* Szaber / The Spoils *(2014) and* Kord / Chord *(2017). She is the recipient of the 2017 Adam Włodek Literary Prize. Her books were shortlisted for the 2015 and 2018 Gdynia Literary Prize in Poetry and for the 2018 Wisława Szymborska Prize in Poetry. She works and lives in Warsaw.*

SPOILS

Some women advise, before you go, to collect what's scattered.
Pyjamas. Plums, yellow and small like forbidden babies.
Slippers in a pattern that pleases the eye, not gaudy.

But – don't collect the abandoned
at the scene of a crash. Don't lay them by. Give them a year
to sober up.

If a year's too little, you can double it. Not at their request.

(The results are clear jars that hold both fruit and vinegar)

Translated by David Malcolm

SZABER

Niektóre kobiety radzą, by przed wyjściem zbierać rozrzucone.
Piżamę. Śliwki, żółte i małe jak zakażone niemowlęta.
Klapki w przyjemny dla oka wzór, nie jaskrawy.

Ale – porzuconych nie zabieraj
z miejsca wypadku. Nie kładź na boku. Daj im rok
na wytrzeźwienie.

Jeśli rok to za mało, można podwoić. Nie na ich wniosek.

(Skutki to przezroczyste weki, do których wejdzie i owoc, i ocet)

ONLY FRAGILE LEFT ALIVE

Yellowish sheep. Guys covered in bristle. Guys with it shaved,
contrary to recent custom. All inhabitants of the northern counties.
Part of the southern ones.

None of the forgetful.
Maybe one of the curious. (I doubt it)
No birds that shit lime. For sure, no women, who till now flaunted feathers.

Translated by David Malcolm

PRZETRWAJĄ NAJWRAŻLIWSI

Żółtawe owce. Faceci pokryci szczeciną. Faceci ogoleni z niej,
w brew niedawnym przyzwyczajeniom. Wszyscy mieszkańcy
północnych powiatów.
Pewna część z południowych.

Nikt z zapominalskich.
Być może ktoś z ciekawskich. (Wątpię)
Żadne ptaki srające wapnem. Na pewno nie kobiety, które dotąd
stroiły się w piórka.

IF WE EAT ASPARAGUS

That means Poland's thinning out.
(Population)
There's more of something else. (An unexpected rash of long-legged girls)

If we eat asparagus, that means from the first of May. You can't eat peaches.
In the blood, no flow of stress hormones.
But probably others.

Translated by David Malcolm

JEŚLI JEMY SZPARAGI

To znaczy, że w Polsce trochę się przerzedziło.
(ludność)
Zagęściło się coś innego. (niespodziewany wysyp długonogich
dziewczyn)

Jeśli jemy szparagi, to znaczy, że od pierwszego maj. Nie można jeść
brzoskwiń.
Nie płynie we krwi tyle hormonów stresu.
Ale chyba inne.

PATHOS

A bird of the cormorant family, with a bold lump
At the gullet. Voracious feeder. Swims fast.

Translated by David Malcolm

PATOS

Ptak z rodziny kormoranów, z widoczną gulą
na wysokości przełyku. Żarłoczny. Szybko pływa.

COVERING

Don't get to know Russians. Don't correct them.
Nor eat with them. (Under the eye of the bodyguard)
And still. Go up with R. to the thirtieth floor. The Gramophone Needle.
The discovery of wind. Today!
– I brushed my teeth and poured the port. You have to know

that our town has shot up
like popcorn. I like it.

Translated by David Malcolm

POKRYWA

Nie poznawać Rosjan. Nie poprawiać.
Nie jadać z nimi. (Pod okiem ochroniarza)
A jednak. Wejść z R. na trzydzieste piętro. Igła gramofonu.
                          Odkrycie wiatru. To dziś.
– Umyłem zęby, nalałem porto. Musisz wiedzieć,

że nasze miasto strzela w górę
jak popcorn. Mnie się to podoba.

FRANCA MANCINELLI (Italy)

Franca Mancinelli (1981) is the author of four books of poetry which have won several prizes in Italy. Two of them, At an Hour's Sleep from Here: Poems 2007-2019 *and* The Little Book of Passage *(from which the prose poems below are selected), were published in the USA, in John Taylor's translation, by The Bitter Oleander Press. Her most recent book is* Tutti gli occhi che ho aperto / All the Eyes that I have Opened *(Marcos y Marcos, 2020). Her poems have been anthologised and translated into several languages.*

'TRAVELLING WITHOUT KNOWING...'

Travelling without knowing what brings me to you. I know you're going beyond the limits of the sheet of paper, of the cultivated fields. It's your way of coming face to face with me: like water in its course, branching off. Looking out the window, I kept reading into your face as long as the light lasted.

Translated by John Taylor

'VIAGGIO SENZA SAPERE...'

Viaggio senza sapere cosa mi porta a te. So che stai andando oltre i confini del foglio, dei campi coltivati. È il tuo modo di venirmi incontro: come un'acqua in cammino, diramando. Guardando dal finestrino, ti ho letto nel viso finché c'era luce.

'IN THE EVENING, A CIGARETTE...'

In the evening, a cigarette between his fingers, watching the sky darken like moistened soil, my father waters his garden. When he's standing down there in the farthest corner, hidden by the tomato plants, I can hear the water pouring from the well, streaming down between the dirt clods to the roots awaiting it. Here, where the flow has trickled out, sprout plants with poisonous fruit, stiff stalks of grass with tiny flowers. I haven't succeeded in hoeing them away, in repairing the water table.

Translated by John Taylor

'LA SERA, CON UNA SIGARETTA...'

La sera, con una sigaretta tra le dita, guardando il cielo scurirsi come terra bagnata, mio padre annaffia. Quando è laggiù, nascosto dalle piante dei pomodori, nell'angolo più lontano del giardino, posso sentire dal pozzo l'acqua versarsi e scendere tra i granuli, fino alle radici dove è attesa. Qui, dove il flusso si perde, crescono erbe dure dal piccolo fiore, piante dal frutto velenoso. Ma non riesco a zapparle via, non riesco a riparare la falda.

'AS IF I ALWAYS HAD ANOTHER NUMBER...'

As if I always had another number, another size, every morning I force myself to put on clothes, shoes. I still grow in the darkness, like a plant drinking from black soil. Getting dressed demands losing the branches extending into sleep, their most tender leaves open. You can suddenly feel them falling like an unexpected winter. At the same time you also lose the tail and the wings you had. You feel it happening somewhere in your body. You're not bleeding, this is a deprivation to which they have accustomed you. Now you only need to look for your clothes. To glide like a sunray, until the light dims.

Translated by John Taylor

'INDOSSO E CALZO OGNI MATTINA FORZANDO...'

Indosso e calzo ogni mattina forzando, come avessi sempre un altro numero, un'altra taglia. Cresco ancora nel buio, come una pianta che beve dal nero della terra. Per vestirsi bisogna perdere i rami allungati nel sonno, le foglie più tenere aperte. Puoi sentirle cadere a un tratto come per un inverno improvviso. Nello stesso istante perdi anche la coda e le ali che avevi. Da qualche parte del corpo lo senti. Non sanguini, è una privazione a cui ti hanno abituato. Non resta che cercare il tuo abito. Scivolare come un raggio, fino al calare della luce.

'UNFINISHED SENTENCES...'

Unfinished sentences remain ruins. You're supporting inside yourself an entire village in danger of collapsing. You know the pain of every tile, every brick. A dull thud in the clearing of your chest. Perhaps it's someone's constant love, a calm chore resounding in the depths of the woods. You who are unpacking your suitcase, you forget to leave.

Translated by John Taylor

'LE FRASI NON COMPIUTE...'

Le frasi non compiute restano ruderi. C'è un intero paese in pericolo di crollo che stai sostenendo in te. Sai il dolore di ogni tegola, di ogni mattone. Un tonfo sordo nella radura del petto. Ci vorrebbe l'amore costante di qualcuno, un lavorare quieto che risuona nelle profondità del bosco. Tu che disfi la valigia, ti scordi di partire.

VLADIMIR MARTINOVSKI (North Macedonia)

Vladimir Martinovski (1974) is a poet, short story writer, essayist, translator and musician. He teaches Comparative Literature at Sts Cyril and Methodius University, Skopje. Former president of the Association of Comparative Literature of Macedonia, and currently vice-president of the Macedonian PEN Centre, he has won a number of literary awards and his poetry has been translated into English, French, Italian, Spanish, Albanian, Turkish, Bulgarian, Greek, German, Chinese, Japanese, Polish, Romanian, Slovenian, Serbian, Croatian, Slovakian and Czech.

THE CITY IS FOLLOWING US

> *This city shall follow you*
> KONSTANTINOS KAVAFIS

We finally understand that we can't escape the city.
    When we headed for the mountain
a hundred new buildings and houses sprang up
    at its foot.
We gave up climbing it, because we knew
    the city would catch up with us
on the way to the top, hell, they have already placed
    the woods in museums that are not open on holidays.

When we headed for the airport we realised
    the runway is passing through the centre of the city
making it pointless to fly: we have a return ticket
    and in every city we go we'll be welcomed by the same
shops employing many of our fellow citizens.
    Though everything else may seem different,
the moon among the skyscrapers shall be the same.
    We'll probably be taken from the airport to the hotel
by a cab driver from our former neighbourhood,
    who, no doubt, will tell us that the world is just one big city.

Translated by Milan Damjanoski

ГРАДОТ НÈ СЛЕДИ

> *Овој град ќе те следи*
> Константин Кавафи

Конечно сфативме дека нема бегање од градот.
    Кога тргнавме кон планината веднаш

изникнаа сто нови згради и куќи
во нејзиното подножје.
Се откажавме од искачувањето бидејќи градот
сигурно ќе нѐ престигне
на патот кон врвот, а и шумите веќе ги ставија
во музеи кои не работат за празници.

Кога тргнавме кон аеродромот сфативме дека
пистата е веќе во центарот на градот и
дека попусто ќе летаме: билетот е повратен,
а и во секој друг град ќе нѐ дочекаат истите
продавници во кои работат многу наши сограѓани.
Дури и сѐ друго да биде навидум различно
месечината меѓу облакодерите ќе биде иста.
Од аеродромот до хотелот веројатно ќе
нѐ вози таксист од нашето поранешно маало и
ќе ни каже дека светот е еден голем град.

THE LAKE EXPANDS

This is no ordinary ebb and flow;
while some lakes recede from
geography and flow into history, one lake expands daily.
It expands a foot in height and width, even more in depth.
The divers have given up all attempts to reach the bottom,
fearing they'll get to the centre, or even to the other side of earth.
Archaeologists have started to boast that they
are sure to find the first home of the first people there.

Yet, further than the deep, expands
the endless silence and the endless blue;
all the things spilled in there never stop it
from being even more blue, more clear, more transparent every new morning.
The blue of the lake expands together with the
blue of the frescoes and the skies. It expands together with the silence.
No matter how loud, noisy or blaring we are in the night,
the lake gets quieter and calmer each morning. The waves
have become silent, quieter than the beating of
a sleeping heart. The silence is expanding to the other side of earth.

Translated by Milan Damjanoski

ЕЗЕРОТО РАСТЕ

Ова не е обична плима или осека:
додека некои езера се селат од учебниците
        по географија во оние по историја едно езеро
секој ден расте. Расте по некоја педа во висина и во ширина
        а најмногу расте во длабина. Нуркачите
се откажаа од идејата да нурнат до неговото
        дно од страв дека ќе стигнат до центарот
а можеби и од другата страна на земјата.
        Археолозите почнаа да се фалат дека длабоко
негде сигурно ќе ја најдат првата куќа од првите луѓе.

Но повеќе од длабочината растат неговата
бескрајна тишина и неговото бескрајно синило:
        што ли не се истури во него а тоа како од
инает секое утро е сè посино, побистро, попрозрачно.
        Расте синилото на езерото заедно со модрилото
на фреските и на небото. Расте заедно со тишината.
        Колку и да сме бучни, гласни, прегласни во ноќта,
езерото секое утро е сè потивко, поспокојно. Далгите
        му станаа безгласни, потивки од биењето на срцето
додека спиеме. Тишината расте до другата страна на земјата.

PORTRAIT OF A POET WITH AN UMBRELLA

Based on the painting 'Portrait of a Poet' by Vane Kosturanov

Some say that a poet has no need for an umbrella
He is sure to leave it somewhere
and get soaked to the bone

And some say he brings it along
to shield himself from some other rain
that not everyone can feel in their bones

An invisible rain of words
for which there is no more space
in his future poems

Translated by Milan Damjanoski

ПОРТРЕТ НА ПОЕТ СО ЧАДОР

Според сликата 'Портрет на поетот' на Ване Костуранов

Некои велат на поет не му треба чадор
Сигурно пак ќе го заборави негде
и пак ќе накисне до гола кожа

А некои велат чадорот со себе го влечка
за некој друг дожд што не може
да го сети секој на своја кожа

Некој невидлив дожд од зборови
за кои нема повеќе место
во неговите идни песни

TRANSFORMATIONS

When you're gone, I suddenly turn into a sunflower without the sun,
A book without letters, a home without doors, rain without drops,
A double bass with no strings, a tricycle without the front wheel,
A clock without hands, a verse without an ancient metric foot,

Into chocolate without the cocoa, a city with no boulevard,
A giraffe without a neck, an orchestra with no conductor,
A condor without feathers, a street without a pavement,
Into a sculpture with neither a head nor a pedestal.

When you're gone, I'm a nut without the kernel,
A bee without a drop of honey, or a selfish
Little cricket that's misplaced its violin.

And when I'm with you, I'm merely
A man who conceals so readily
All the things he used to be.

Translated by Kalina Janeva

ПРЕОБРАЗБИ

Кога те нема се претворам за час во сончоглед без сонце,
во книга без букви, во дом без врати, во дожд без капки,
во контрабас без жици, во тротинет без предно колце,
во часовник без стрелки, во стих без антички стапки,

во чоколадо без какао, во главен град без булевар,
во жирафа без врат, во оркестар без диригент,
во кондор без перја, во улица без тротоар,
во скулптура без глава и без постамент.

Кога те нема станувам орев без јатка,
пчела без ронка мед или себичен
скакулец без виолина в рака.

А кога сум со тебе сум обичен
човек кој знае да крие вешто
дека порано бил сѐ и сешто.

NINO MICK (Sweden)

Nino Mick (1990) is a poet and train driver in Gothenburg, Sweden. In 2013 they won the Swedish poetry slam nationals, and in 2018 their first book, Tjugofemtusen kilometer nervtrådar / Twenty-five-thousand Kilometres of Nerve Fibres, *was published.*

'FIRST VISIT...'

First visit.

I'm here because I want to be left alone

Translated by Christian Gullette

'FÖRSTA BESÖKET...'

Första besöket.

Jag är här för att jag vill bli lämnad ifred

'GENDER IDENTITY CLINIC...'

Gender Identity Clinic:

In order to proceed, I need access to
your body i.e. brain
your life i.e. sex life
your medical history
your stories

Translated by Christian Gullette

'KÖNSUTREDNINGEN...'

För att det ska ske behöver jag tillgång till
din kropp inkl hjärna
ditt liv inkl sexliv
din medicinska historia
dina berättelser

'SECOND VISIT...'

Second visit.

Have I completed a gender survey so I can cope with being a poet
or am I a poet in order to cope with the Gender Identity Clinic
so used to narrating myself
in exchange for fees and care

The glossy floors and the large window
upon arrival I leave
my name and agency at the reception
I want to narrate myself as complex and human and for people to narrate
                                                        me as respectable
to line up the words on the table in front of the psychologist
so we can look at them and pretend we're equal

A gatekeeper may deny access
a sword can burn against the throat
can still be called angel
fear's throbbing anatomy

the throat artery's defiant disposition
highlights a sample of beautiful truths
the same obedience as usual
the same hands folded in my lap

Translated by Christian Gullette

'ANDRA BESÖKET...'

Andra besöket.

Söker jag till könsutredningen för att klara att vara poet
eller är jag poet för att klara könsutredningen
så van att berätta mig själv
i utbyte mot arvode och vård

Blankgolven och det stora fönstret
vid ankomst lämnar jag
namn och agens i receptionen
jag vill berätta mig komplex och människa vill berätta mig respektabel
radar upp orden på bordet framför psykologen
så vi kan titta på dom och låtsas jämlikhet

En grindvakt kan neka tillträde
ett svärd kan brinna mot halsen
kan ändå kallas ängel
rädslans dunkande anatomi
halsåderns trotsiga läggning
framhäver ett urval av vackra sanningar
samma lydnad som vanligt
i knäet samma knäppta händer

'THIRD VISIT...'

Third visit.

Gender Identity Clinic:
Describe your social situation

Translated by Christian Gullette

'TREDJE BESÖKET...'

Tredje besöket.

Könsutredningen:
Beskriv din sociala situation

'SAW A SNAKE...'

Saw a snake in the woods today
winding across the gravel on its stomach
as if nothing hurt
and every obstacle it met on the way
it slid right around

What if my body could help me like that?

Translated by Christian Gullette

'JAG SÅG EN ORM...'

Jag såg en orm idag i skogen
ringlande på magen över gruset
som om inget gjorde ont
och varje motstånd den mötte på vägen
gled den bara runt

Tänk om min kropp kunde hjälpa mig så där

'FOURTH VISIT...'

Fourth visit

I cancel

Translated by Christian Gullette

'FJÄRDE BESÖKET...'

Fjärde besöket

ställer jag in

'I'VE CONSTRUCTED EVERYTHING...'

I've constructed everything
the boy the girl and the autistic one
documented the fatigue and depression

With the diagnosis as a veil a shield I slid through the corridors.
In the middle of puberty, I escaped sexuality

got out of slumber parties and boy problems
got out of punishment and ostracism
avoided learning from the group
how women apply make-up to put on a face

The group of girls I tried to belong to
didn't work out and lost interest
the punishments ricocheted against the mirrors
newly awakened, I cut myself on the shards
without a clear direction or sender

So the girl was kept intact
floated across the school yard, slid through
high school corridors
rape cultures
mostly unscathed

Women were formed there
I understand now, as protection and strategy
formed groups there
dancing in a circle around feminist totebags
they became women
I did not become body

Translated by Christian Gullette

JAG HAR EFTERKONSTRUERAT ALLT

Jag har efterkonstruerat allt
pojken flickan och autisten
men utmattningsdepressionen har jag papper på

Med diagnosen som en slöja ett skydd skred jag genom korridorerna
mitt i puberteten slapp jag könet
slapp tjejfester och pojkproblem
slapp bestraffningar och utfrysning
slapp lära mig av gruppen
hur kvinnor målas fram i ansiktet

Flickgängen jag försökte tillhöra
misslyckades och tappade intresse
bestraffningarna rikoschetterade mot speglarna
yrvaken skar jag mig på splittret
utan tydlig riktning eller avsändare

Så behölls flickan intakt
svävade över skolgården, skred genom
högstadiekorridorerna
våldtäktskulturerna
knappt kantstött

Kvinnor formades där
förstår jag nu, som skydd och strategi
formade grupper där
dansar i en cirkel runt FATTA!-tygpåsarna
dom blev kvinnor
jag blev inte kropp

ADULTS CAN'T GRASP THE SITUATION

Adults can't grasp the situation
and instead refuse to let go of breasts
after all, you shouldn't throw away gifts

She says some people regret it
who realize the urge is about something else

Mum is right
my anxiety is not my breasts
it came from somewhere else
the only body parts that bother me
are other people's brains
and I can't correct those

Translated by Christian Gullette

VÅRA VUXNA SOM INTE KAN GREPPA LÄGET

Våra vuxna som inte kan greppa läget
som istället vägrar släppa taget om brösten
och en ska inte kasta bort gåvor

Hon säger att det finns dom som ångrar sig
som kommer på att det handlar om nåt annat

Mamma har rätt
min ångest är inte mina bröst
den kom nån annanstans ifrån först
den enda kroppsdel som besvärar mig
är andra människors hjärnor
och dom kan jag inte korrigera

'WE...'

We:

In order to lift the gaze from my gender
I need a liveable future
to which I can attach the horizon

Translated by Christian Gullette

'VI...'

Vi:

För att jag ska kunna lyfta blicken från mitt kön
behöver jag en levbar framtid
att fästa horisonten vid

DOIREANN NÍ GHRÍOFA (Ireland)

Doireann Ní Ghríofa (1981) is author of six critically-acclaimed books of poetry. Her awards include the Rooney Prize for Irish Literature and a Seamus Heaney Fellowship (Queen's University). Her first book of prose is the bestselling A Ghost in the Throat, *which finds the 18th-century poet Eibhlín Dubh Ní Chonaill haunting the life of a contemporary young mother, prompting her to turn detective.*

WHILE BLEEDING

In a vintage boutique on Sullivan's Quay,
I lift a winter coat, with narrow bodice,
neat lapels, tight waist, a fallen hem.
It is far too expensive for me,
but the handwritten label
      [1915]
brings it to my chest in armfuls of red.

In that year, someone drew a blade
through a bolt of fabric
and stitched this coat
into being. I carry it
to the dressing room, slip my arms in.
Silk lining spills against my skin.
I clasp the belt and draw a slow breath
as a cramp curls again,
where blood stirs and melts.
In glass, I am wrapped in old red –

      red pinched into girl cheeks,
      and smeared from torn knees,
      lipstick blotted on tissue, scarlet
stains concealed in pale sheets –
      all the red bled into pads and rags,
      the weight of red, the wait for red,
      that we share.

In the mirror, the old coat blushes.

This pocket may once have sheltered something
precious: a necklace, a love letter, or

a fresh egg, feather-warm, its shell brittle
around a hidden inner glow, held loosely
so it couldn't crack, couldn't leak through seams,
so it couldn't stain the dress within.

Written in English

CRAQUELURE

Her tracksuit is pink velour,
her earlobes prettily golden-hooped,
and she shivers, as we all do,
in this dim bus queue.

> At 5.56, some glitch, some distraction
> some finger twitch, slips the phone
> from her grip and sends it smashing
> into the pavement. We all flinch.

Soon, the bus moves us through streets
and suburbs and into the dark.
Night makes a mirror of the window
and makes me a spy. I sit behind her and pry.

> I watch her fingers, fast over that fractured glass,
> jabbing its lattice of cracks where digits progress,
> still, splintered italics eclipsing her child's smile,
> his face grown suddenly lined.

A little ink begins to leak from the rifts,
and it grows dark. Oh, it grows dark
and darker. Take us back, driver.
Lurch this bus into reverse.

> As a conservator rewinds the lines
> from a painting's tempera eyes,
> bring us back. Let her lift her phone
> from the path, unharmed.

Let her shiver, check the time,
sigh at her child's smile, then
slide the phone back in her pocket,
its digits slipping to 5.59.

Written in English

CALL

No slender thread,
                    no telephone cord
binds us any more.
Now that our computers call each other,
            I can't
press your voice to my ear.
No longer can I hear you breathe. Now, we are bound only
by a weak connection
and we break   up
        and break up
                and break up.

Translated by the poet

GLAOCH

Ní cheanglaíonn
            aon chorda caol,
aon sreang theileafóin sinn níos mó.
I réimse na ríomhairí,
        ní thig liom
do ghuth a bhrú níos gaire do mo chluas.
Ní chloisim ag análú thú. Anois, is í an líne lag seo
        an t-aon cheangal amháin atá eadrainn
agus titimid
            as a chéile
        arís
            is
        arís eile.

TATTOO REMOVAL

I thought they would simply delete you,
as a child might find an error in homework,
frown, lift a pink eraser, and rub it out.
I was wrong. Everything's worse now.

To take your name from my skin, lasers
split it into a million particles of pigment.
My flesh bled, absorbing that broken ink,
letting your name fall deeper still. Sink.

Sink. Sunk. Now, you're stuck
in there, wedged somewhere in my innards'
disarray, between my arteries, my shame,
my quivering veins, and I, I must live
with your syllables, smashed, astray.

OK, OK. If you're inside me now, lost,
invisible, it's my fault. I'm sorry,
it was me who made us indivisible.

Translated by the poet

LE TATÚ A BHAINT

Shíl mé nach mbeadh ann ach go scriosfaí thú
sa tslí chéanna go gcuirfeadh gasúr grainc air féin
ag breathnú dó ar chóipleabhar breac le botúin,
á shlánú in athuair lena ghlantóir:
bhí dul amú orm.

Nuair a baineadh d'ainmse de mo chraiceann,
bhris na léasair an tatú ina mílte cáithníní líocha.
Shúigh mo chorp do dhúch scoilte, scaoilte. Anois,
is doimhne fós ionam siollaí d'ainm, táid daite im' chealla;
táim breac leat.

Tá tú laistigh díom anois – caillte, dofheicthe.
Mé féin is tú féin, táimidne do-dhealaithe.

ANTONIJA NOVAKOVIĆ (Croatia)

Antonija Novaković (1979) is a poet and short fiction writer who lives and works in Zagreb. Her poetry collection, Lako mi je biti lošija / It's Easy for Me to be Worse *(2008), won the International Bridges Award at the 47th Struga Poetry Evenings, the unpublished manuscript having previously won the Goran poet-debutant award at the Goranovo Proljeće festival.*

'YOU SAID IT RIGHT...'

you said it right, a dog can look
like any second it's about to speak, but everyone knows
it won't
it took you several hours and a bit of alcohol to guess what I'm like
why I am so prejudiced when it comes to animals
and why I'd never have a pet
why I'd never take off my nylons
in some staircase
only to do you good
so that you can type in peace for the next few days
and chase people around
with what it is you chase them
for your apartment utilities and those few cds
I'm no longer capable of miracles (silence
metastases into knees resting in my arms) you'll never
find me on a poster
with my eyes pierced with needles
I swallowed all cold weapons, there they are in my throat
dreaming of bears (well, do you
punk?)
just as you consent to my sorrow which everyone else
thinks is contagious, just as you patiently let
the foam recede and the blinds
bury the headlights
you can't extinguish my untouched beautiful veins, their
inhuman yearning
for a hero, a dirty syringe

Translated by Tomislav Kuzmanović

'DOBRO SI REKAO...'

dobro si rekao, pas može izgledati
kao da će svakog trena progovoriti, ali svi znaju
da neće
trebalo ti je nekoliko sati i nešto alkohola da me pročitaš
zašto sam tako zadrta kad je u pitanju životinjsko
i nikad ne bih imala kućnog ljubimca
zašto se neću skinuti u najlonke
na nekom stepeništu
samo da ti učinim dobro
da možeš sljedećih par dana u miru tipkati
i ganjati ljude
već onim čime ih ganjaš
za stan režije i par cd-ova
nisam više sposobna ni za kakvo čudo (tišina
metastazira u rukama obgrljena koljena) nećeš me
naći na plakatu
očiju probodenih špenadlama
progutala sam
sve hladno oružje, eno ga u grlu
sanja medvjede (well, do you
punk?)
to kako pristaješ na moju tugu za koju svi drugi
misle da je zarazna, kako strpljivo puštaš
pjenu da se spusti i rolete
da sahrane farove
ne može ugasiti moje netaknute lijepe vene, njihovu
nečovječnu žudnju
za herojem, nekom prljavom špricom

'ON THE PHONE...'

on the phone you sound like you've just found a lump
(mouth
full of snow, your transatlantic
eyes, neither brown
nor completely yellow. we'll talk
when I get there) what I'd like most is to
sink my face into jarmusch's sleeve and bite
the fabric, bring everything down to swallowing face-washing breathing
and so on (postcoital
smoke)
what I'd like most is to get away from here

I'll get you some
trinkets, a fridge magnet or a new
shower cap (you're simple, you can touch
exactly what you want to touch)
while driving I'm working on the sturdiness
of verses (I write best
when I'm naked, sleep deprived and hungry, but that's not now, now
there's everything): *a downpour is*
an autogenous practice for the poor. or something like that.
the girl in the car next to mine is hassling the window
she makes faces at the old lady that got splashed as happily
as gummies, red and yellow
bottles of baby coke. the only thing still alive
is the stuffed animal in the back seat, I no longer know
whose. if I were closer
I would light her cigarette. everyone else on the road thinks
they're travelling to cleveland.

Translated by Tomislav Kuzmanović

'PREKO TELEFONA...'

preko telefona zvučiš kao da si napipala kvržicu
(usta
puna snijega, tvoje prekooceanske
oči, ni smeđe
ni posve žute. razgovarat ćemo
kad dođem) najradije bih
zarila lice u jarmuschev rukav i grizla
štof, svela sve na gutanje umivanje disanje
i tako redom (postkoitalni
dim)
najradije bih se maknula
kupit ću ti usput
neku glupost, magnet za frižider ili novu
kapu za tuširanje (jednostavna si, možeš dotaknuti
baš ono što želiš dotaknuti)
vozeći se radim na žilavosti
stihova (najbolje pišem
kad sam gola, neispavana i gladna, a to nije sad, sad
ima svega): *pljusak je*
autogeni trening za siročiće. ili tako nekako.
curica u susjednom autu gnjavi staklo
babi koju je zalilo krevelji se radošću
gumenih bombona, crvenožute

flašice baby coca-cole. živa je još samo
plišana životinja na zadnjem sicu, ne znam više
čija. da sam bliže
pripalila bih joj cigaru. svi drugi na cesti misle
da putuju u cleveland

'WE GET DRUNK...'

we get drunk and then say we're posthumans
it sounds like later we'll
fuck so hard that all electric appliances in the apartment
start working again
and all the lights turn on, on their own
it's good that there's comfort still
I can't even tell you how much I stopped loving
these sweaty people
their alcohol tears
at home the flower is waiting for me to water it
it stands on the window and subverts
my constant desire
to drop dead
if you see it don't tell it what made its leaves turn
yellow (the truth is
but a flesh wound)
there could hardly be a living being as tolerant
to the merciless way of showing
affection, look
away when you see me
again, don't
search for what isn't there

Translated by Tomislav Kuzmanović

'NAPIJEMO SE...'

napijemo se pa govorimo da smo postljudi
zvuči kao da ćemo se kasnije
jebati tako da prorade svi mali kućanski
aparati u stanu
i upale se svjetla, sama od sebe
dobro da još postoji utjeha
ne mogu ti ni reći koliko sam prestala voljeti

ove znojne ljude
njihov alkoholni plač
kod kuće čeka cvijet da ga zalijem
stoji na prozoru i subverzira
moju neprestanu želju
da crknem
ako ga vidiš nemoj mu reći zbog čega mu je požutjelo
lišće (istina je
samo površinska rana)
teško da još postoji živo biće toliko tolerantno
za nemilosrdan način pokazivanja
nježnosti, okreni glavu
u stranu kad me ponovo
vidiš, nemoj
tražiti ono čega nema

'AT THE HEART OF THINGS...'

At the heart of things lies pain.

It is clearer if I say: between the bed and the table I make cameo appearances.

The laws of physics bring the postman to my door.
Good morning.
Best of all is the meagreness of the water bill.

And the sudden loss of memory.

That's when my eyes dilate and all things seem familiar and dear.

Translated by Mirza Purić

'U OSNOVI STVARI...'

U osnovi stvari leži bol.

Jasnije je ako kažem: na liniji između kreveta i stola pojavljujem se u
ulozi same sebe.

Zakoni fizike dovode poštara pred vrata.
Dobro jutro.
Od svega je najljepša oskudnost računa za vodu.

I iznenadni gubitak pamćenja.

Tada mi rastu oči i sve se čini poznato i drago.

SANDEEP PARMAR (UK)

Sandeep Parmar (born in Nottingham and raised in Southern California) is a poet, editor, novelist and a BBC New Generation Thinker. She has published two collections of poetry: The Marble Orchard *and* Eidolon, *which won the Ledbury Forte Prize for Best Second Collection. Her essays and reviews have appeared in the* Guardian, The Los Angeles Review of Books, *the* Financial Times *and the* Times Literary Supplement. *She teaches at the University of Liverpool and co-directs Liverpool's Centre for New and International Writing.*

ARCHIVE FOR A DAUGHTER

November 1972, Derby
A dance card embalmed in sweat.   Her ruthless curve of palm
mowing the carpet into sheaves before a gas fire.

Liquidescent virgin in a purple dress.
                          Oil paint, shaded avocado, umbrella sun-wings.
Box 2, folder 20 'Early Married Life'
a single page:
        recto
            a fashionable centre-parting
        verso
            consonants: midnight affair nuclear affair bleach affair
        watermark indecipherable

[But here we are jumping ahead]

The archivist notes that no exact birth date is known.
An already Western dressed 6-year-old reads the headlines of English
                          newspapers for party tricks.
Her black eyes are blunt and unequivocal like the prophecies of pharaohs.
In a Punjabi village, she and her impeccable mother, gemstoned, oracular,
                          princess a vernal causeway.

Box 1, folder 2 'Emigration'

The BOAC stewardesses Max Factor crinkled baskets
of sweets to soothe the girl's swinging, impatient feet.
Aviation – a risky endeavour in 1963 – levels a curse at her progeny.
Aerophobia – her own daughter's – fear of the air between home and
                                                 exile collapsing.

Box 1, folder 7 'Education'

Homelands Grammar School For Girls

Miss Moore leans across an oak sea and parquets a line of future mothers.
Her bovine sympathies, neatly pressed, tentacle towards the only Indian
                                                           in the class.
The Georgian battlecross marking her forehead, kindly and thoughtfully,
                                                           segregates.

The girl bounds wildly through the Public Library – Huxley to her
                                                 11-year-old mind
suggests individuality – but the Savage's feet recommend no one specific exit.

folders 8-17

[Unbound Notebook, mostly unreadable]

I thought I could become a doctor and asking found I could not think to ask to
                                                       become anything

The archivist notes that these pages are not continuous. Refer to Box 2, folder 10
   'Correspondence'.
                        A photograph of a prospective husband and several
                                          handwritten credentials.

Box 3, folder 1 'Notes on Motherhood'

Nursery – pram – groceries – pram – doctor's visit – cucumbers in half-lengths –
– over each shoulder some conspicuous intellect –

Husband-academic, wife-typist.
She door-to-doors Hoovers, Avon, thick rosaries of factory lace,
while her children pop tic-tacs for invented ailments in plastic houses.

Nottingham hurls snowballs at her black turbaned gentleman.

    Soaked typescript, fair copy of a life –

When she asked her parents for a spare suitcase for an exodus, they replied
    my child, nothing is ever spare

Box 4, folder 1 'Exile'

1985, Vancouver – ablaze with cherry blossoms from here to the kindergarten.
We arrived with one steel pot, a bag of lentils and an onion.

    folder 2

1987, North Hollywood – submarine fences root Thanksgiving potatoes,
        one a piece.
My daughter reads Laura Ingalls Wilder to her menagerie of dolls. Raft
        sails calmly on.

    folder 3

1989, Oxnard – Gifted children are purse strings. We mind their collegiate years
        with interest.
El Rio wizens to a stockpile of citrus and rental agreements.

    folder 4

1995, Ventura – Bibled to real estate, gold blazers cinch round a wade of
        blonde, leathered adulterers.
The neighbours tend their god-plots of lawn and hedge.

Box 5, folder 1 'Drs Parmar'

She saunas with the ladies of the Gold Coast –
one Japanese ex-comfort woman, one savvy señora goldbuckled and
multifranchised.

Stanford, Northwestern, Harvard, London, Cambridge – and when my
husband's sisters wept
because I had no sons I said I have two doctors (one of body, the other of mind)
and sent my uterus via Federal Express to the village, with my compliments!

On the verso, written in ink, is a page from Box 1, folder 8 [misplaced]

I remember clearly when I knew that I would one day die.
I was on the toilet and I was 11.
The bathroom was white and oblivious.

from **EIDOLON**

I

It was not me, but a phantom
whose oath
a variable star
moldering in the reliquary
is doubt.

I have not unsealed love, its taproot
mouthing blackness
nor seized the fairer woman
to purge from her her song –

> *This hell-house of primogeniture, bookish*
>   *and pale*   *quartering what is also*
>   *its own and only rule*
>   *this: fire*
> *and the fire that comes*   *from fire.*

    II

Helen, dispirited
      camera-bound   Helen
fetching the paper from the front lawn in her dressing gown a lot
  of the time
      and knowing when the phone will ring
      seconds before   by the click of its current

Demi-goddess – not woman, not god
      disembodied like a bowl turned over and its loaf
  thumping out
            Helen
    Queen of never-mind-the-time, of *you can't run on gin for*
  all the
     everlasting
     And such

    moths, broiling airlessly in a sodium bulb
      smell of it on her front porch
        lights on   home

    XXV

Helen is   instrumental

Laws permit me to refuse your advances
although I have eaten the salt from your table

As for your hospitality –
I like it anywhere just fine
      so long as I'm coming or going

Helen   is not all but
     scattered like grain

     Vituperate   ghost meaning

     to greet herself   to make room
         for herself   at the table

to eat a meal of dry meat and vinegar

Helen is not vital

   xxx

I am not the virgin mother   *lamenting in the hills above*
   Ephesus

I am the invective   *injuring these dry plains studded with stone pines*

I am the lateral commemorate   *of war*
    as the steps up to my hiding place suggest
      I am the birther of sacrifice *received back into*
      the earth   *heavenly rockface*

    if you knew my real name   *you would not*
     use it so lightly

XXXVII

You are wild-eyed
You are Helen

The grey-blue dawn
the Rosy-fingered Dawn
turning the snaking cloud
into the body of a goddess
raising her thin spear

we glide across
the blue-eyed morning
changing flags
as a woman changes
her lover as often
as another
lover permits
we glide across
zones of conflict

The wind lays down a road
across the waves
hiding us in a mooring of fog
flanks of earth lighten
like fantasy   like Leda's body
to make way for our white ship
of a hundred tiers
and some thousand men

This parthenous soup
of buried cities
held close   we make out
the scent of their joints
the only real thing
in an invented eschatology
of free will

Did I mention the Indiana corn
from whence I came
and its hot unendingness?

      Proud like crosses on a prairie landscape.
Corn madness
industrial corn a devil
bleating like a harp
made of 22 karat gold
High Fructose Syrup
infantile mass delusion   god
sugar fix of empire

Helen makes out the morning freeze
in the stillness of a suspended harvest
what eviction has nature made
in retaliation for these unkillable crops?
Out out for the outing acres of frozen heads.

XLVI

'*Put first before the rest as light for all and entrance-song of all,*
That of eidolons.' [Whitman]

No one alive
remembers
the unrecordable
warmth of my
breath

JOSEP PEDRALS (Spain / Catalonia)

Josep Pedrals (1979, Barcelona) has, since 1997, been performing his poetry on stages throughout Europe, Asia and America at numerous literary festivals and has received many awards, including one from the Osaka International Slam in 2009. For two years, from 2010-2012, he published a sonnet every day in the newspaper Ara. *He works in poetry education.*

THREE SONNETS, 7

No wonder she came over queer.
In that pox-ridden, clap-ridden den,
only the breeze of a ceiling-fan
and a palm-leaf to stir the air.
Everything stifled in there:
thick, heavy vapour, spice-laden,
smoke haze, soft glances through hair,
jalousies, style half-Persian,
half wild Paraguay,
with a parrot's cry.
The tragedy's summarization
of dull and prosaic stagnation.
And plumb-centre in the mosaic,
the muse gone inert, apoplectic.

Translated by Anna Crowe

TRES SONETS, 7

No fou d'estranyar el desmai.
En aquell cau de venèries,
només amb l'airet d'una hèlice
i el ventar-se amb un pai-pai.
Tot ofegava en l'espai:
vapors espessos, espècies,
fum quiet, mirades de xai,
gelosies d'entre Pèrsia
i selva del Paraguai
i un guacamai.
El resum de la tragèdia
de l'estancament prosaic.
I al bell mig d'aquest mosaic,
la musa, inerta, apoplèctica.

ART OF THE TROUBADOURS

I always know I can – if I want – find,
gleaning through doings with a sieve:
I measure the ballistics beforehand
and then do exactly the opposite.

I can scour the sordid warmly,
tracking the emptiness of alone
through tunnels thick with phony dark
that turn up on the prettiest postcards.

I can gaze down the gaping precipice
loving the love of those who jumped.

Translation by Ronald Puppo

ART DE TROBAR

Ja sempre sé que puc, quan vull, trobar-hi,
espigolant pels tràfecs amb sedàs:
mesuro l'embranzida abans del pas
i faig, precisament, tot el contrari.

Podré recórrer el sòrdid amb escalf
seguint ressons al buit del solitari
per túnels plens d'un fosc artificial
que acaben en postals de calendari.

Podré mirar pel tall de l'estimball
amant l'amor d'aquells que van saltar-hi.

I FALL INTO PERPETUAL GRAVITY

I fall into perpetual gravity,
like the unreachable sleep
eyelids support
or faeces that poke
but constipation curbs;
I fall with the pains of the body.
And it's the practice of falling
– I've got to learn but haven't a clue how –

easy, I find, taken in abstraction
virtualizing sensations,
but in no way tolerable
as a state with no comfort.
I fall living it like a trauma
accepted unconditionally,
like a fact inseparable
from a stay in this world,
where everyone's a human cannonball,
and vaginas, cannons
where life shoots out
at a slope of horizons.

Translation by Ronald Puppo

CAIC EN GRAVETAT PERPÈTUA

Caic en gravetat perpètua,
com el son inassolible
que sostenen les parpelles
o bé l'excrement que fibla
prò el restrenyiment el frena;
caic amb les penes del cos.
I és l'exercici de caure
-que he d'aprendre no sé com-
el que em costa menys d'abstraure
virtualitzant sensacions,
prò em resulta intolerable
com a estat sense confort.
Caic vivint-ho com un trauma
admès sense condicions,
com un fet indissociable
de l'estada en aquest món
on tot home és home bala,
i les vagines, canons
per on la vida es dispara
cap a un pendís d'horitzons.

THREE SONNETS, 9

Into his eye death has contrived to creep.
Since then, with lid macabre, ill-fated,
his glance resembles olives left to steep:
black and dead and sad, debilitated.
It doesn't even cry! No whim to weep.
Glassy, about to be check-mated,
it doesn't let a single tear-drop seep,
the olive-press is dry, soul dehydrated.
But we're all waiting for the day we reap
the flow of olive-juice that's generated
by woe now grounded on a reef and deep.
We'll even lick his face – well-lubricated!
Till then, old olive-press, given up to grippe,
with olive-stones your eyes will fill, instead of sleep!

Translated by Anna Crowe

TRES SONETS, 9

Se li va ficar la mort a l'ull.
De llavors ençà, parpre macabre,
té un mirar d'olives en remull:
negres, mortes, tristes i aixafades.
Mes, no plora, no! No té l'antull.
Vidriós i a punt per la trencada,
no deixa anar llàgrima, té el trull
sec i l'ànima deshidratada.
Tots comptem que algun dia, curull,
regalimarà suc d'olivada
d'una pena encallada a l'escull.
I encara s'hi lleparà la cara!
Fins llavors, molí que mai no mols,
se't faran lleganyes com pinyols!

MALTE PERSSON (Sweden)

Malte Persson (1976) is a poet, novelist, children's book author, translator, columnist and literary critic. He has published four books of poetry, among them the sonnet collection Underjorden / The Underground, *(2011) and* Till dikten / To Poetry *(2018) and also writes satirical verse. He has been awarded a number of literary prizes, and is featured in a recent anthology of Swedish poetry through the ages. He currently lives in Berlin.*

ENTERTAINMENT

When we grow ashamed of the amount of poetry we've been reading and feel the need to engage in something more serious, we turn on the TV. We watch, perhaps, a news programme about the global situation, which is extremely serious, if not acutely alarming; or perhaps a drama series with a complex narrative structure, which, over the course of several seasons, portrays the development of a number of fictive characters though the use of long *story arcs*; or perhaps a documentary film about owls, those wisest of animals that have never learned to read but are deep into networking and mindful presence. The TV has both sound and image, which poetry mostly pretends to – not only that, but our modern televisions and computer screens on which we stream our TV programmes are able to display an enormous number of different colours, which they make use of to depict a multitude of objects and events – whereas poetry, for the most part, only has two: black, and white, with which it desperately tries to give itself airs. Poems are often short (such as *limericks*, a kind of ludicrous joke told in rhyme, and *haikus*, which are the same thing, but without the rhyme or any sense of fun) so that even an idiot can read all the way through without losing concentration, whereas TV programs, for example awards ceremonies in which significant contributions to the television-related arts are celebrated, can go on for hours, if not days. However, we aren't as smart as we like to pretend we are, and generally fall asleep in front of the TV before it is quite done showing us what it intended to show – or else, more often than not, we quickly go back to reading poetry.

Translated by Olivia Olsen

UNDERHÅLLNING

När vi skäms för att vi läst så många dikter och vill göra
något seriösare så tittar vi på teve. Kanske är det nyheter
om världsläget, som är djupt allvarligt, för att inte säga
akut oroväckande; eller kanske en serie med komplex
berättarteknik, som under flera säsonger skildrar en mängd
fiktiva gestalters utveckling genom långa story arcs; eller
kanske en dokumentär om ugglor, det allra klokaste djuret,
som aldrig lärt sig läsa, men som jobbar med nätverkande
och medveten närvaro. Teven har både ljud och bild,
medan dikten mest låtsas ha det, och dessutom har dagens
teveapparater och datorskärmar på vilka vi streamar
teveprogram massvis av färger, som de använder för att visa
en mångfald av ting och händelser, medan dikten för det
mesta bara har två, svart och vitt, som den förgäves försöker
göra sig märkvärdig med. Dikterna är oftast korta (till
exempel "limerickar", ett slags små löjliga skämt på rim, och
"haiku", som är samma sak, men utan rim och humor) för att
även den som är dum i huvudet ska orka koncentrera sig på
dem, medan teveprogrammen, till exempel en gala där olika
framstående insatser inom de teverelaterade konstarterna
prisas, kan pågå nästan hur länge som helst. Vi, däremot, är
inte så smarta som vi låtsas vara, och somnar därför framför
teven innan den är klar med vad den har att visa, eller så
återgår vi allt som oftast inom kort till dikten.

THE POETS

Poets are the partisans of language.
They ponder this
in the pale light of their laptop camp-fires.

Afar they see great shadows move
and hear
a thunderclap that they believe is language.

Translated by Olivia Olsen

POETERNA

Poeterna är språkets partisaner.
Så tänker de,
vid sina laptopskärmars svala lägereldar.

I fjärran rör sig stora skuggor
och de hör
något som de tror är språkets åska.

IN HELL

One must imagine Sisyphus is happy.
Pushing his stroller up the street
Writing another weekly column.
Hades is like Twitter: all the others.
Hades is like Tinder: all the same.
Hades is a haiku without end.
Where demography meets demagoguery.
Where the Netflix series is the new novel.
Caught in a near unreadable diagram.
From a market research survey.
That someone calls about at dinner.
Is hell another looping GIF
where a cute animal gets hurt.
Is hell another insipid meme:
"You know you're in hell when..."
Is hell an open office space.
An inbox with no spam filter.
Do you want to meet hot singles in your area?
Like hell I do. Now take this quiz:
Which Patriarch are you most like?
Which vintage Tupperware product?
Which character from *Enoch Arden*?
Lucky I'm a genius, you see.
Lucky the mainstream audience
has a perfect ear for irony.
We say in hell (*JK!*).
In hell we argue about poetry
but nobody remembers any poetry.

All there is to read are editorials.
All there is to read is copy.
All there is to read are end-user license agreements.
All there is to read are letters of rejection.
All there is to read are milk cartons
of milk way past its sell-by date,
like a millennium ago,
when Tetrapaks were first domesticated.
In hell they play a pan-flute cover
of Sex Pistols' "Holiday in the Sun".
In hell the coffee machine only takes bitcoins
and nobody has any bitcoins.
In hell they show a live-feed of heaven
24/7 in pretty shitty resolution.
Overall the figurative language
isn't all that great in hell.
No matter how modern it seems.
Because hell is only a craze.
But what a craze it is!

Translated by Olivia Olsen

I HELVETET

Man måste tänka sig Sisyfos som lycklig.
Där han knuffar fram sin barnvagn.
När han skriver veckans krönika.
Hades är som Twitter: de andra.
Hades är som Tinder: det samma.
Hades är en haiku som aldrig tar slut.
Där demografin möter demagogin.
Där tvserien är den nya romanen.
Fångad i ett nästan oläsbart diagram.
Från en marknadsundersökning.
Som någon ringer om när du ska äta.
Är helvetet ännu en loopad GIF
med ett gulligt djur som gör sig illa.
Är helvetet ett ganska tjatigt meme:
"You know you're in hell when..."
Är helvetet ett öppet kontorslandskap.
Ett mejlkonto utan spamfilter.
Vill du träffa heta tjejer nära dig?
Så i helvete heller. Testa dig själv:
Vilken kyrkofader är du mest lik?

Vilken vintage Tupperware-produkt?
Vem är du i Fänrik Ståls sägner?
Det är tur att man är ett geni.
Det är tur att den breda publiken
har ett perfekt öra för ironi.
Säger vi "på skoj" i helvetet.
I helvetet pågår poesidebatter
men ingen minns någon poesi.
Allt man får att läsa är ledarsidor.
Allt man får att läsa är copy.
Allt man får att läsa är användaravtal.
Allt man får att läsa är refuseringsbrev.
Allt man får att läsa är mjölkkartonger
vars mjölk passerat bäst före-datum
för cirka ett millennium sedan,
då tetrapacken först domesticerades.
I helvetet spelas en lounge-version
av Ebba Gröns "800 grader".
I helvetet tar kaffemaskinen bara bitcoin
och ingen har några bitcoin.
I helvetet visas en livefeed från himlen
24/7 med ganska dålig bild.
Överhuvudtaget är bildspråket
inte jättebra i helvetet.
Hur modernt det än kan tyckas vara.
För helvetet är bara en fluga.
Men vilken fluga det är!

MEMENTO MORI

Wanderer, now listen up:
An iPhone is a tiny tombstone
made from some black and shiny mineral.
Maybe from a cemetery for small pets.
Armoured guinea pigs and dancing
parrots and other viral triumphs.
All equal in the face of dissolution.
Even Grumpy Cat will die one day!
Each lapidary epigraph
maxed at 140 characters.
Once. You. Got. Ten. Thousand. Likes./
Now. No. One. Evermore. Says. Lol.

Translated by Olivia Olsen

GRAVDIKT

Vandringsman, hör på nu här:
En iphone är en mycket liten gravsten
i något blankt svart stenslag.
Kanske från en kyrkogård för smådjur.
Marsvin i rustning och dansande
papegojor och andra virala succéer.
Alla inför förgängligheten lika.
Också Grumpy Cat skall en gång dö!
Varje inskription i stenstil
får vara max 140 tecken.
En. Gång. Fick. Du. Tiotusen. Likes. /
Nu. Säger. Ingen. Mera. Lol

EPITAPH / or Elegie for faire POESY / That in Our Age at Long Last hath Expired

O, hear me, Passer-by! For resting here –
no, rest is really not the fitting word :
Here lies fair murdered Poetry interred.
Like the from misshot arrows wounded deer
that dashes through the forest unbeknownst
to both the hunter and the bow he drew*
so Poetry to Lethe, bleeding, flew:
fell silent to its whiteout-waters' flow,
and left poor language – wretched shard of Babel –
the sad fields of utility to till.
Now Poetry is dead, and dead it will
weigh upon each word, it's absence able
to haunt unspoken, and forever chill
the souls of the damned thugs that got her killed.

* Aen. IV: 69-73

Translated by Olivia Olsen

EPITAPHIUM / eller Klage-Kling-Dicht öfwer POËSIEN / som i wårt Tidehwarf ändteligen aflidit

Hör upp, o vandrare! Här nedan vilar –
om vilar alltså är det rätta ordet –
den hulda poesin. Vems skuld var mordet?
Likt hjorten sårad av förlupna pilar
igenom skogen springer, utan att den
bland jägarna som höll i bågen vet det*,

stöp poesin tyst blödande mot Lethe,
mot glömskans kalla tip-ex-bleka vatten,
och lämnar språket, arma Babelsskärv,
åt nyttohjonens trista jordbruksvärv...
Nu ligger dikten grunt begravd i tjälen;
dess frånvaro i varje ord och nerv
skall alltid spöka outsagd i själen
hos skurkarna som tanklöst haft ihjäl den.

* *Aen. IV : 69–73*

REGARDING THE SITUATION OF POETRY IN OUR DAY AND AGE

Poetry: there isn't much to recommend it, really.
It lacks, for instance, awesome special effects.
Such as giant balls of fire. Furthermore:
The line too labours, and the words move slow,
– or whatever Elvis sang in Vegas.
Hark the vaudeville poet's cry:
With verse I used to entertain,
but now I entertain in vain;
I was a well-known, well-liked bard,
but being that is now too hard.
Poetry is not a social medium.
Mme. Blavatsky was. Poetry, no.
Sometimes poetry gets a grant. A small one.
Then it runs off right away and spends it on something dumb.
Poetry sometimes gets recited by Morgan Freeman.
It really shouldn't be.
But what happens, happens.
And yet – yet: Poetry.

Translated by Olivia Olsen

RÖRANDE POESINS BELÄGENHET I VÅRT NUVARANDE SAMHÄLLE

Mycket talar emot dikten.
Till exempel saknar den häftiga specialeffekter.
Såsom stora bollar av eld. Vidare:
Dikten är icke som blommornas doft,
som färgade bågen i skyar.
Och inte som Elvis i Las Vegas heller.

Hör estradpoetens klagan:
En gång var jag estradör,
nu minns jag inte hur man gör;
jag var en känd estradpoet,
nu är jag inte längre det.
Dikten är inget socialt medium.
Mme Blavatsky var ett. Inte dikten.
Ibland får dikten pengar. Bara lite.
Då springer den genast iväg och gör något dumt.
Dikten blir ibland uppläst av Stina Ekblad.
Det borde den inte bli.
Men det som sker, det sker.
Och ändå: poesin.

ALDO QURESHI (France)

Aldo Qureshi (1975) started writing poems in the early 1990s. They first appeared on the internet, then in chapbooks and literary reviews. His three published collections are Made in Eden *(2018),* Barnabas *(2018) and* La Nuit de las graisse *(2019). He is also known for his readings and public performances.*

NON-DUALITY

my wife and I we decided to quit calling each other nicknames.
I won't go by the name of *rabbit* any more, nor will she answer to
sweety, cupcake, honey, etc. We decided to both call
each other god. It makes talking easier, and,
in a way, it sets us on equal footing.
But then, you know what they say about what's bred in the bone.
And there she goes, she's at it again, giving me orders.
She calls them *self-begotten streams of consciousness,*
but mind you, I can still tell the difference between
Satan Trismegistus and a jar of Nutella.
Every morning she turns up with a schedule for me, she says
do this and do that, don't eat in between meals,
avoid fry-ups, exercise, and she leaves telling me
make sure you hang the laundry and emphasizes
that I'm too old now to be playing *World of Warcraft*
In the evening my feelings are black with a red tail,

feelings that are attuned to the night.
And whenever I do the shopping list, she double-checks
and crosses out: beer, potato chips, Kinder
Buenos. When we're in the store I go *Ok now what
should we get?* And she says: *I can't be making all
the decisions all the time... take the initiative, will you*

Translated by Alexis Bernaut

LA NON-DUALITÉ

avec ma femme on a décidé d'arrêter les diminutifs.
Moi de ne plus me faire appeler *mon lapin*, et elle *ma
biche, bibiche, mimine,* etc. On a décidé de s'appeler
tous les deux dieu. Ça simplifie les entretiens, et,
d'une certaine façon, ça nous met sur un pied d'égalité.
Seulement vous savez ce qu'on dit à propos du naturel.
Et là ça y est elle s'est remise à me donner des ordres.
Elle appelle ça *des flux de conscience auto-engendrés,*
mais je suis encore capable de faire la différence entre
Satan trismégiste et un pot de Nutella.
Le matin elle déboule avec mon planning, elle me dit
de faire ça et ça, de ne pas manger entre les repas,
d'éviter les fritures, de faire du sport, de dire en partant
pense à étendre le linge et de me faire remarquer
que j'ai passé l'âge de jouer à *World of Warcraft.*
Le soir j'ai des sentiments noirs à queue rouge, des
sentiments qui vont dans le même sens que la nuit.
Et quand je fais la liste des courses elle passe derrière
moi, elle raye le pack de bières, les chips, les Kinder
Bueno. Une fois dans le magasin *Bon alors qu'est-ce
qu'on achète?* Et elle: *J'en ai marre que ce soit tout
le temps moi qui décide de tout... prends des initiatives*

THE GENERAL STATES OF SWISS CHEESE

Véronique and Jean-Claude, kids just aren't their thing.
Problem is, Véronique is a real breeder, and Jean-Claude,
well, he just can't help it: when it itches, he'll
scratch. Hey I got an idea you know what we're going to do
we're going to put them in the cellar. And Véronique says
damn right, they'll be comfortable down there, they'll do as
they please. And they'd send every new one

in the cellar. But then came the time when they
started getting a little squashed in and the children
started to get out and to overrun the main floor, the 1st floor,
and Véronique would go: "There goes my kitchen!" And
Jean-Claude would go: "It feels like we're strangers
in our own house." And they would hold on to each other,
and scream, and jump on their feet, and trample,
and holler – saying: "This-is-ooouur-HOME!
This-is-ooouur-HOME! This-is-ooouur-HOME!"

Translated by Alexis Bernaut

LES ÉTATS GÉNÉRAUX DU GRUYÈRE

Véronique et Jean-Claude les mômes c'est pas leur truc.
Seulement Véronique est une vraie pondeuse et Jean-Claude
ne peut pas se retenir à chaque fois que ça le démange il faut
qu'il se gratte. Au bout d'un moment j'ai une idée tu sais ce
qu'on va faire on va les mettre à la cave. Et Véronique dit
t'as raison, ils seront bien en bas, ils pourront faire ce qu'ils
veulent. Et à chaque fois qu'il y en avait un nouveau,
ils l'envoyaient à la cave. Et puis il y a eu un moment où ça
a commencé à devenir ric-rac au niveau place et les enfants
se sont mis à sortir et à envahir le rez-de-chaussée, le 1er étage,
et Véronique disait: «Je reconnais plus ma cuisine!». Et
Jean-Claude disait: «On a l'impression d'être des étrangers
dans sa propre baraque». Et ils se prenaient dans les bras
et ils gueulaient en sautant sur place et en trépignant
et ils gueulaient – ils disaient: «On-est cheez NOUS!
On-est cheez NOUS! On-est cheez NOUS!»

THE LOBBY OF ANGUISH

I have a purse-shaped swimming suit.
Actually, it isn't – *shaped*, it is a purse. It doesn't
cover my nakedness but bumps along between my thighs
and I must walk as if I had a horse between
my legs. And it strikes me that not only is the swimming pool
full of people but that every one of them
has the flu. Every time their heads stick out of the water in step
you can spot the vermicelli hanging from their noses
or they sneeze and it squirts out. Now

that I'm here, I can't walk back, lest I should
insult the swimming teacher. This swimming pool with
its infectious swimmers beckoning me to join them,
as if they were just waiting for somebody to share their
microbes, this swimming pool pretty much
sums up my life. I swim a little, like I'm not really
there, I try not to think of the purse, of the horse
which is meant to be between my legs, and whenever I
get my head under the water, I see the dander and the filaments
which spot my presence right away, and when I
stick my head out again I see swimmers all around me,
with ringed eyes, waiting for someone to replace them, and,
behind them, the swimming teacher who is pushing microbes
and points at me with a squeegee

Translated by Alexis Bernaut

LE LOBBY DE L'ANGOISSE

j'ai un maillot de bain en forme de sac à main.
En fait, il n'est pas *en forme*, c'est un sac à main. Il ne
couvre pas ma nudité, mais ballotte entre mes cuisses
et m'oblige à marcher comme si j'avais un cheval entre
les jambes. Et je réalise que non seulement la piscine
est pleine à craquer mais en plus les baigneurs ont tous
chopé la grippe. Ils sortent la tête en cadence et à chaque
fois qu'ils remontent on voit les vermicelles qui pendent
ou alors ils éternuent et ça sort d'un coup. Maintenant
que je suis là, je ne peux plus revenir en arrière, sinon
le maître-nageur va se sentir insulté. Cette piscine, avec
les nageurs infectieux qui me font signe de les rejoindre,
comme s'ils n'attendaient que ça, que quelqu'un vienne
partager leurs miasmes, cette piscine, c'est un peu le
résumé de ma vie. Je fais quelques brasses en essayant de
ne pas être là, de ne pas penser au sac à main, au cheval
que je suis censé avoir entre les jambes, et quand je
mets la tête sous l'eau je vois les squames, les filaments
qui détectent immédiatement ma présence, et quand je
remonte à la surface je vois les baigneurs autour de moi,
les yeux cernés, l'envie que quelqu'un les remplace, et,
derrière, le maître-nageur qui pousse les microbes
en me désignant avec la raclette

RACIAL PROFILING

the cashier watches the *Herta* 10 ham slices package and then looks
at the ham and looks at my ID, and then she
looks at me again, and again at the ham, as if
she were seeking to compare, to make a connection, or to find
a balance that would justify my purchase. One senses that the poem
might stop
in its tracks right now, but
it continues – bravely or foolishly, never mind,
the important thing is that it continues. The other customers twitch
their eyebrows, waiting for her reaction,
and the cashier resumes her inspection. She compares
my skin with the ham's skin; she squints.
And then – she turns the packaging over, looking for something
at the back of the package – she hits the button
and the emergency light above the checkout starts
to blare and rotate in the shop.

Translated by Alexis Bernaut

CONTRÔLE AU FACIÈS

la caissière observe le jambon *Herta* 10 tranches et regarde
alternativement le jambon et ma carte d'identité, puis elle
me regarde à nouveau et à nouveau le jambon comme si
elle cherchait à comparer ou à établir un lien, ou à trouver
une adéquation justifiant mon achat. On sent bien qu'à cet
instant précis le poème
pourrait s'arrêter brutalement, mais
il continue – courageusement ou stupidement, peu importe
l'important c'est qu'il continue. Les autres clients font sauter
leurs sourcils en attendant de savoir quelle sera sa réaction
et la caissière de reprendre son examen. Elle compare
ma peau avec la peau du jambon, elle plisse les yeux.
Puis – retournant l'emballage, cherchant quelque chose
au dos de l'emballage – elle appuie sur le bouton
et le gyrophare situé au-dessus de la caisse se met
à hurler en tournoyant dans le magasin

LOU RAOUL (France)

Lou Raoul (1964) is a French poet with a bilingual French-Breton background which influences her writing. She has published ten books since 2010, and was awarded the Poés Yvelines Prize in 2013 for Else avec elle / Else with Her *(Editions Isabelle Sauvage, 2012). Lou Raoul gives public readings, takes part in literary encounters and writing residences and works in collaboration with other artists*

'ON THE PILLAR...'

on the pillar there it's perched this bird
pichig-ruhig robin

pichig-ruhig chomit un tamm
robin stay a while
ho tiwaskell skañz war ma c'halon
your two light wings on my heart
pichig-ruhig chomit amañ
robin stay here
ganeoc'h e teu un amzer all
another time comes with you

all birds
various passerines thrushes too
when the sun has reached the west
the whole Stanco throbs
on the turned-up earth of the corral
two doves

both one and the other

> *Translated by Ian Monk*

'SUR LE PILIER...'

sur le pilier il est perché c'est cet oiseau
pichig-ruhig rouge-gorge

pichig-ruhig chomit un tamm
rouge-gorge restez un peu
ho tiwaskell skañv war ma c'halon
vos deux ailes légères sur mon cœur
pichig-ruhig chomit amañ

rouge-gorge restez ici
ganeoc'h e teu un amzer all
avec vous vient un autre temps

tous les oiseaux
divers passereaux des grives aussi
quand le soleil est tout à l'ouest
c'est tout le Stanco qui palpite
et sur la terre retournée du courtil
deux tourterelles

et l'une et l'autre

'IN THE YARD THAT DAY...'

in the yard that day
seizh eur da noz 'son
seven pm sounds
and the crows in the ploughed fields opposite

and right then too a woman comes over
yes that one there, this young brunette
just there looking at me
she's standing near
the low wall
of the vegetable garden
the cows coming back to be milked

and around all around around
the voices taking off that day
the voices of all the other days taking off
my head spinning my head

Translated by Ian Monk

DANS LA COUR CE JOUR-LÀ

dans la cour ce jour-là
seizh eur da noz 'son
sept heures du soir sonnent
et les corneilles dans les labours d'en face

et aussi bien une femme s'approche
oui celle-là même, cette jeune femme brune
se tenant là me regardant
elle est debout près
du muret
du potager
des vaches qui reviennent pour la traite

et autour tout autour autour
les voix envolées de ce jour-là
les voix de tous les autres jours envolés
ma tête tourne ma tête

MA'AÏ

in her heart
in the April blue sun
firstly she keeps
a few sentences, words one after the other and while walking she
adds others to them, words, sentences
all one after the other
it's in her heart
that she warms up in the April blue sun

and they note note note down by hand or on their
keyboards
otherwise they forget them all one after the other
or else forget
in their brimming hearts
in their hearts a clutter
and you too, Else, like them
and to order your days you write lists
this and that in lists

then you join her on the bench, sitting
it's so as to join her on the bench, sitting
on the little schist bench in front of the house
which is a maisonette with holes in the roof
it's in her heart
quietly

and gradually the years, sentences words do all that
a hundred and fifty long long songs *gwerzio*
in her heart by heart, their melodies too
and without hesitation standing she, singing
a series around her many people

you watch her sing in your heart, you say her name and it's
Ma'aï
you join her in your heart that comes and goes, that comes and goes
you see that they pass by at 14kph in their vehicles
you look away
you watch her in your heart, you say her name and she's called
Ma'aï

an April blue for everyone listening to her

'vit tout re a selaou un ebrel glas
un ebrel glas 'prof Ma'aï
profañ 'ra Ma'aï
ya profet 'vez se ganti

Ma'aï offers
yes she offers this
an April blue for everyone listening to her

Translated by Ian Monk

MA'AÏ

dans son cœur
au soleil bleu avril
d'abord elle garde
quelques phrases, des mots bout à bout et en marchant elle
en rajoute d'autres, des mots, des phrases
tout bout à bout
c'est dans son cœur
qu'elle réchauffe au soleil bleu avril

et eux ils notent notent notent écrivent à la main ou avec des
claviers
sinon ils oublient tout mis bout à bout
oublient sinon
dans leurs cœurs tout pleins

dans leurs cœurs un encombrement
et toi aussi, Else, comme eux
et pour ordonner tes journées t'écris des listes
ceci cela des listes

puis tu rejoins celle qui se tient sur le banc, assise
c'est pour rejoindre celle qui se tient sur le banc, assise
sur le petit banc de schiste devant sa maison
qui est maisonnette et toit troué
c'est dans son cœur
tranquillement
et peu à peu les années, des phrases des mots ça fait tout ça
cent cinquante longues longues chansons *gwerzio*
dans son cœur par cœur, leurs mélodies aussi
et sans hésiter debout elle, chante
une assemblée autour d'elle beaucoup de monde

tu la regardes chanter dans ton cœur, tu dis son nom et c'est
Ma'aï
tu la rejoins dans ton cœur qui va et vient, qui va et vient
tu vois qu'ils passent à 140 leurs véhicules à eux
tu détournes la tête
tu la regardes dans ton cœur, tu dis son nom et elle s'appelle
Ma'aï

un bleu avril pour tous ceux qui l'écoutent

'vit tout re a selaou un ebrel glas
un ebrel glas 'prof Ma'aï
profañ 'ra Ma'aï
ya profet 'vez se ganti

Ma'aï offre
oui elle offre ça
un bleu avril pour tous ceux qui l'écoutent

AN AMZER O TONT / THE COMING WEATHER

tonight it's so close
it isn't the russet horse that hauls the caravan, which knows
you are there
which, from afar, can hear you, you can see its ears, between the branches
ha ne ra nemet glav
and it does but rain

may he who is looking at tomorrow's weather in the sky turn
around, return
ruz da noz glav pe avel antronoz, red at night rain or wind
the next day
but he who is looking at tomorrow's weather in the sky is
further off, not with the russet horse either

may he who places in the hearth the very large log which should not
be entirely consumed turn around, return
he who holds the poker
for he warms up the souls of the dead who come back from time
to time
who come to the places where they lived
kef Nedeleg pe skod Nedeleg, the Yule log, yes,
not like a Swiss roll of a log, no, not at all
a wooden log
the cold poker, wrapped up in paper, in a cloth
the poker in the cupboard, between piles of sheets, all year

still standing the russet horse which listens to you, beyond the mound
may he who approaches be able to say as well
ar marc'h glas 'zo deuet maes, the blue horse is out
still looking at the sky
the sky which is clearing, after the rain

you no longer know, Else
if you observed the tomorrow of he who watches the weather
returning souls, such sunny periods
this day you see the threads the flows of light
as well as the fast trains honking long before they arrive
near the men on the track
in the earth of the graveyard, the mixing dusts
and with them, yours too

but before
when the night falls, into the full moon you look
not at the man with the charriot
you look at the man in front of his red caravan outside inside
his bandoneon

Translated by Ian Monk

AN AMZER O TONT / LE TEMPS VENANT

cette nuit c'est tout près
ce n'est pas le cheval roux qui tracte la caravane, lui qui sait
que tu es là
qui, de plus loin, t'entends, tu vois ses oreilles, entre les branches
ha ne ra nemet glav
et il ne fait que pluie

que celui qui regarde le temps du lendemain dans le ciel se
retourne, s'en retourne
ruz da noz glav pe avel antronoz, rouge à la nuit pluie ou vent
le lendemain
mais celui qui regarde le temps du lendemain dans le ciel est
plus loin,
pas avec le cheval roux non plus

que celui qui pose dans l'âtre la bûche très grosse qui ne doit
pas entièrement se consumer se retourne, s'en retourne
celui qui garde le tison
car il réchauffe les âmes des défunts qui reviennent de temps
en temps
qui reviennent sur les lieux de leur vie
kef Nedeleg pe skod Nedeleg, la bûche de Noël, oui,
pas un dessert, non, du tout
de bois la bûche
le tison froid, emballé dans du papier, dans du linge
le tison dans l'armoire, entre les piles de draps, toute une année

debout encore le cheval roux qui t'entends, au delà du talus
que celui qui s'approche peut dire aussi
ar marc'h glas 'zo deuet maes, le cheval bleu est de sortie
en regardant le ciel encore
le ciel qui s'éclaircit, après la pluie

tu ne sais plus, Else
si tu as observé le lendemain de celui qui regarde le temps
le retour des âmes, de telles éclaircies
ce jour tu vois les fils les flots de lumière
aussi les trains rapides qui klaxonnent bien avant d'arriver
à proximité des hommes sur la voie
dans la terre du cimetière, les poussières qui se mêlent
et avec elles, la tienne aussi

mais avant
à la nuit venue, dans la lune pleine tu regardes
pas l'homme à la charrette
tu regardes l'homme devant sa caravane rouge dehors dedans
son bandonéon

JOHAN SANDBERG McGUINNE (Sweden)

Johan Sandberg McGuinne (1987) grew up speaking Swedish, English, South Saami and Scottish Gaelic, and writes in all his languages. He has translated a number of Gaelic and Saami poets into English and Swedish and his verse novel And I Never Truly Knew Whom I Was Talking To *won the Swedish Saami Youth Organisation's Young Writers' Award.*

'THAT SUMMER YOU SHOWED ME...'

That summer you showed me
how you spun sinew into swans, aided by your songs,
how you, effortlessly, snared each spoken syllable
        of   ours
as we once again
made up lies about translations,
you wrote
a book with blood drawn from your heart
on the backbone of our people

Translated from the South Saami by the poet

GIESEGE GUJHTH VUESIEHTIH

giesege gujhth vuesiehtih
guktie njoktjh vueline sneerhkedh
guktie gïeleb gealojne gïelh
gosse jorkestimmiej bïjre
vihth slognestimh,
die gärjab vïrrine
saepmien lïhtsegisnie
tjeelih

'O SEA, REST BESIDE ME...'

O sea, rest beside me
on the borderland of oceans
and teach me another song
Music came to me through you;
each verse, each chorus from your lips
like flocks of birds in flight under the stars,
the murmur of your waves
washing over my head.

Translated from the Scottish Gaelic by the poet

'A MHUIR, SUIDH SÌOS RI M' THAOBH...'

A mhuir, suidh sìos ri m' thaobh
air iomall an stuadh,
is leig dhomh òran eile.
Bha e tromhad an dàinig ceòl thugam;
gach rann 's gach sèisd bho d' bhilean
mar ealt eun nar itealaich fo na reultan,
do ghàir-thuinn binn
nar barcadh mu m' cheann

PAATA SHAMUGIA (GEORGIA)

Paata Shamugia (1983) published his debut collection Panther's Skin *in 2006. His second collection,* Preference (2010) *met with wide acclaim and in 2012 his collection* Acatiste *was published and named book of the year, receiving the prestigious SABA literary prize. In 2015 he again won the SABA literary prize for his book* Schizo National Anthms, *also named book of the year. Since 2018, Paata Shamugia has been president of the Georgian PEN Centre.*

ORDERS

Let there be houses for the homeless,
millions for the broke,
inspiration for the poets,
a skeleton for the tongue,
sheep for the sleepless – one sheep, two sheep, three sheep...

let there be strength for those in love
to spread themselves in each other,
let there be toys for the kids,
for the dictators too,
let there be freedom for the imagination
and food for the hungry,
let there be trees for the winds
to get some rest in the branches,
let there be nothing at all for the politicians.

Translated by Kristian Carlsson and Manana Matiashvili

ბრძანება

დაე, მიეცეთ უსახლკაროებს სახლები,
უფულოებს – მილიონები,
პოეტებს – შთაგონება,
ენას – ძვალი,
უდიდლოებს – ერთი ცხვარი, ორი ცხვარი, სამი ცხვარი...
შეყვარებულებს მიეცეთ ძალა,
გაიფანტონ ერთმანეთში.
ბავშვებს მიეცეთ სათამაშოები, დიქტატორებსაც.
ფანტაზიას მიეცეს გასაქანი, მშივრებს – საკვები,
ქარებს მიეცეთ ხეები, რომ ტოტებზე ჩამოისვენონ პოლიტიკოსებს
არ მიეცეთ არაფერი.

A BUSY POET

No visa is required from my language,
I obtain business contracts from verbs and nouns,
I use intermissions for interjections,
I'm a busy poet.
I lead diplomatic negotiations with binary oppositions,
I stand after a prefix – like a gentleman,
but I turn a blind eye to the past – impudent!
I check my base – I have to stand strong,
I'm a busy poet.
I practise all forms of interrelations – I'm in shape.
I rebuild the crumbed infrastructure of my body – I run.
For leisure I invest my hormones in the first girl I meet – oops!
Nothing personal, just poetry,
I'm a busy poet.

I set everyone free
from a life in the prison of ready-made answers.
It's time to be sentenced to peace!
It's time to be sentenced to love!
We deserve even worse!
Zero tolerance for petty obsessions!
I'm a busy poet.
I try to eliminate the separatism –
the separation of language (*aka* the State)
and human beings (*aka* human beings).
The one who speaks is always lying.
The one who writes is always
exposed by the lies he writes.
52
My lies are ordinary,
my poems extraordinary.
I'm a busy poet.

Translated by Kristian Carlsson and Manana Matiashvili

საქმიანი პოეტი

მიმოვდივარ ენაში (უვიზოდ),
ვდებ საქმიან კონტრაქტს ზმნებთან და არსებით სახელებთან,
შორისდებულებს შორის ვდებ ზავს.
მე საქმიანი პოეტი ვარ.
ვაწარმოებ დიპლომატიურ მოლაპარაკებებს ბინარულ
                                       ოპოზიციებთან,
ზმნისწინის უკან ვდგები – თავაზიანი ვარ,
მაგრამ წარსულ დროს ზურგს ვაქცევ – თავხედი!
ფუძეს ვუსინჯავ საკუთარ თავს –
მყარად უნდა ვიდგე.
მე საქმიანი პოეტი ვარ.
ვხვეწ ურთიერთობის ფორმებს – ფორმაში ვარ.
ვაწესრიგებ ჩემი სხეულის ჩამოქცეულ ინფრასტრუქტურას –
დავრბივარ. განტვირთვის მიზნით, პირველსავე შემხვედრ გოგოში
ვდებ ჰორმონების ინვესტიციას – ოჰო!
არაფერი პირადდული, მხოლოდ ლექსი.
მე საქმიანი პოეტი ვარ.
ის, ვინც წლობით ცხოვრობდა მზა პასუხების ციხეში,
ყველა ამნისტიით გამოვუშვი.
დროა, ყველას მოგვესაჯოს მშვიდობა!
დროა, ყველას მოგვესაჯოს სიყვარული!
ახია ჩვენზე!
ნულოვანი ტოლერანტობა წვრილმან გატაცებებს!

მე საქმიანი პოეტი ვარ.
ვცდილობ აღმოვფხვრა სეპარატიზმი –
გაუცხოება ენას (ანუ სახელმწიფოს)
და ადამიანს (ანუ ადამიანს) შორის.
ის, ვინც ლაპარაკობს, ყოველთვის ტყუის.
ვინც წერს, მას კი მუდამ ამჯდავგნებს
ის, რასაც წერისას ტყუის.
ჩემი ტყუილი საშუალოა,
ჩემი ლექსები – უშუალო.

A TELEVISION COMMERCIAL

Yearning for home.
Yearning for tea.
Yearning for coffee.
Yearning for sex.
Yearning for sex in Cleopatra's bathroom.
Yearning for a television commercial.
Yearning for the second volume of psychoanalysis by Sigmund Freud,
and the third volume of psychoanalysis by Sigmund Freud,
and the fourth volume of psychoanalysis by Sigmund Freud.
I need evolution.
I need psychological mutation.
I need for me to be Walt Whitman
and for you to be terrorists.
Need Dada.
Need Daddy.
Need the EU and the EU standards in repair works.
Yearning for fizzlings,
for fine fieldfares,
for Fred and the fortress,
for *It's Far to Gurjistan*
for a furious man with black fur hat.
I need black asphalt.
I need Linda.
I need pandas.
Yearning for inclusive angels
and exclusive BBC programmes.
Need to have 100 million in my private bank account
and an appointed private meeting with Miss USA.

I need coffee.
I need coffee,
a cup of coffee on wasteland islands.
Yearning for asymmetrical gods
and symmetrical friendship.
I need to know the formula for economic collapses
and for human happiness too.
I need cheap vodka
and a yacht in the Pacific.
I need The Goncourt Prize and after that
I need The Booker Prize and after that
I need The Nobel Prize as well.
I need prizes to buy a house,
to buy dolls for my wife,
to buy myself a tranquil death,
to buy a small piece of land in Paradise
where I could oversleep.

Translated by Kristian Carlsson and Manana Matiashvili

სარეკლამო პაუზა

მინდა სახლი
მინდა ჩაი
მინდა ყავა
მინდა ფული
მინდა სექსი მინდა სექსი კლეოპატრას აბაზანაში
მინდა სარეკლამო პაუზა
მინდა ფროიდის ფსიქოანალიზის მეორე ტომი
და ფროიდის ფსიქოანალიზის მესამე ტომი
და ფროიდის ფსიქოანალიზის მეოთხე ტომი
მინდა ევოლუცია
მინდა ფსიქიკური მუტაცია
მინდა მე უოტ უიტმენი ვიყო და თქვენ იყოთ
ტერორისტები
მინდა დადა მინდა დედა
მინდა ევროკავშირი და ევრორემონტი
მინდა შიშინი
 შავი შაშვი შიო შორაპანი
შორია გურჯისტანამდე შავსა კაცსა შავქუდოსანსა
მინდა ასფალტი
მინდა ლინდა მინდა პანდა
მინდა ინკლუზიური ანგელოზები
და ექსკლუზიური გადაცემები `ბი-ბი-სი-"ზე
მინდა პირად ანგარიშზე მილიონი მეხადეს

და კალთაში "მის ამერიკა" მეჯდეს
მინდა ყავა მინდა ყავა მინდა ყავა და უკაცრიელი კუნძულები
მინდა ასიმეტრიული დმერთები და სიმეტრიული მეგობრები
მინდა ეკონომიკური კოლაფსის ფორმულა
და ადამიანური ბედნიერების ფორმულა
მინდა იაფფასიანი არაყი
და იახტა დარდანელის სრუტეში
და იახტა წყნარ ოკეანეში
მინდა გონკურების პრემია
მერე ბუკერის პრემია
მერე ნობელის პრემია
რომ ვიყიდო სახლი
რომ ვიყიდო თოჯინები ჩემი ცოლისთვის
რომ ვიყიდო მშვიდი სიკვდილი
რომ ვიყიდო სამოთხეში პატარა ფართი
სადაც კარგად გამოვიძინებ.

DANAE SIOZIOU (Greece)

Danae Sioziou (1987) is a multilingual poet, cultural manager and educator. Recipient of the National Prize for Young Writers and the Hellenic Writer's Association Jiannis Varveris' Prize for Young Writers, her first poetry collection was Useful Children's Games. *Her poems have been translated into thirteen languages and published in national and international journals. She has participated in many literary festivals as a poet and performer. She has translated German, post-colonial, aboriginal and African-American poetry. Her new collection,* Possible Landscapes, *appeared in 2020.*

AROUND THE HOUSE

She wasn't paying attention
maybe she didn't even notice
she simply continued cutting
beyond the pears she was peeling
her hands

Blood ran gently
from the lines of fate
of life of love
and into the sink
and swirled around among the dirty dishes
and the scraps of food

Her cat, uneasy,
ran up to her
and with sincere fellow feeling
licked her wounds
while she

for a split second
saw herself
through its glassy cat eyes
a stranger

imprisoned in a filthy cage
a ceiling without sunrise
little beetles on the floor
in the sink a dark lake
she soaked her hands in
and now it shines, crowned with
the white frost of detergent

From the depths of the sink
rise full moons brilliant white
she thought
let me at least
finish the dishes today

Translated by Rachel Hadas

OIKIAKA

Δεν πρόσεξε
ίσως και να μην το κατάλαβε
απλά συνέχισε να κόβει.
Το αίμα κύλησε ήσυχα
απ' τις γραμμές της τύχης
στο νεροχύτη.
Η γάτα της ανήσυχη
έτρεξε κοντά της
ενώ εκείνη
για μία σύντομη
μια ακαριαία στιγμή
είδε τον εαυτό της

μέσα απ' τα γυάλινα γατίσια μάτια,
ξένο,
μες σε βρώμικο κλουβί φυλακισμένο.
Οροφή δίχως ανατολή
στο πάτωμα μικρά σκαθάρια
στο νεροχύτη η σκοτεινή λίμνη
που μέσα μουλιάζουνε τα χέρια της
και τώρα αστράφτει πια στεφανωμένη
από πάχνη λευκή, απολυμαντική:
σκέφτεται να τελειώνει σήμερα
τουλάχιστον με τα πιάτα.

THE SPIDER

Dear Sir,

I watch you from the ceiling,
your coffee requests more sugar.
Something about the clothes and the shoes is off,
you shouldn't have patched up all the holes.
Grab the day like a knife,
the weight of your life keeps growing,
the agreement with the mirror has been cancelled
and you are turning fat.
Tomorrow I will hang before your nose,
perhaps you could please feed me?

Sincerely,
The Spider

Dear Spider,

just yesterday the bat gave birth in a corner of the attic, her tasty
eggs float in the air.
I haven't learned to drive, to debone fish, to read newspapers.
I have two useless dog teeth and a BB gun.
I have made a deal with the morning coffee,
I respect the decision of the mirror.

I no longer set traps for birds,
each day I head to the river and shoot the waters.

Yours,
C.

Translated by Panagiotis Kechagias and Mania Meziti

Η ΑΡΑΧΝΗ

Αγαπητέ Κύριε,

σας παρακολουθώ από το ταβάνι
ο καφές ζητάει ολοένα περισσότερη ζάχαρη
κάτι με τα ρούχα και τα παπούτσια πάει λάθος
δεν έπρεπε να μπαλώσετε τις τρύπες
αρπάξτε τη μέρα σαν μαχαίρι
το βάρος τη ζωής σας αυξάνεται
η συμφωνία με τον καθρέφτη ακυρώθηκε
κι εσείς παχαίνετε
αύριο θα κρεμαστώ μπροστά στη μύτη σας
θα μπορούσατε ίσως να με ταίσετε;

Φιλικά,
η Αράχνη

Αγαπητή Αράχνη,

μόλις εχθές η νυχτερίδα γέννησε σε μία γωνιά της σοφίτας,
τα λαχταριστά αυγά της αιωρούνται σχεδόν στον αέρα.
Δεν έμαθα να οδηγώ, να ξεκοκαλίζω ψάρια, εφημερίδες.
Έχω δύο άχρηστους κυνόδοντες κι ένα φλόμπερ.
Έχω κάνει συμφωνία με τον πρωινό καφέ, σέβομαι την
    απόφαση του καθρέφτη.
Δεν στήνω πια παγίδες για πουλιά, όρθιος στην όχθη
    πυροβολώ το ποτάμι.

Δικός σας,
Κ.

SUNDOWN

Alexandra newly married, her husband's joy
and pride (my bird, my little bird)
she went up on the roof
to get yesterday's laundry.
But maybe the clothes billowing on the line
the doves' choreographed flight
the sun that forced eyes to blink
as it tumbled on the slit of successive
mountain ridges
redeeming the day
it was somehow like this that Alexandra became
like sun like bird
her white cardigan a sail.

Translated by Panagiotis Kechagias

ΗΛΙΟΒΑΣΙΛΕΜΑ

Νιόπαντρη η Αλεξάνδρα, του αντρός της η χαρά
και το καμάρι (πουλί, πουλάκι μου)
ανέβηκε στην ταράτσα
για τη χτεσινή μπουγάδα.
Μα θες τα απλωμένα ρούχα που φουσκώναν
οι χορογραφίες των περιστεριών
ο ήλιος που ανοιγόκλεινε τα μάτια
καθώς κυλούσε στη σχισμή των αλλεπάλληλων
κορυφογραμμών
εξαργυρώνοντας τη μέρα
κάπως έτσι έγινε κι η Αλεξάνδρα
σαν ήλιος σαν πουλί
με την άσπρη ζακέτα της πανί.

BROKEN INTO

As I unlock my front door
I keep thinking that poetry is a privilege
like the expensive toys of childhood
or listening to your favourite song
100 times in ideal acoustic conditions
like french kissing the love of your life
like millions of shiny ponies
like life on other planets
like honey dissolving in tea
like herds of thunders from a distance
and I enjoy writing poems
the way I enjoy lying on the grass
caressing dogs
eating apricots and cream
and if people don't particularly enjoy
listening to poetry
I like this sound of the way

words are arranged into order
like the way someone breaks into a home
I enjoy writing poems
the way cats enjoy licking themselves in the sun
and I want to get good at this
I want to get good at this.

Tramslated by the poet

ΔΙΑΡΡΗΞΗ

Καθώς ανοίγω την πόρτα του σπιτιού μου,
σκέφτομαι ότι η ποίηση είναι ένα προνόμιο
όπως τα πολύ ακριβά παιχνίδια της παιδικής ηλικίας
ή η εκατοστή ακρόαση του αγαπημένου σου τραγουδιού
σε ιδανικές ακουστικές συνθήκες
σαν φιλί με γλώσσα με τον έρωτα της ζωής σου
σαν εκατομμύρια λαμπερά πόνυ
σαν τη ζωή σε άλλους πλανήτες
σαν το μέλι που διαλύεται εντελώς μέσα στο τσάι
σαν κοπάδια κεραυνών από απόσταση
κι εμένα μου αρέσει να γράφω ποιήματα
όπως μου αρέσει να ξαπλώνω στο γρασίδι

να τρώω κρέμα με βερίκοκα, να χαϊδεύω σκύλους
κι αν στους ανθρώπους δεν αρέσει να ακούνε ποιήματα
εμένα μου αρέσει αυτός ο ήχος
ο τρόπος να βάζεις τις λέξεις στη σειρά
ο τρόπος ν' ανοίγεις την πόρτα κρατώντας κλειδιά
για ένα απαραβίαστο σπίτι
μου αρέσει να γράφω ποιήματα
όπως στα γατιά αρέσει να γλείφονται στον ήλιο
και θέλω να γίνω καλή στη δουλειά
θέλω να γίνω καλή στη δουλειά.

MICHAŁ SOBOL (Poland)

Michał Sobol (1970) debuted with the collection Lamentacje /
Lamentations *for which he received the Kazimiera Iłłakowiczówna Award
for best first book in 2001. This was followed by* Działania i chwile /
Actions and Moments *(2007) and* Naturalia / Naturals *(2010). In 2013,*
Pulsary / Pulsars *received the Literary Award of the Town of Radom and,
in 2014, was nominated for the Wisława Szymborska Poetry Award. In
2016 he received the Zbigniew Herbert Foundation Award and in 2017, the
Gdynia Literary Award.*

BANKS

Let's not pretend that anyone can simply get up and ask:
What's this? And answer: The world. The monetary system

would not have appeared if not for the comforting thought that banks
exist. It isn't out of the question that only concern about money

now stops us from sailing away when this burning question
is debated. One way or another, we feel safer ever since

the famous gold was placed in bunkers carved in
the Swiss Alps. The bank's customer need not ask about it.

Translated by Antonia Lloyd-Jones

BANKI

Nie udawajmy, że da się ot tak po prostu zapytać:
Co to jest? I odpowiedzieć: Świat. System monetarny

nie powstałby, gdyby nie pocieszająca myśl, że istnieją
banki. Niewykluczone, że już tylko troska o pieniądz

nie pozwala nam odpłynąć przy roztrząsaniu tej palącej
kwestii. Tak czy owak, czujemy się bezpieczniej, odkąd

w wykutych w szwajcarskich Alpach bunkrach złożono
to słynne złoto. Klient banku nie musi o nie pytać.

LABORATORIES

Laboratories exist to enable us to talk about ourselves again. While enzyme
chases enzyme in a warmed-up flask and we patiently await the outcome

of a reaction that will change us, we can give several examples of
marital infidelities that ended in the ritual of silence and take on board

the tale, tiresome in other circumstances, of an undesirable pregnancy
and some missing eyes. Not just Oedipus learned the truth, but today we

can only put it in words in passing, while shaking the retort,
predicting the results of many years' research, propped on columns of figures.

Translated by Antonia Lloyd-Jones

LABORATORIA

Laboratoria są po to, byśmy znów mogli o sobie mówić. Gdy enzym
goni enzym w podgrzewanej kolbie i cierpliwie czekamy na wynik

reakcji, która nas odmieni, można podać kilka przykładów
małżeńskich zdrad zakończonych ceremonią ciszy i przyswoić

nużącą w innych okolicznościach opowieść o niechcianej ciąży
i braku oczu. Nie tylko Edyp poznał prawdę, lecz wypowiedzieć

ją dzisiaj możemy jedynie mimochodem, potrząsając retortą,
przewidując rezultaty wieloletnich badań, w oparciu o słupki cyfr.

LIBRARIES

By now we know there's nothing to fear. But when sleep
assumes the watch, admitting to us only the things we really do

desire, suddenly we start up the feverish exploration of
library buildings, in which words stripped of images

will be able to hide. Ignored in the daytime, changed into rooms
for playing the virtual flute and PlayStation, they don't deserve the
attention

of scurrying tourists awarding prizes to ogee arch and architrave
rather than reinforced concrete beams. At night they regain their missing
title.

Translated by Antonia Lloyd-Jones

BIBLIOTEKI

Już wiemy, że nie ma czego się bać. Lecz gdy sen
przejmuje wartę, dopuszczając do nas jedynie to, czego naprawdę

pragniemy, nagle rozpoczynają się gorączkowe poszukiwania
bibliotecznych gmachów, w których ogołocone z obrazów słowa

będą mogły się skryć. Lekceważone w dzień, zmieniane w sale
do gry na wirtualnym flecie i PlayStation, nie zasługują na uwagę

zabieganych turystów premiujących raczej ośli grzbiet i architraw
niż żelbetonowe belki. Nocą odzyskują utracony tytuł.

LABOUR EXCHANGES

No, for we'd have been like a dream, like thoughts that don't put pressure
on the body. No, for the advantage would go to the bookkeeper, the
caretaker,

the warehouseman and the inspector, and nobody wants any peeping
under his worker's tunic before he's even started. No, for we'd have to

lay our hammers, pliers and multi-purpose spanners on the threshold
like weapons after a lost battle, but nothing testifies more forcibly

to the fact that it's lost than the laying down of arms. No, for such
retraining for another job will destroy us, even if we're going to be rich.

Translated by Antonia Lloyd-Jones

URZĘDY PRACY

Nie, bo bylibyśmy jak sen, jak myśli, które nie napierają
na ciało. Nie, bo przewagę zyskałby księgowy, cieć,

magazynier i lustrator, a nikt nie chce, by mu zaglądano
pod roboczy fartuch, jeszcze nim zaczął. Nie, bo musielibyśmy

nasze młoty, obcęgi, klucze wielofunkcyjne złożyć na progu
jak broń po przegranej bitwie, a o tym, że jest przegrana,

nic nie świadczy dobitniej niż składanie broni. Nie, bo takie
przekwalifikowanie zniszczy nas, nawet jeśli będziemy bogaci.

CEMETERIES

Whenever we need urgent confirmation that it is in fact possible
to die, we visit cemeteries. These rare moments of stopping –

we only remove the yellowed wreath adorned with a Christmas
bauble in the spring, when catkins are in bloom – from year to year

last for several minutes longer. Digital music even comes in
here from cars parked behind the wall, and anger

prompted by the tasteless joke that the mind will live on, only
the body won't, softens the sight of grave pits, but not always any more.

Translated by Antonia Lloyd-Jones

CMENTARZE

Gdy na gwałt potrzebujemy potwierdzenia, że jednak możliwe jest
umrzeć, odwiedzamy cmentarze. Te rzadkie chwile postoju –

pożółkły wieniec udekorowany bożonarodzeniową bombką
usuwamy dopiero wiosną, gdy kwitną bazie – z roku na rok

trwają kilka minut dłużej. Cyfrowa muzyka dobiega
nawet tu z zaparkowanych za murem samochodów i gniew

wywołany tym niesmacznym kawałem, że umysł przetrwa, tylko
ciało nie, łagodzi widok ziemnych grobów, ale już nie zawsze.

TZVETA SOFRONIEVA (Bulgaria / Germany)

*Tzveta Sofronieva (1963) is a multilingual poet, born in Sofia, now at home
in Berlin. Among her poetry collections are* Landscapes, Shores *(2013),*
Anthroposcene *(2017) and* Multiverse *(2020). Her poetry has been translated
into French, English, Hungarian, Finnish, Dutch, Japanese, Serbian, Russian,
Polish and Spanish. Sofronieva was recipient of the Adelbert-von-Chamisso
Förderpreis (2009) and a Max-Kade-Writer-in-Residence at MIT (2012). Her
book* A Hand full of Water *was translated by C. Wright with a PEN American
Translation Fund Award (2009).*

RIEN NE VA PLUS

a glass of water nurses flowers
chairs stare at us, and far off
a table could accommodate food
or traces of poems
but there is nothing, only emptiness
measuring the temperature
between inside and out
setting the snapdragons on the roses
air streams in inflating the lampshade
anxiety-free fraying sense of home
dreamweed the smile of an absent angel
it is too empty to feel comfortable
gingerly the mountain loses its grip
and silence shakes the sky

Translated by the poet

RIEN NE VA PLUS

ein Glas Wasser hütet Blumen
Stühle starren auf uns, und in die Ferne
der Tisch könnte Essen beherbergen
oder Gedichtabdrucke
doch nichts, gar nichts
die Leere ist der Beobachter selbst
misst die Temperaturen zwischen Innen und Außen
hetzt die Löwenmäulchen auf die Rosen
Luft strömt ein, bläst den Lampenschirm auf
angstfreie Fransen Heimatgefühl
Traumkraut das Lächeln eines abwesenden Engels
zu viel Leere um sich geborgen zu fühlen
behutsam verliert das Gebirge Halt
von dieser Stille erbebt der Himmel

CLONING

Snow rushes towards me
asking questions.
Its whiteness is still. The snow's
breath is like a liquid nitrogen
found in the laboratory of the self.
Frost waits for someone. Burns
the skin and the eyes.
Time snows disrupted:
Quantum-question – quantum-silence,
quantum-question – two quanta silence,
splitter of Is. And nitrogen turns to love
in the crystal-melting hair.
Quantum is a unit of light
as a snowflake is a unit of snow.
The road spends its breath
on my efforts to clear the snow-drifts.
The nitrogen has already vanished. And
what about me? Me and the snow...
The light is fixed.

Translated by the poet

ICH

Der Schnee läuft mir entgegen, stellt Fragen.
Das Weiß schweigt. Der Atem des Schnees
ist flüssiger Ich-Stoff in irgendeinem Labor.
Die Kälte wartet auf jemanden: Stich-Stoff
durchdringt Haut und Augen. Die Zeit schneit
in Splittern: Quant-Frage – Quant-Schweigen,
Quant-Frage – zwei Quanten-Schweigen.
Der Stick-Stoff verwandelt sich in Liebe
in den Kristall gewordenen, tauenden Haaren.
Ein Quant ist eine Einheit Licht wie
eine Schneeflocke eine Einheit Schnee ist.
Vergeblich verführt mich der Weg,
ihn von den Schneewehen zu befreien.
Der Erstick-Stoff ist bereits verdunstet.
Ich, ich... oder ich und der Schnee?
Das Licht ist unbeweglich.

SUN

Who draws eyes and eyebrows
who makes no incisions,
gentle, luminous, who burns,
who can't burn out.
Who swings like a bird,
who flies away from the face
of the traveller.
He's going east.
Tender fire,
I caress you,
I am still alive.
No trace of ash or thirst.
You are a child's drawing
sun

Translated by Chantal Wright

SONNE

Zeichnest Augen und Augenbrauen,
stichst nichts aus,
sanft, leuchtend, brennst,
kannst nicht ausbrennen.
Schwingst wie ein Vogel,
fliegst vom Gesicht
des Fahrenden ab.
Nach Osten fährt er.
Zartes Feuer,
ich liebkose dich,
noch lebe ich.
Keine Spur Asche oder Durst.
Eine Kinderzeichnung bist du
Sonne

UN-LOST IN TRANSLATION

The window at the front and right of my compartment
reflects the scene on the left at my rear.
I can see what is passing superimposed on
what is coming, and it is as though the light
likes this game, irrespective of where the sun is,
or where the train is heading.

Translated by Chantal Wright

UN-LOST IN TRANSLATION

Im Fenster vorn rechts in meinem Abteil
spiegelt sich das linke hintere Bild.
Ich sehe im Kommenden das Entrinnende
völlig überlagert, und es ist als ob das Licht
dieses Spiel mag, unabhängig davon, wo
die Sonne steht, und wohin der Zug reist.

HABITS

I can't love myself
that's why I love people like me

was something I heard from a girl with orange hair
on an evanescent evening

Her name was Clara, she was
a clear being, like crystal –
I think that's still her name,
she paints with lots of colour and water,
adores professors

Outstretched trees knock at my window
I will have to consider whether I love myself

whether I can forgive myself the nervousness, the twilight realizations,
the abortive attempts to catch my heartbeat

I am seduced by the charm of chaotic friendships
and attracted by ancient gestures

In the rhythm of a new game
I erase words and write lines
I wr I te l I nes I wr I

Translated by Chantal Wright

GEWOHNHEITEN

Ich kann mich nicht lieben,
deswegen liebe ich mir ähnelnde Menschen,

hörte ich von einem Mädchen mit orangenen Haaren
an einem verblassenden Abend.

Sie hieß Klara und war
ein wie Kristall klares Wesen,
ich glaube, sie heißt noch immer so,
malt mit viel Farbe und Wasser,
liebt Professoren.

An meinem Fenster klopfen sich ausbreitende Bäume,
ich muss nachdenken, ob ich mich selbst liebe,

verzeihe ich mir die Änsgte, die Dämmerungen,
die vergeblichen Versuche, meinen Herzschlag einzufangen?

Ich lasse mich auf den Charme chaotischer Freundschaften ein,
werde von uralten Gesten angezogen,

im Rythmus eines neuen Spiels
radiere ich Worte und schreibe Gedichte
diiiiicht iiiiiichtdi

THOMAS TSALAPATIS (Greece)

Thomas Tsalapatis (1984) received the National Prize for the best emerging author in 2012 for his first collection Daybreak is Slaughter, Mr. Krak. *His second collection,* Alba, *was published in 2015 and* Geographies of the Fritzs and the Langs *was published in 2018. In 2018 he won the 'Premio InediTO-Colline di Torino' for his poetry. His poems have appeared in a number of anthologies and have been translated into English, French, Spanish, Italian and Arabic.*

CITY OF LONELINESS

This neighbourhood is inhabited primarily by Nietzsches. Fatigued by their infinite return, lingering afar from good and evil, strolling romantic promenades, looking listlessly at idols and twilight, drawing moustaches on posters of Wagner, conversing aloud about the little hunchback, the eagle and the snake.
They kiss horses on the lips, they kiss time on the cheeks, they generally do what Nietzsches do. And dawn smiles with all its broken teeth.
One day, three Nietzsches were found murdered. Their bodies covered in knife wounds, their age untouched and all their apples eaten. Even when authorities allured to a revenge killing, we knew, with sufficient certainty, that this incident was far more important than a mere mention on the news.

Translated by Elena Anna Mastromauro

ΠΟΛΙΤΕΙΑ ΤΗΣ ΜΟΝΑΞΙΑΣ.

Στη γειτονιά αυτή κατοικούνε αποκλειστικά Νίτσε. Εξαντλημένοι από την αιώνια επιστροφή τους, μετεωρίζονται πέρα από το καλό και το κακό, περιπατούν ρομαντικούς περιπάτους χαζεύοντας είδωλα και λυκόφως, ζωγραφίζοντας μουστάκια στις αφίσες του Βάγκνερ, συζητώντας μεγαλόφωνα για τον καμπουράκο, τον αετό και το φίδι. Φιλάνε τα άλογα στο στόμα, φιλάνε τον χρόνο στα μάγουλα, κάνουνε γενικά όσα οι Νίτσε κάνουν. Και το ξημέρωμα χαμογελά με όλα τα σπασμένα του δόντια.
Μια μέρα 3 Νίτσε βρέθηκαν δολοφονημένοι κάτω από μια μηλιά. Τα σώματά τους μαχαιρωμένα, η ηλικία ανέπαφη και όλα τα μήλα της χτυπημένα. Ακόμα και όταν οι αρχές κάνανε λόγο για ένα ακόμη ξεκαθάρισμα λογαριασμών, εμείς γνωρίζαμε με αρκετή βεβαιότητα πως το περιστατικό ήταν σαφώς σημαντικότερο από μια απλή καταχώρηση στα δελτία.

(SUBLINGUAL)

This morning I woke up. 20 words poorer. When it all began, I only lost five a day. But inside me the silence accelerates. With every sentence, an unpleasant surprise. And I, for a while now, talk less and less.
I realized it once when I tried to complain. The mouth. A void with teeth. And the voice would not come out. In the end I said thank you and returned home. I felt the words slipping through the teeth. I sought help. Visited a functional linguist-orthodontist. He examined me. My condition is irreversible, he said. I suffer from pause. Worst still, from silence.
The objects around me decrease.
I am getting used to it. I can talk, avoiding certain words. I will not say _ _ _ _ _ _ _.
This word I've lost. I do not know, cannot recall, just feel the void it left behind. I cannot say _ _ _. I have to rephrase my sentence. Instead I will say "It's pretty, what you're wearing on your head". The objects around me _ _ _ _ _ _ _ _.
In a moment of despair, I thought I could latch one word onto the other and save _ _ _ _.
Soitriedtolatchonewordontotheother.

Theonlythingiaccomplishedwastolosethemallatonce.
Lately the _ _ _ _ _ _ _ _ _ _ has become even more dire. Recently
_ _ _ articles disappeared as well. Few at present, but this all
points to me entering _ _ _ end stage.
_ _ _ objects around me _ _ _ _ _ _ _ _.
All within _ _ in pieces. _ _ _ _ _ _ _ _ _ _ getting harder. _ _ tongue
separated from _ _ life. Wind whisks away _ _ _ consonants.
Whispers suffocating _ _ _ vowels. How _ _ _ _ _ _ _ _ _ _ _ _
another? Now unexpectedly _ _ _ _ _ old age _ _ _ sorrow.
_ _ _ _ _ _ _ _ _ _ _ _ _ _ me _ _ _ _ _ _ _ _ _.
_ _ _ _ _ _ _ _ _ _ whispers. _ life _ _ _ _ cannot be expressed
with words and yet _ _ is _ _ life. _ _ _ _ _ _ _ _ _ _ _ _ _ _ _ _ _
_. Anonymous _ _ _ _ _ _ nameless _ _ _ _ _ _ _. Devoid of sense.
_ _ _ _ empty _ _ _ _ _ _ _ _.

_ _.

Translated by Elena Anna Mastromauro

(ΥΠΟΓΛΩΣΣΙΑ)

Σήμερα ξύπνησα. Με 20 λέξεις λιγότερες. Όταν ξεκίνησε
έχανα μόλις πέντε τη μέρα. Μα μέσα η σιωπή επιταχύνει.
Κάθε πρόταση μια δυσάρεστη έκπληξη. Και γω, εδώ και
καιρό, μιλώ όλο και πιο λίγο.
Το κατάλαβα μια φορά που πήγα να διαμαρτυρηθώ. Το
στόμα. Ένα κενό με δόντια. Και φωνή δεν έβγαινε. Είπα
τελικά ευχαριστώ και γύρισα σπίτι. Ένιωσα τις λέξεις να
γλιστρούν απ' τα δόντια. Ζήτησα βοήθεια. Επισκέφτηκα
έναν γνωσιακό γλωσσολόγο-ορθοδοντικό. Με εξέτασε. Η
κατάσταση είναι μη αναστρέψιμη, είπε. Πάσχω από παύση.
Ακόμα χειρότερα, από σιωπή.
Τα αντικείμενα γύρω μου αραιώνουν.
Άρχισα να συνηθίζω. Μπορώ να μιλήσεις χωρίς κάποιες
λέξεις.. Δε θα πω _ _ _ _ _ _. Τη λέξη αυτή την έχασα. Δεν
γνωρίζω, δεν θυμάμαι, μόνο νιώθω το κενό που άφησε
πίσω. Πίνακας που τον ξεκρεμάς χρόνια μετά και βλέπεις
στον τοίχο το αποτύπωμά του. Δεν μπορώ να πω _ _ _ _ _ _.
Θα αναγκαστώ να μιλήσω περιφραστικά. Θα πω «Όμορφο
αυτό που φοράτε στο κεφάλι σας».
Τα αντικείμενα γύρω μου _ _ _ _ _ _ _ _ _.
Σε μια στιγμή απελπισίας σκέφτηκα πως θα μπορούσα να
γαντζώσω τη μία λέξη απ' την άλλη και να

_ _ _

σώσω. Πρπαθησανακολλησωμιαλεξημεμιααλλη.
Τομονοπουκαταφεραειναινατισχανωολεςμαζι.
Τελευταία η _ _ _ _ _ _ _ _ _ έγινε απελπιστική. Πρόσφατα
άρχισαν να φεύγουν και _ _ άρθρα. Λίγα προς _ _ παρόν,
μα όλα δείχνουν πως βρίσκομαι σε τελικό στάδιο.
_ _ αντικείμενα γύρω μου _ _ _ _ _ _ _ _ _.
Όλα μέσα _ _ _ σε κομμάτια. _ _ _ _ _ _ _ _ _ _ γίνονται
δύσκολα. Χωρίζει _ γλώσσα από _ _ ζωή. Αέρας σαρώνει _
_ σύμφωνα. Ψίθυρος πνίγει _ _φωνήεντα. Πώς _ _ _ _ _ _
_ _ _ _ _ _ τον άλλο; Τώρα _ _ _ _ _ _ _ ξαφνικά γερατειά _
_ _ θλίψη.
_ _ _ _ _ _ _ _ _ _ _ _ _ _ γύρω μου _ _ _ _ _ _ _ _ _.
_ _ _ _ _ _ _ _ _ ψίθυρο. _ _ _ ζωή _ _ _ δεν εκφράζεται _ _
λέξεις και όμως είναι _ ζωή μου. _ _ _ _ _ _ _ _ _ _ _ _ _ _
_. Ανώνυμος _ _ _ _ _ _ _ _ _ ανώνυμα _ _ _ _ _ _ _ _ _ _ _.
Χωρίς νόημα.
_ _ _ _ _ _ _ _ _ _ _ στεγνά.
_ _

POACHERS

Lord lord how I want to write a little poem
(Bon dieu de bon dieu que j'ai envie d'écrire un petit poème)
RAYMOND QUENEAU

It is oh so hard
To catch a poem
Just common knowledge
Poems prefer
to distance themselves from humans

You watch them from afar and all seems calm, but beware:
Ever alert
– even while drinking water –
They will detect the slightest sound
They'll run from the hunter
And they'll hide
Behind the silence

Poems habitually move alone:
Self-referential and selfish creatures
They feast on grass in savannahs and in solitude

Much easier:
To catch
A sonnet
Cumbersome figures, rhymed breaths
They choose to move in packs.

After capturing a poem:
First you remove their thorn.
Then you rephrase them
You explain them
You assort them
And you let them roam
Next to self-improvement guides
And cookery books.

Though placid by nature you can never be too sure:
It's in all the books
It's been a long time since poems last attacked a human
Yes, it's been a long time
Since poems were killing humans

"I respect poems, therefore I kill them"

For years, humans have hunted poems

They're worth a fortune
on the black market
They impart prestige
A matter of style and sophistication

The power
The constant amazement
The razzle-dazzle
Facing the literary conquest of our days:
A living room adorned with poet's heads

Translated by Elena Anna Mastromauro

ΛΑΘΡΟΘΗΡΕΣ

> χ θεούλη μου, τι ωραία που θα' ταν να' γραφα ένα
> ποιηματάκι
>
> PAYMON KENΩ

Είναι δύσκολο πολύ κανείς
να πιάσει ένα ποίημα
Όλοι το γνωρίζουν
Στα ποιήματα αρέσει
Να μένουν μακριά απ τους ανθρώπους

Από απόσταση τα παρατηρείς και όλα μοιάζουν ήσυχα,
μα προσοχή:
Με τις αισθήσεις τεντωμένες,
– ακόμη και τις ώρες που πίνουνε νερό –
Θα αντιληφθούν τον ελάχιστο ήχο,
θα τρέξουνε μακριά από τον θηρευτή
και θα χαθούνε
πίσω απ τη σιωπή.

Τα ποιήματα συνήθως κινούνται κατά μόνας:
Πλάσματα αυτοαναφορικά και εγωιστικά
Μασούν χορτάρι σε σαβάνες και σε μοναξιά.

Το πιο εύκολο:
Να πετύχει κανείς
Ένα σονέτο
Μορφές δυσκίνητες, ανάσες ομοιοκατάλληκτες.
Συνήθως επιλέγουν να μετακινούνται σε αγέλες.

Αφού αιχμαλωτίσεις τα ποιήματα:
Αρχικά τους αφαιρείς το αγκάθι.
Ύστερα τα παραφράζεις
τα επεξηγείς
τα ταξινομείς
Και τ' αφήνεις να τριγυρνούν
Δίπλα σε βοηθήματα
Και οδηγούς μαγειρικής.

Αν και φιλήσυχα ποτέ δεν μπορείς να είσαι σίγουρος:
Όλα τα βιβλία το γράφουν
Πως πάει καιρός από τότε που ένα ποίημα επιτέθηκε σε ανθρώπους
Ναι, πάει καιρός,
από τότε που τα ποιήματα σκοτώνανε ανθρώπους.

«Σέβομαι τα ποιήματα, γι αυτό και τα σκοτώνω»

Εδώ και χρόνια οι άνθρωποι κυνηγούνε τα ποιήματα

Στην μαύρη αγορά
Πληρώνει κανείς όσο όσο
Προσθέτει κύρος
Είναι ζήτημα κυρίως στυλ και ύφους

Το γόητρο
η μόνιμη έκπληξη
η φαντασμαγορία
Μπροστά στο λογοτεχνικό απόκτημα των ημερών:
Ένα σαλόνι στολισμένο με κεφάλια ποιητών.

INDRĖ VALANTINAITĖ (Lithuania)

Indrė Valantinaitė (1984) won the first prize in the poetry category of the 2006 First Book Contest of the Lithuanian Union of Writers with her debut book Of Fish and Lilies. *Her second book* Tales About Love and Other Animals *(2011) won the Young Yotvingian Prize in 2012. The Featurettes was published in 2017 and* Clothed with the Sun *in 2020. In addition to writing poems, Indrė is a former singer and a journalist and producer.*

HOTEL ROOM

He travels a lot.

Every night it seems
that the rented room
urges him to take
all seven roads.

There is, though,
a Bible and a mini bar:

Two ways to grasp at
tomorrow.

Translated by Rimas Uzgiris

VIEŠBUČIO KAMBARYS

Jis daug keliauja.

Kiekvienąkart jam rodos,
kad išnuomotas kambarys
primygtinai siūlo
visus septynis kelius.

Nors jame tėra
mini baras ir Biblija.

Du būdai
įsitverti rytojaus.

SIGHT

There are days when it's so hard –
so vain – to swallow even a gulp,

Days when I lack the strength to be dazzled
by the fragrance of flowers leaning towards you.

All of it exists for a moment to remain,
as when a bee flies by with advice:
one, two, three – open your eyes!

And you see the taut, shining
strings of being –

quivering, diaphanous threads
stretching up high from every
animate thing.

Later, there will be more
long days…

(But some gifts are too large
to be nicely wrapped.)

Translated by Rimas Uzgiris

REGĖJIMAS

Būna dienų, kai nuryti gurkšnį –
toks sunkus, bergžias darbas.

Dienų, kai svaigintis į tave linkstančio
žiedo kvapų derme nėra jėgų.

Visa tai tam, kad ištiktų akimirkos,
kai praskrendanti bitė perspėja:
viens, du, trys – atsimerk!

Ir pamatai įtemptą,
švytinčią būties stygą.

Tuos vos virpančius, perregimus siūlus,
besidriekiančius aukštyn nuo kiekvienos
krutančios gyvasties.

Paskui vėl būna ilgos
ilgos dienos…
(Juk esti dovanų, per didelių,
kad būtų dailiai įpakuotos.)

ANGKOR WAT

The dancer of the shrine
with a bullet
in her belly of stone

Turns and turns and
twists her hips and wrists
repeating eternal

Movements of veneration
for implacable gods
in crumbling frescos

While their resold heads
are comfortably ensconced
in the wealthy interiors of this world

Translated by Rimas Uzgiris

ANGKOR WAT

Šventyklos šokėja
su kulka
akmeniniame pilve

Vis sukasi ir sukasi
raitydama klubus ir riešus
kartoja amžinus

Nepermaldaujamų dievų
garbinimo judesius
ištrupėjusiose freskose

Kol jų perparduotos galvos
patogiai įsitaisiusios
šio pasaulio turtingųjų interjeruose

SHELL

From the time I moved out of you,
I slithered like a snail,
with sharp shards of its broken shell
stuck to its slimy body.

An unfeeling trail left behind.

Millions of the world's hotels – made of ice, ivory, stone, salt –
awash in unknown languages, faces, customs, seas –
would hide me, would open their doors.

I would return to where, twenty years ago, I mangled a dead jellyfish –
a transparent cloud the colour of water.
At a time when I didn't have to wear my bathing suit top.

My fingers poked its formless body.
Plasticine.

This would be called "starting over",
moulding yourself from the very first words,
from the tips of your toes.

Where my heart once was – a sharp shard of glass,
In time it will grow over with petals of woven muscle

with each heartbeat it won't sting so much
it will remind me less of fault, provenance, native language.

Translated by Ada Valaitis

KIAUTAS

Nuo tada, kai iš tavęs išsikrausčiau,
šliaužiu lyg sraigė,
prie kurios glitaus kūno vis dar prilipę
aštrūs sulūžusio kiauto likučiai.

Bejausmė šliūžė driekiasi iš paskos.

Milijonai pasaulio viešbučių – iš ledo, dramblio kaulo, akmens druskos –
skalaujamų nežinomų kalbų, veidų, papročių jūrų –
paslėptų mane, atvertų savo duris.

Grįžčiau ten, kur prieš dvidešimt metų maigiau negyvą medūzą –
vandens spalvos skaidrų debesį.
Paplūdimyje dar nedėvėjau viršutinės maudymuko dalies.

Mano pirštai smigo į beformį jos kūną.
Plastilinas.

Tai vadintųsi „viską pradėti iš naujo",
sulipdyti save nuo pirmųjų žodžių,
nuo kojų pirštų nagų.

Ten, kur būta mano širdies – aštri stiklo šukė,
ilgainiui apaugs raumens audinio žiedlapiais:

sulig kiekvienu tvinktelėjimu vis mažiau gels,
vis rečiau primins kaltę, kilmę, gimtąją kalbą.

BIOLOGICAL CLOCK

Passed down from generation to generation. An antique.
But I cannot take it to the pawnshop –
It's embedded too deeply within me.

My biological clock is ticking
like an explosive in a terrorist's hand.

One day I will give birth.
One day I will throw a small fish into a shark aquarium.

I will be my son's first compartment, with darkened windows,
I will let him off at a station of light, but

there are more and more articles in newspapers
about floods and suicides,
storms, accidents, and other punishments.

And my biological clock is ticking
like an explosive in a terrorist's hand.

Translated by Ada Valaitis

BIOLOGINIS LAIKRODIS

Paveldėtas iš kartos į kartą. Antikvarinis.
Tik užstatyt jo lombarde negaliu –
Per giliai many įmontuotas.

Mano biologinis laikrodis tiksi
kaip sprogmuo teroristo letenoj.

Kada nors aš pagimdysiu.
Kada nors aš įmesiu žuvelę į ryklių akvariumą.

Būsiu sūnui pirmoji kupė užtamsintais langais,
išlaipinsiu jį šviesos stotelėje, bet

vis daugiau žinučių laikraščiuose
apie potvynius ir savižudybes,
audras, avarijas ir kitas bausmes.

O mano biologinis laikrodis tiksi
Kaip sprogmuo teroristo letenoj.

GLORJANA VEBER (Slovenia)

Glorjana Veber (1981) holds a Ph.D. in Literary Studies and has published two poetry collections, The Free Fall *(2013) and* Someone Before in Italy *(2015), and a book of selected poems,* In Proximity of Silence in Bangladesh *(2019). In 2020, she published* Blueye, *a book of 500 akasha wisdom quotes. Translated into 30 languages, her poetry has received a number of Slovene and international awards. She is founder and director of the IRIU Institute which was engaged in the development of experimental poetry projects.*

IN GOD'S PROXIMITY

They bring God to the funeral parlour
precisely at four
the minister hangs himself as well
and there's dirt everywhere
no one to hear their confessions
and their bodies get covered with bugs
no one to bury them
how to bring god to a funeral parlour
Stephen Hawking
just when you write down
God does not exist

Stephen at four I counted
three thousand letters on a single page
in a book with a thousand pages
to date we have published one hundred and fifty million books
which is approximately five hundred billion letters
and that means the universe has one hundred and fifty billion stars more
than the number of all the letters in books

Stephen how can anyone capture god in a calculator
and trustingly forget Chopin's ballad in F minor
and convert life percentage into death percentage without dread
mister Hawking when I was little
I used to carry a brown suitcase with arm bands
and a towel to the cemetery
an association of words with the ideal weight

I don't know I don't know Sir what it's like to die until the end
but when a bug lands on my coat in front of the funeral parlour
it seems to me
that god isn't so silly that he'd prove himself

Translated by Petra Meterc

V BLIŽINI BOGA

V mrliško vežico pripeljejo boga
točno ob štirih
se tudi duhovnik obesi
in je vsepovsod zemlja
nikogar da ju spove
in njuni telesi prekrijejo hrošči
nikogar da ju pokoplje
kako v mrliško vežico pripeljati boga
Stephen Hawking
točno takrat ko zapišeš
Bog ne obstaja

Stephen ob štirih sem izračunala
da je na eni strani knjige tri tisoč črk
v knjigi s tisoč stranmi tri milijone črk
da smo do danes izdali sto petdeset milijonov knjig
kar je približno petsto bilijonov črk
in da ima vesolje sto petdeset bilijonov več zvezd
kot imamo vseh črk v knjigah

Stephen kako lahko kdorkoli v kalkulator ujame boga
in zaupljivo pozabi na Chopinovo balado v f-molu
in brez groze pretvarja odstotke življenja v odstotke smrti
gospod Hawking ko sem bila majhna
sem na po-kopališče nosila rjav kovček z rokavčki in brisačo
asociacijo besed z idealno težo

Ne vem ne vem gospod kako je umreti do konca
a ko na moj plašč v mrliški vežici prileti hrošč se mi zdi
da bog ni tako trapast da bi se dokazal

UNIVERSE

I hear music and feel no other need
I see a girl in the corner playing my grandfather's piano
with my own fingers
we shall all meet again
and the silence will explain the meaning of the universe

there are revolutionary alleys overlooked by many
fugitives in all directions of our new cities
I want to stand on the expanding land
I want a smile with an explanation

as on the face of a foreign land
my essence is crying at the point where others awake
starving in misery without a dog's chance in life
in another place high above us

concerned with our own smallness
a temporary consolation
I need to listen to the screams
sometimes it's all I need

Translated by the poet

VESOLJE

slišim glasbo in nobene druge potrebe ne čutim
v kotu vidim deklico – z mojimi prsti igra dedkov klavir
vsi se bomo ponovno srečali
in molk nam bo razložil smisel vesolja

so revolucionarne ulice ki jih mnogi spregledajo
kot ubežniki v vse smeri naših novih mest
hočem stati na zemlji ki se širi
hočem nasmeh ki nam bo razložil

kot na obrazu neke druge dežele
se moja bit zjoče prav tam kjer se prebujajo drugi
v stradanju in bedi brez pasje priložnosti
v nekem drugem kraju visoko nad nami

nas skrbi lastna majhnost
v naval v tolažbo za nekaj časa
moram poslušati krike
včasih je to vse
kar potrebujem

HUMAN

I love the way solitude is arranged at night
book edges cat half-closed window
when the silence has the most space to be seen
slippers peel smell of lilies
and the body releases the chained soul and starts to walk
are we most human when we sleep?

like tea or soup in winter
cold fingers frosty windowpanes covered roads
I could believe that warmth is the only love
footsteps smell of colour shifted branch
from a distance we are all ready for life
for a fall for a run for hands legs and sight
and then?

If there really is an incredible silence at the end of darkness
a straight wall its edge and the edge of this edge
yet I fall somewhere
somewhere where someone before me fell

Translated by the poet

ČLOVEK

Ljubim kako se samota razporeja ponoči
robovi knjig mačka priprto okno
ko ima tišina največ prostora da se jo vidi
copati olupek vonj lilij
in telo izpusti vklenjeno dušo in shodi
smo ljudje najbolj človeški ko spimo?

kot pri čaju ali juhi pozimi
zmrzli prsti zaledenele šipe prekrite ceste

lahko bi verjela da je toplota edina ljubezen
stopinje vonj barve premaknjena veja
od daleč smo vsi pripravljeni na življenje
na padec na tek na roke noge in vid
in zatem?

če je na koncu teme zares neverjetna tišina
ravna stena njen rob in rob tega roba
nekam vendar padem
nekam kamor je padel nekdo pred mano

MIKAEL VOGEL (Germany)

Mikael Vogel (1975) has published six books of poetry: Kassandra im
Fenster *(with Friederike Mayröcker and Bettina Galvagni, 2008);* O
Wildnis Dunkelheit! – Nachtgedichte *(2009);* Massenhaft Tiere
(2011); Morphine *(2014);* Dodos auf der Flucht. Requiem für ein
verlorenes Bestiarium *(2018); and* zum Bleiben, wie zum Wandern
– Hölderlin, theurer Freund *(with José F. A. Oliver, 2020). He was
awarded the Medienpreis RAI Südtirol from Lyrikpreis Meran in 2016 and
in 2019, received the Literaturstipendium from the German state of Baden-
Württemberg.*

THE GOLDEN TOADS

Discovered in
Just a few square miles
Of cloudy elfin forest in Costa Rica
Between crawling boughs, stirring roots, dripping leaves
In 1964: unfathomably luminousneonorangegold, posing sublime in
Unbridled stillness before sex.. lived underground
Above only in
April for a few days of orgy to greet the rain.
Males rose
First, awaited females, bodies taut.
Any movement an advance – the first twitching limb provoked hops and cries
Throughout the mass; whoever managed to mount another's back clung on
For hours, regardless of rivals' violence. Coincidental lovers
Left seafoams of fertilized eggs in puddles under roots.

Last sighting: May 15, 1989 when
For the second year in a row only one single, golden male emerged.
Nullified by
Human-spread fungal infection, chytridiomycosis, on a
Warming globe

Translated by Jon Cho-Polizzi

DIE GOLDKRÖTEN

1964 in
Wenigen Quadratkilometern
Von Nebelschwaden durchzogenen Elfenwalds in Costa Rica
Zwischen knorrigen Bäumen, verschlungenen Wurzeln,
        tropfenden Blättern ent-
Deckt: unbegreifbar leuchtendneongoldorange, erhaben
        posierend
In ungezügelter Regungslosigkeit kurz vor dem Sex.. lebten
        unterirdisch
Nur im April
Die Regenzeit oberirdisch ein paar Tage lang mit einer Orgie
        begrüßend.
Die männlichen kamen
Als erste hervor, erwarteten angespannt die weiblichen.
Bewegung war Anmache – sobald *ein* Körper zuckte ging ein
        Hüpfen und Schreien
Durch die Menge; wer irgendjemandes Rücken besprungen
        hatte klammerte sich
Stundenlang darauf fest, egal wieviele Prügel. Die zufälligen Paare
Ließen Meeresschäume befruchteter Eier in Regenpfützen unter
        Wurzeln zurück.
Letzte Sichtung 15. Mai 1989 als
Im zweiten Jahr in Folge nur eine einzige männliche Goldkröte
        auftauchte.
Global erwärmt durch die
Von Menschen in Umlauf gebrachte epidemische Pilzinfektion
        Chytridiomykose zu-
Nichtegemacht

THE STELLER'S SEA COW

Dragging along the bottom on its
Stumps, grazing kelp, stolid colossus
Thirty feet in length, weighing in more than ten tons, tree-bark skin,
              40 pounds of heart.
Toothless, only mammal without finger bones, incapable of self-defence
When Vitus Bering's ship wrecked on its solitary shore
Seeking a land bridge between Asia and America
In the name of Czar Peter the Great, hungry seamen savaged
Sea cows alive. Bering died of scurvy, the naturalist accompanying him
Georg Wilhelm Steller announced their existence on his return to
Mainland Russia. Buffet opened – 27 years after discovery, seal
Hunters clubbed to death its last of kin. Victuals and oil.
Some, Steller describes, *hewed great pieces from the*
Still living beast. The female's vulva is located eight inches above the anus
One can easily fit five fingers in the vaginal opening
Without constraint

  Translated by Jon Cho-Polizzi

    ### DIE STELLERSCHE SEEKUH

    Auf Stümpfen zog sie sich über den
    Boden, weidete Seetang ab, behäbige Kolossin
    Neun Meter lang, zehn Tonnen schwer, Borkenhaut, 18 Kilo Herz.
    Zahn- und als einziges Säugetier fingerknochenlos konnte sie
               sich nicht wehren
    Als Vitus Berings Schiff, von Zar Peter dem Großen auf
           Entdeckungsreise befohlen
    Eine Landbrücke zwischen Asien und Amerika zu suchen
    Auf ihrer abgelegenen Insel Schiffbruch erlitt, die Mannschaft hungrig
    Über sie herzufallen begann. Bering starb an Skorbut, der ihn
           begleitende Naturforscher
    Georg Wilhelm Steller aber verkündete nach seiner Rückkehr auf
           dem russischen Festland
    Ihre Existenz. Das Buffet war eröffnet – 27 Jahre nach ihrer Entdeckung
    Erschlugen Robbenjäger die Letzte ihrer Art. Wegproviant und Öl.
    Einige, beschrieb Steller, *schnitten dem noch lebenden Thiere*
    Grosse Stücken aus. Die weibliche Scham stehet acht Zoll über dem Hintern.
    In die Spalte selbst gehen fünf zusammen geschlagene Finger
    Ohne Zwang

THE LABRADOR DUCK

Almost nothing known about
It.. though it spent its winter months
By New York City, on the North Atlantic coast.
Tender lateral flaps protruded from a flattened bill
Likely for feeling prey beneath the waves: shellfish
Crustaceans, molluscs.. lamellae in its lower jaw to sieve the sand
When burrowing. Drowned on hooks fishermen hauled in with their catch.
On the markets of Manhattan, Brooklyn, Baltimore, Philadelphia
Its flesh disesteemed, festering unpurchased for its fishy taste.
Nesting grounds never located
No one knows why they died out, though they probably
Like other ducks, slept with one open eye –
The last Labrador duck surprised December 12, 1878
Elmira, Southern Tier, New York, a hunter's rifle blast.
From autumn 1875, Long Island: the last corpse to be preserved
Wears a plastic bag upon its head
Sheds feathers now
When touched

Translated by Jon Cho-Polizzi

DIE LABRADORENTE

So gut wie nichts über sie be-
Kannt.. obwohl sie die Wintermonate
Nahe New York an der nordostamerikanischen Küste verbrachte.
Ihr vorn flacher Schnabel lief seitlich in weiche Ränder aus
Mit denen sie unter Wasser vermutlich Beute ertastete: Muscheln
Schalentiere, Mollusken.. im Unterkiefer Lamellen, beim Wühlen
Den Sand auszusieben. Am Haken ertrunken zogen Fischer sie an Bord.
Auf den Märkten Manhattans, Brooklyns, Baltimores, Philadelphias
War ihr Fleisch unbeliebt, verdarb oft ungekauft, habe fischig geschmeckt.
Nistgründe nie lokalisiert
Niemand weiß warum sie ausstarb obwohl sie
Wahrscheinlich wie andere Enten mit einem offenen Auge schlief –
Die letzte Labradorente wurde am 12. Dezember 1878
Bei Elmira, New York vom Gewehrschuss eines Jägers überrascht.
Die späteste erhaltene Leiche aus dem Herbst 1875 von Long Island
Trägt eine Plastiktüte über dem Kopf
Bei jeder Berührung
Fallen ihr Federn aus

THE THYLACINE

Tasmania was its and its alone.. raised
Sheltered in its mothers' pouch, eschewing no
Fight, it mostly played victor. Hunting in long forays for
Wombats, wallabies, possums, potoroos, trout. Then
Arriving settlers from Europe. Clear-cut woods for pastureland
Drove it away, its prey grown scarce. Could open its jaws to
90° – but its bite was too weak to kill a sheep
The sheep industry accused it of this crime. Eradicated for bounty
Van Diemen's Land Company, colonizing its island, hid its own
Mismanagement from stockholders in London, bounty
Rising with the bodies settlers turned in – soon the government
                                        determined budgets
Maintained annihilation pressure on thylacines, posting annual savings
As sightings became rare. Also called *Tasmanian Tiger*
Exaggerating danger. Alleged vampirism on ovine throats, locking
Jaws in scholarly literature. Its threats resembled yawns.
The final thylacine died the night of September 7, 1936 in a
Cage at Hobart Zoo, locked from sleeping quarters in winter cold.
The government had declared it a protected species 59 days before. Birth of
Offspring in captivity: a one-time success

Translated by Jon Cho-Polizzi

DER BEUTELWOLF

Tasmanien war ganz und gar sein.. geschützt
Im mütterlichen Beutel aufgewachsen scheute er keinen
Kampf, ging meist als Sieger hervor. Jagte auf langen Streifzügen
Wombats, Wallabys, Possums, Kaninchenkängurus, Forellen. Dann
Ankunft der Siedler aus Europa. Rodeten Wälder für Weideflächen
Drängten ihn ab, seine Beute immer rarer. Konnte den Unterkiefer
90 Grad weit aufklappen – sein Biss jedoch zu schwach für die Schafe
Die zu reißen die Schafindustrie ihm vorwarf. Per Kopfgeld
                                        beseitigt worden
Die seine Insel kolonialisierende Van Diemen's Land Company so ihr
Missmanagement vor den Aktionären in London verschleiernd, die
                                        Abschussprämie
Mit der Zahl vorgelegter Kadaver steigernd – bald beschloss die
                                        Regierung Budgets

Zur Aufrechterhaltung des Vernichtungsdrucks, verbuchte
jährlich Einsparungen
Weil der Beutelwolf auszubleiben begann. Auch *Tasmanischer
Tiger* genannt
Seine Gefährlichkeit übertreibend. Angeblicher Vampirismus
an Schafshälsen ver-
Biss sich in der wissenschaftlichen Literatur. Sein Drohen sah
wie Gähnen aus.
Der letzte Beutelwolf starb in der Nacht des 7. September 1936
in einem
Zookäfig in Hobart, bei Wintertemperaturen aus seinem
Schlafquartier ausgesperrt.
Die Regierung hatte ihn zur geschützten Art erklärt 59 Tage
zuvor. Eine
Nachzucht war in den Zoos ein einziges Mal gelungen

ABOUT THE EDITOR

PHOTO: GILLES ORTLIEB

PATRICK McGUINNESS is a poet and novelist, and Professor of French and Comparative Literature at the University of Oxford. His books include the *The Last Hundred Days*, longlisted for the Man Booker Prize and winner of Wales Book of the Year, the memoir *Other People's Countries: A Journey into Memory*, which won the Duff Cooper Prize, and the novel, *Throw me to the Wolves*, which won the Royal Society of Literature's Encore Award. He is the author of two books of poems, *The Canals of Mars* and *Jilted City*. He has translated volumes by Stéphane Mallarmé, Hélène Dorion, and Jorge Manrique into English, and is the editor of the *Everyman Anthology of French Poetry: from Medieval to Modern Times*.

ABOUT THE TRANSLATORS

Lars Ahlström works as translator (Swedish / English) and literary critic in Stockholm and specializes in Australian literature (Gerald Murnane, Gillian Mears, David Brooks, and John Kinsella) and Australian children's literature. He has translated Swedish poetry for the American literary journal *Verse*.

Alexis Bernaut is a poet, editor and translator (French / English). His first collection, *Au matin suspendu / Suspended in the morning* was published in 2012, and his poems have appeared in anthologies and international journals.

Madeleine Campbell is Teaching Fellow in Language Education at Edinburgh University. Her recent book *Translating across Sensory and Linguistic Borders* (2019), co-edited with Ricarda Vidal, challenges traditional notions of literary translation through the embodied perspective of practitioners working in a range of media, including dance, film, materials and the visual arts.

Karo Caren is an American poet and translator, mainly of Polish and Ukrainian poetry into English. She has published a poetry collection, *I Am Air*, a poetic memoir, *Life in Footnotes* and a novel, *Roman and Julian*.

Kristian Carlsson is a writer, translator, video artist and cultural curator. He has published 20 books in Swedish, ranging from poetry to prose to conceptual pieces and as a translator (English / Swedish) he introduces contemporary Swedish poetry in English and women beat poets from the US in Swedish. He has also translated a number of Bengali poets into Swedish.

Želika Černok is a Croatian poet who studied creative writing in Sweden and in 2005, published a collection of poetry *When You Lean Too Far from a Train Window*. She translates from Swedish, Norwegian and English and is a member of the Society of Croatian Literary Translators.

Jon Cho-Polizzi is a literary and academic translator, travel writer and professional photographer, currently teaching at East Bay German International School, Emeryville, California.

DAVID COLMER is an Australian writer and translator, mainly of Dutch-language literature. He translates novels, poetry and children's literature and is the current English translator of Radna Fabias, Gerbrand Bakker, Dimitri Verhulst, Annie M. G. Schmidt, and Nachoem M. Wijnberg.

PATRICIA CRAMPTON (d. 2016) was a prize-winning British literary translator who served as a translator at the Nuremberg War Crimes Trials.

ANNA CROWE is a British poet, trained linguist and translator of primarily Catalan and Castilian poetry. She has published poetry pamphlets and three poetry collections, the latest of which is *Not on the Side of the Gods* (Arc, 2019) and has translated her own poetry into Catalan.

MILAN DAMJANOSKI is a freelance interpreter and literary translator (Macedonian / English) and teaches at Ss. Cyril and Methodius University of Skopje. He is editor of *Blesok Prose*.

CHRISTIAN GULLETTE is a poet and translator (Swedish / English) of fiction, non-fiction, young adult literature and poetry, currently lecturing at the University of California, Berkley.

RACHEL HADAS is an award-winning American poet, teacher, essayist, and translator (Greek / English). Her most recent essay collection is *Classics: Essays* (2007), and her most recent poetry collection is *The Ache of Appetite* (2010).

JENNIFER HAYASHIDA is a poet, translator (Swedish / English) and visual artist whose poetry and translations have been widely published in US literary journals.

TIM AP HYWEL is an artist, poet and translator (Welsh / English) with an interest in ancient Welsh history in poetic, written form, particularly the *Book of Taliesin*.

JOHN IRONS has been a professional translator for twenty years, His poetry translations have mainly been from Dutch and the Scandinavian languages. He lives in Odense, Denmark.

HENRY ISRAELI is a poet and playwright. His books include a collection of poetry, *New Messiahs* (2002) and *Fresco: The Selected*

Poetry of Luljeta Lleshanaku (2002), which he edited and co-translated from the Albanian.

KALINA JANEVA is a literary translator (Macedonian / English) and an active member of the Macedonian Translators Association.

OLENA JENNINGS is a poet and translator (Ukrainian / English). Her poetry collection *Poems from an Apartment* appeared in 2017 and her translation of Iryna Shuvalova's collection *Pray to the Empty Wells* in 2019.

LENA KALLERGI is a poet, linguist and translator (Greek / English). She has published two books of poetry: Κήποι στην άμμο / *Gardens on Sand* (Gavrielides, 2010) and Περισσεύει ένα πλοίο / *One Ship Apart* (Gavrielides, 2016).

PANAGIOTIS KECHAGIAS is a writer and translator (Greek / English). His translations include the short story collection *Prodigals* by Greg Jackson (2017).

TOMISLAV KUZMANOVIĆ is a translator (Croatian / English) whose translations include *Smrt Djevojcice sa žigicama* / *The Death of the Little Match Girl* by Zoran Feric and, with Russell Valentino, *Dvorac u Romagni* / *A Castle in Romagna* by Igor Štiks.

FRANCESCO LEVATO is a poet, a translator (Italian / Spanish / English), and a new media artist. His first poetry collection, *Marginal State*, appeared in 2006.

ANTONIA LLOYD-JONES is a full-time translator of Polish literature into English including novels, short stories, crime fiction, poetry and children's books. She was the 2018 winner of the Transatlantyk Award for the most outstanding promoter of Polish literature abroad.

GIAN LOMBARDO is a prose poet, publisher, editor, and literary translator. He has published a number of prose poetry collections and his translations include works by Michel Delville, Eugène Savitzkaya and Aloysius Bertrand. He teaches publishing at Emerson College.

OKSANA LUTSYSHYNA is a Ukrainian writer, poet, literary scholar, and translator. She is author of four poetry collections, one collection of short stories, and two novels.

David Malcolm is Professor of English at SWPS University, Warsaw and translates from Polish to English. He has published many books and articles, including *On John Berger: Telling Stories* (2016).

Elena Anna Mastromauro is a professional translator and a journalist. She translates from English, German, Spanish, French and Italian into Greek, English and German.

Manana Matiashvili is a Georgian poet, translator and journalist. A recipient of the 2010 Vakjushti Kotetishvili prize for young translators of poetry, she now teaches Translation Theory and Practice at Caucasus University, Tbilisi.

Petra Meterc is a freelance journalist and film critic, based in Slovenia. She writes and reports on film and literature for the radio, in magazines and other media outlets.

Mania Meziti is a professional translator and runs the poetry platform poets.gr.

John Minahane is a full time translator of literary, musicological, art-historical, ethnological, and other writings from Slovak (and occasionally Czech) into English. He has lived in Slovakia since 1996.

Ian Monk is a British writer and translator (French / English, both ways) based in Paris. He won the prestigious [British] Society of Authors Scott Moncrieff Prize in 2004 for his translation of *Monsieur Malaussène* by Daniel Pennac.

Ciaran O'Driscoll is a member of Aosdána and has published nine books of poetry, including *Gog and Magog* (1987), *Moving On, Still There* (2001), and *Surreal Man* (2006).

Olivia Olsen is a freelance writer and translator (Swedish / English) and works as a book editor in Stockholm.

Renée von Paschen is a professional literary translator, bilingual poet and scholar. A bilingual book of her poetry *Vice Versa: Poetry in English & French* was published in 2017. She mainly translates from English into German and German into English as well as from French into German.

Ronald Puppo translates from Catalan and teaches Translation and English Studies at the University of Vic, Catalonia. His book *Selected Poems of Jacint Verdaguer: A Bilingual Edition* (2007) is the first English translation of the poetry of this Catalan poet.

MIRZA PURIĆ is a literary translator working from German and BCMS. He is a contributing editor of *EuropeNow* and in-house translator for the Sarajevo Writers' Workshop. He has published several book-length translations into BCMS and his translations into English have appeared in international journals and anthologies.

JUSTIN QUINN is an Irish poet, critic and translator (Czech / English) who lectures at Charles University, Prague and the University of West Bohemia. He has published seven poetry collections and translates extensively from Czech, in particular the poetry of Petr Borkovec, Bohuslav Reynek and Ivan Blatný.

PAWEŁ SAKOWSKI is a writer and professional translator (Polish / English) specialising in conference interpretation and literary translation. He is also a playwright and theatre and television actor.

JOEL SCOTT is a poet and translator, originally from Sydney. He co-runs the Berlin-based magazine and reading series *artiCHOKE*. His translation of the second volume of Peter Weiss's *Die Ästhetik des Widerstands* appeared in 2020.

IRENA ŠKARICA is a professional translator (Croatian / English) who has published translations of novels by Anthony Doerr, Nathan Fiuler, Susan Spencer-Wendel and Lois McMaster Bujold among others.

JAMES SUTHERLAND-SMITH is a poet and translator living in Slovakia. He has published seven collections of his own poetry and translates poetry from Slovak and Serbian for which he has received the Slovak Hviezdoslav Prize and the Serbian Zlatko Krasni Prize.

PAULI TAPIO is a poet and translator (Finnish / English). His poetry collection *Varpuset ja aika / Sparrows and Time* (2017) won the Helsingin Sanomat Literature Prize for the best debut collection and his poetry has been published in English, Macedonian, Norwegian and Romanian. He also translates works by Russian novelists and poets.

JOHN TAYLOR is an American writer, translator (English / Modern Greek / Italian / French) and polyglot literary critic living in France. He is the author of eleven collections of stories, short prose and poetry and his work has been translated into more than a dozen European languages. He mainly translates poetry.

CHARLOTTE THIESSEN is a poet and translator. She co-runs the magazine and reading series *artiCHOKE* in Berlin and also edits the internationalist feminist poetry publication *Virgulentxs*.

RIMAS UZGIRIS is a poet, translator, editor and critic and teaches translation at Vilnius University. His work has appeared in numerous international journals and he is primary translator of *How the Earth Carries Us: New Lithuanian Poets* and of the poetry of Ilzė Butkutė, Judita Vaičiūnaitė and Gintaras Grajauskas.

ADA VALAITIS came to Lithuania in 2007 to study and translate Lithuanian literature. Her translations have appeared in numerous collections and journals, including the *Vilnius Review* and *The Dedalus Book of Lithuanian Literature*.

RADU VANCU is a Romanian writer, editor, scholar and translator (Romanian / English). His publications include eight books of poems and a novel and he has translated poetry by Ezra Pound and John Berryman and prose by W. B. Yeats.

KARLIEN VAN DEN BEUKEL is a poet and Course Director of the BA in Creative Writing at London South Bank University. Her research interests include modernist poetry and twentieth-century dance, and digital poetics in translation.

MARILYA VETETO REESE is Professor of German at Northern Arizona University in Flagstaff, and translator of the poetry and prose of Anant Kumar since the 1990s. She is the recipient of many grants for her decades-long research on minority authors in Germany.

PAUL VINCENT studied at Cambridge and in Amsterdam. Until 1989 he was a professor at the Dutch department of University College London. Since then he has worked as a freelance translator.

CHANTAL WRIGHT is a literary translator who has twice been shortlisted for the Marsh Award for Children's Literature in

Translation. She translates literary and academic texts from German and French into English and teaches literary translation at the University of Warwick.

MONIKA ZOBEL is the author of two books of poems and her writing has appeared in many English-language poetry magazines as well as publications in Germany and Austria. She works as a translator in Bremen, Germany.

JERNEJ ŽUPANIČ is a Slovenian writer, with a poetry collection and two novels to his name, and a translator (English / Slovene). His translations of English-language writers have won him many awards, including the Radojka Vrančič Award.

LIST OF POETS BY COUNTRY & BY NOMINATING FESTIVAL

ALBANIA –
'Genoa International Poetry Festival'
Luljeta Lleshanaku

AUSTRIA –
'Literatur & Wein'
Renate Aichinger
Helwig Brunner

BELGIUM –
'Felix Poetry Festival'
Geert Buelens
Moya De Feyter
Andy Fierens
'Ars Poetica'
Michel Delville

CROATIA –
'Goran's Spring'
Alen Brlek
Marijo Glavaš
Monika Herceg
Davor Ivankovac
Antonija Novaković

CZECH REPUBLIC –
'Literatur & Wein'
Peter Borkovec

FINLAND –
'Poetry Moon'
Sanna Karlström

FRANCE –
'Le Printemps des Poètes'
Aldo Qureshi
Lou Raoul
Aurélia Lassaque (Occitan)

GEORGIA –
'Tbilisi International Festival of Literature'
Paata Shamugia

GERMANY –
'Hausacher LeseLenz'
Zehra Çirak
Lütfiye Güzel
Tzveta Sofronieva (Bulgaria / Germany)
Mikael Vogel

GREECE –
'Athens World Poetry Festival'
Thanos Gogos
Thomas Tsalapatis
'Struga Poetry Evenings'
Danae Sioziou

IRELAND –
'Ledbury Poetry Festival'
Doireann Ní Ghríofa

ITALY –
'Genoa International Poetry Festival'
Valentina Colonna
Tiziano Fratus
Franca Mancinelli

LITHUANIA –
'Druskininkai Poetic Fall'
Aušra Kaziliūnaitė
Indrė Valantinaitė

THE NETHERLANDS
'Felix Poetry Festival'
Radna Fabias

NORTH MACEDONIA –
'Struga Poetry Evenings'
Nikolina Andova
Vladimir Martinovski

POLAND –
'The European Poet of
Freedom Literary Festival'
Barbara Klicka
Natalia Malek
Michal Sobol

ROMANIA –
'Poets in Transylvania
Festival'
Ana Dragu

SLOVAKIA –
'Ars Poetica'
Eleni Cay
Michel Delville (Belgium)
Michal Habaj
Eva Luka

SLOVENIA
'Days of Poetry and Wine'
Veronika Dintinjana
Kristina Kočan
Glorjana Veber

SPAIN –
'Poetas Festival Madrid'
Carmen Camacho
Josep Pedrals (Catalonia)

SWEDEN –
'Littfest'
Athena Farrokhzad
Sanna Hartnor
Nino Mick
Malte Persson
Johan Sandberg McGuinne

UK
'Ledbury Poetry Festival'
Liz Berry
Vahni Capildeo (Trinidad &
Tobago)
Kayo Chingonyi
Mererid Hopwood (Wales)
Helen Ivory
Sandeep Parmar

UKRAINE –
'Lviv International Literature
Festival'
Olena Huseinova
Kateryna Kalytko
Halyna Kruk

ACKNOWLEDGEMENTS

The Editor, Patrick McGuinness, writes: "It has been an honour as well as a pleasure to edit this anthology, and to be bringing it to an international audience through a collaboration between a British and a Slovenian publisher. I'm especially grateful to Petra Kavčič at Beletrina and to Aleš Šteger, *fons et origo* of Versopolis as idea and as reality, for their invaluable help with information and material.

I'm grateful to Angela Jarman at Arc for her indefatigable work on a complex and finicky project, to Tony Ward at Arc for his helpful advice and to Jimmy Symonds for the cover."

The Publishers would like to thank all poets and translators and other copyright-holders who have given us permission to include poems and translations in this anthology.

Poems previously published include: Geert Beulens' 'Dogma' Poetry International website 2006 and 'Zero Hour / Uur nul', translated by David Colmer with the support of Flanders Literature; Vahni Capildeo's 'In A Dream' and 'Utter', reproduced with the permission of Peepal Tree Press and 'Going Nowhere, Getting Somewhere' reproduced with the permission of Carcanet Press; Eleni Cay's 'Oranges are the Only Fruit' in *Poetry Ireland Review*, 'Soldiers' Graves' in *Glasgow Review of Books* and 'Welcome Digital! / Vitaj digitálno!' in *A Butterfly's Trembling in the Digital Age* (Parthian Books, 2017); Radna Fabias' 'Opening Scene / Openingsscene', 'Bride / Bruid' and 'Roosting Tree / Roestplaats' in David Colmer's translation in the English edition of *Habitus* (forthcoming, Deep Vellum, 2021); Tiziano Fratus' 'St Francis at Oxford Street / San Francesco a Oxford Street' in *Creaturing: Selected Poems* (Marick Press, 2010), and 'The Seed of God / Il seme di Dio' and 'Every Seed carries a Journey Within / Ogni seme ha dentro un viaggio' in *Arborgrammaticus: Poems in Shape of a Seed* (Mondadori, 2015); Helen Ivory's 'In a Time Before Maps', 'Streets of the Abandoned City', 'Nights in the Abandoned City', 'Luncheon in the Abandoned City'. 'The Birds', and 'The

Cartographer Unmakes' in the chapbook *Maps of the Abandoned City* (SurVision, 2019); Aurélia Lassaque's 'Pantais', 'Lo sòmi d'Orfèu', 'Sa pèl escura e cauda…' and 'De sa maire beguèt lo lach…' in *Pour que chantent les salamandres* (Editions Bruno Doucey, 2013) in a new translation by Madeleine Campbell © 2020; Sandeep Parmar's 'Archive for a Daughter' in *The Marble Orchard* (Shearsman, 2012) and sections i, ii, xxv, xxx, xxxvii and xlvi of 'Eidolon' in *Eidolon* (Shearsman, 2015); Lou Raoul's 'on the pillar… / sur le pilier…' and 'in the yard that day / dans la cour ce jour-là…' in *Roche Jagu / Roc'h Ugu* (Éditions Encres Vives, 2010), and 'Ma'aï' and *'An amzer o tont* / The Coming Weather / Le temps venant' in *Else avec elle* (Éditions Isabelle Sauvage, 2012); Danae Sioziou 'Around the House / Οικιακά' in *Austerity Measures: The New Greek Poetry* (Penguin; 2016), 'The Spider / Η αράχνη' (*Ilanot Review*, 2019) and 'Sundown / Ηλιοβασίλεμα' and 'Broken Into / Διάρρηξη' in *Useful Children's Games* (Antipodes, 2016); Tzveta Sofronieva's 'Cloning / Ich', ' Sun / Sonne', ' Un-lost in translation' and 'Habits / Gewohnheiten' in *Landschaften, Ufer* (Carl Hanser Verlag GmbH & Co. KG, München, 2013); Mikael Vogel's 'The Golden Toads / Die Goldkröten', 'The Steller's Sea Cow / Die Stellersche Seekuh', 'The Labrador Duck / Die Labradorente' and 'The Thylacine / Der Beutelwolf' in *Dodos auf der Flucht. Requiem für ein verlorenes Bestiarium* (Verlagshaus Berlin, 2018).